Myrna Orenstein, PhD

Smart But Stuck
Emotional Aspects of Learning Disabilities and Imprisoned Intelligence

Revised Edition

Smart But Stuck

Emotional Aspects
of Learning Disabilities
and Imprisoned Intelligence

Revised Edition

Smart But Stuck

Emotional Aspects of Learning Disabilities and Imprisoned Intelligence

Revised Edition

Myrna Orenstein, PhD

The Haworth Press®
New York • London • Oxford

The Haworth Press, Inc., 10 Alice Street, Binghamton, NY 13904-1580

Cover design by Marylouise E. Doyle.

Library of Congress Cataloging-in-Publication Data

Orenstein, Myrna.
    Smart but stuck : emotional aspects of learning disabilities and imprisoned intelligence / Myrna Orenstein.—Rev. ed.
       p. cm.
    Includes bibliographical references and index.
    ISBN 0-7890-1466-1 (hard)—ISBN 0-7890-1467-X (soft)
    1. Learning disabled—Psychology. 2. Learning disabled—Mental health. 3. Learning disabled—Intelligence levels. 4. Learning disabilities. I. Title.
RC394.L37 O74 2001
616.85'889—dc21
                                                                  00-047283
                                                                       CIP

To Al

for being there

ABOUT THE AUTHOR

Myrna Orenstein, PhD, LCSW, BCD, ACSW, is a psychotherapist in private practice and Adjunct Instructor at Oakton Community College in Illinois. Dr. Orenstein is a former Vice President of the Mental Health Association in Evanston. She has presented many workshops and presentations on the subject of imprisoned intelligence and undiagnosed learning disabilities in adults and is the author of *Imprisoned Intelligence: The Discovery of Undiagnosed Learning Disabilities in Adults.* Her affiliations include the National Association of Social Workers, the Mental Health Association of Evanston, the Illinois Society for Clinical Social Work, and the Primary Prevention Task Force of Evanston.

CONTENTS

Series Editor's Comments

We are pleased to publish Dr. Orenstein's book, *Smart But Stuck: Emotional Aspects of Learning Disabilities and Imprisoned Intelligence*, as part of The Haworth Social Work Practice in Action textbook series. Dr. Orenstein's historical review, insightful analysis, theoretical perspectives, and practical guidelines are helpful for all professionals working with people with learning difficulties. Any professionals who have worked with such individuals and heard them describe how as children they were significantly delayed in some learning areas while advanced in others, and was puzzled as to how this could be, will be aided in their understanding by this book.

Carlton E. Munson, PhD
Editor in Chief
The Haworth Press
Social Work Practice in Action

Foreword

This book is a tribute to adults who belatedly discover they have an unidentified learning disability. It is also an inspiration to others who struggle to understand the sources of some of their difficulties, not knowing that they too may have an unidentified learning disability. These are adults who as children struggled academically but remained undiagnosed for one reason or another. As the subjects studied in this book demonstrate, their struggle to understand themselves and the sources of their difficulties was obscured by the absence of a clear diagnosis.

Significant advances have been made in recent years both in the diagnosis of learning disabilities and in understanding their effects on a person's development. School systems are now mandated to test children who struggle academically. Schools must provide services to those who meet the legislative criteria indicating that a child has a learning disability. However, the diagnosis of a learning disability only begins a long process of addressing the deficits themselves and dealing with the emotional repercussions of those deficits. The consequences of both sets of difficulties carry over into adulthood.

We may think of adults with learning disabilities as falling into two groups: those who were diagnosed as children and those who were not. Those in the first group, who were diagnosed as children, faced the task of incorporating into their sense of self and their identity the meaning of having a learning disability, and often of being so labeled. In addition to having to deal with the problems their deficits presented, they had to confront whatever stigma was associated by their social group with that label, and live with their feelings about themselves as being different. Some came to terms with their strengths and deficits. They found ways of compensating for and accommodating to their disabilities. Some eventually found their way into careers that were satisfying and achieved success in spite of the disability. Yet, even for those who found success, the disability did not leave them unscathed. For some, the experience led to a sense of shame they never seemed able to overcome; they carried the diagnosis as a secret to be hidden at all costs, a secret they shared with no one. This secret may have formed the nucleus of a low self-esteem regardless of their successes. In spite of being perceived by colleagues as intact and as leading productive lives, they inwardly carried the conviction of fraudulently deceiving others with their competence. They carried the conviction that their success was due to an accident of circumstance or to pure luck.

The more fortunate of these adults were exposed to teachers or caregivers who gave them the means to cope with both the deficit and the resulting self-perception of being flawed. Aside from acquiring the means to compensate for their deficits, they regarded their sense of difference as a handicap to be overcome rather than as only a source of shame. They discovered that to be different was not equivalent to being less of a human being; as human beings we all have strengths and weaknesses. An appreciation of their assets and deficits provided them with the inner strength and determination to overcome life's obstacles. The less fortunate in this group were crushed by the burden of the deficit and the stigma they perceived as attached to it. As children they withdrew, feeling defeated or unable to cope with the demands of a highly competitive society. In adulthood, they faced the difficulties of finding jobs commensurate with their intelligence, and of addressing the intricate task of dealing with their emotional confusion. Clinical experience reveals that even for this group, all hope should not be lost. Some become "late bloomers" who in their late twenties or early thirties find an area of interest that leads to a productive career.

For the second group of children, who, like the adults discussed in this book, grew up without having their learning disability identified, their lives took a different turn. It is difficult to estimate the number of undiagnosed adults in the population today. Many of these adults grew up at a time when school systems had little awareness of learning disabilities. For some, the mystery of the reasons for their school failure remained hidden until circumstances led to its discovery. As children who did not perform according to expectations, they were perceived and labeled as either unmotivated or not very bright. As children they may have been considered discipline problems because they dealt with their failures by creating disturbances in the class-room rather than being compliant students. A few took the alternative of silently withdrawing from the fray. These children, often girls, were considered nice kids who would never make it in the competitive world of academics. For most in this group, as adults, the puzzle of their failure to achieve in school continued to burden them. If they achieved successful careers, they could not understand the reasons for the problems of their early school years. Some attributed those problems to being in the wrong school, the wrong community, or to conflicts with their parents or between their parents. They externalized the sources of their problem; for them the sources of the difficulties lay outside of themselves. The emotional cost of the stigma they carried into adulthood is quite different from that of the children who were identified and labeled early. Some knew they were smart in spite of being called lazy or unmotivated. They silently held within them a conviction that given the opportunity, they would show the world what they could accomplish. Some turned to sports where they excelled; others turned to business where their good business sense led them to find success with their entrepreneurial skills; others turned to nonacademic pursuits such as the arts, music, or acting where their talents could find expression.

Those who were more introspective and who looked inward found only feelings of embarrassment or shame. They attributed their failures to flaws within themselves, although they remained at a loss as to the nature of those flaws. The confusion drained their self-confidence and produced a variety of personality traits to cover their sense of being flawed.

The diagnosis, however late, brings not only a sense of relief at having solved the puzzle of earlier failures but also its own set of anxieties. These anxieties are often related to the task of dealing with the bewilderment involved in integrating the newly discovered facts. Even when the diagnosis occurs in childhood, the task of integrating that knowledge into a view of one's sense of self as an adult is complex. People who suffer from physical handicaps at least have the option of directly pointing to their handicap as evidence for their disability. This does not mean that their task is any easier. However, those with learning disabilities cannot concretely point in any direction to justify their inability to perform. To say, "There is something wrong with my brain that does not allow me to spell correctly!" is to open oneself to ridicule.

Central to both groups is the feeling of shame engendered by the experiences to which the children are exposed. As Myrna Orenstein poignantly describes, the "chasm" that her subjects continually faced was the fear of being exposed, of unexpectedly encountering a situation in which their deficits would become evident to others. Orenstein's orientation as a self-psychologist leads her to be exquisitely attuned to these feelings in her subjects.

How then to integrate the handicap? When the diagnosis is made in adulthood, the integration is much more difficult than it is when made in childhood. Rewriting one's history after all those years to include the new knowledge entails making a fundamental change in one's sense of self and one's identity. It entails viewing the past very differently than it had previously been interpreted. It also entails facing the possibility that it is too late now to do anything about the disability. Perhaps the only thing that can change under those circumstances is the person's feelings about himself or herself. Dealing with the shame becomes central to the healing process.

This book provides examples of such struggles. It offers adults with academic histories of school failures the opportunity to seek testing to determine whether those failures were due to a learning disability. The discovery that such a disability did exist may then make it possible to begin healing the wounds caused by earlier experiences.

Joseph Palombo, MA
Founding Dean
Institute for Clinical Social Work (Chicago)

Acknowledgments

Publishing this book was like giving birth. Although it is my creation, many kept me moving during the lengthy creative process.

First Connie Goldberg and Joe Palombo's input was decisive and always thought provoking.

A special heartfelt thanks to my friends and colleagues who were kind enough to read my manuscripts when I was feeling stuck and in my own personal chasm: Kenan Heise, Lois Roewade, Ruth Rootberg, Susan Sholtes, Jeanne Hanson, and Janice Wiley. Furthermore, my children have always been a source of support.

I wish to thank my editors, Lynelle Morgenthaler and Cindy Pineo, who have the ability to turn complicated ideas into elegant, easy-to-read sentences. Special thanks to Cindy for her invaluable help with the revised edition. Thanks to Lorraine Anderson for her many talents and beautiful artwork, to Kevin Robnett for a tremendous Web site design, and to David Block for his great ideas, contagious enthusiasm, and sociological insights.

Thanks to editors Peg Marr and Karen Fisher of The Haworth Press for their intelligent, sensitive input, and to Andy Roy and Melissa Devendorf for their helpfulness and support. Thanks also to Sandy Sickels, Margaret Tatich, and Bill Palmer, who were instrumental in creating the revised edition. Their insight and vision helped this book live up to its potential.

Of course the participants in my research form the backbone of this book. Their ability to persevere in the face of many obstacles was the fuel that propelled the writing of their story. Much gratitude to Thomas Kenemore, Patrick Curtis, Amy Eldridge, and Dennis Shelby of the Institute for Clinical Social Work for encouraging and supporting my research.

Finally, heartfelt thanks to my analyst, mentor, and friend, Fred Levin, without whom this book would not have been written.

Introduction

Why Does Imprisoned Intelligence Happen?

My curiosity about the experience of living with learning gaps led me into a world I could not possibly have imagined. It began with a simple question. I asked adults who finally learned about their previously undetected learning disabilities, "What's it like to know *now* that you lived with an undiagnosed learning disability?" Almost everyone interviewed answered with one word: "Frustrating." This was the tip of the iceberg.

Exploring this frustration became an adventure. As the participants shared their experiences, they described "the chasm"—an impasse frustrating their desire to learn. They also described the exhilaration that comes from the ability to persist against seemingly impossible odds. This success, unfortunately, barely clothes a secret world of shame and exposure. My reverence, therefore, for the courage and dignity of these individuals increased with each interview.

The story of overcoming the chasm needs to be told. Here is a snippet from one interview.

Participant: They said it was a mild learning disability. I had trouble, they said, with certain decoding skills. I know the words, but, I make little errors, or I'll leave a word out occasionally, or I'll skip over words a lot of times. What I *know* I do is, I'll draw a conclusion without reading it.

Interviewer: How do you mean?

Participant: I'll read a bunch of stuff, and I'll say I want to read this, and this is what I think, where I think it's going to go, you know? I'll do that a lot and [laughs] sometimes I'm right, and sometimes I'm not, although I'm right better than half the time. They said had I chosen some other line of work, it would have been [laughs] nothing! I might not have even noticed. But even though I've always been promoted at work, I've had to do more and more reading and my frustration level got higher and higher.

It is so interesting that some very smart people:

- feel intrinsically flawed and are afraid of being "found out";
- can be successful, yet feel stupid inside; and
- can be considered goof-offs rather than underachievers.

This book is about people who struggle with frustrating learning gaps: people who are gifted in some areas but seemingly incompetent in others. It is about the absent-minded professor, the engineer who gets A's in math but fails English, or the gifted writer who cannot spell. It is about the paralegal who takes work home every night because she just cannot finish at the office, and the secretary who uses the dictionary a thousand times a day.

People such as this shared what it was like living with what they called the chasm. They describe the invisible nature of learning gaps and how this hidden problem constricts intelligence. They also share reasons why the chasm can create serious emotional distress if one's innate ability is either overlooked or misunderstood.

This book shows the courage of those who have been willing to admit what is missing in themselves. Their strength and perseverance resulted in finding fulfilling outlets for their potential.

The participants in the study found that they had learning disabilities. Other factors, of course, can also cause learning gaps. For example, some people unfortunately missed out when certain skills were taught in school. Others may have emotional problems that constrict their learning. *But no matter what the cause, if intelligent individuals are missing skills vital for achievement, they may end up being left out in the cold.* Clearly, life can be difficult for people who seem very bright in some areas of learning and curiously "out of it" in others. These areas of weakness can interfere with using, or even knowing, one's strengths and even oneself. What is not clear is how these discrepancies can imprison intelligence and constrict potential.

Many people struggle with this problem. One out of five children have learning disabilities. That is 20 percent of the population in this country who suffered or continue to suffer. The chances are, therefore, that there are individuals with frustrating learning gaps in most families. The problems differ from person to person, however. Here are some examples.

Musically, Mozart was incredibly gifted. In fact, according to historians he wrote music the way one eats ice cream. It was easy for him. Yet, as seen in the movie *Amadeus,* he could never figure out how to act around people and ended up alienating himself from everyone.

These discrepancies are quite common. A mechanic I knew, for example, could hardly read but he was gifted too. When a car broke down, he was the man of the hour. His ability to solve difficult mechanical problems was uncanny. And it was usually inexpensive. Obviously it would have been tragic if this mechanic ended up writing music or if Mozart's only option was to fix cars. Everyone needs to find a niche in life and many are not as lucky as Mozart and the mechanic. Each could use his intelligence without always tripping over his weaknesses.

For people with learning gaps, strengths can often be hidden by weaknesses. Teachers, bosses, or family may *not* be able to see their strengths because deficits get in the way. This problem of discrepancies (unless one is very lucky) is no trivial matter.

As a music major in high school and college, only the bare necessities in math and science were required of me. The geometry teacher, for example, called me the most inept student she had ever passed. Yet this was not a deterrent for me in a professional career as a singer, where no one cared about biology. In earning a PhD in social work, however, I discovered that "getting around" learning gaps was indeed challenging. A tutor, for example, was a necessity in order to deal with statistics.

To this day, my areas of weakness continue to be confounding. It is not only math. A persistent lack of a sense of direction causes difficulties. New environments are especially troublesome. Driving alone across the country is not even possible. If a crisis required reading a diagram or building a bicycle in five minutes (or even five hours), trouble would be afoot.

Think about the bright people in this country who are floundering in school. How many of us have heard: "How can someone as bright as you flunk this test?" or "You must not care," or "You're lazy."

To people who struggle with these problems, this book is not a hand-holder. The focus of this book involves (1) taking responsibility for one's strengths and weaknesses, and (2) recognizing and defending oneself when others inadvertently sabotage one's motivation.

Clearly, as the research in this book shows, undiagnosed learning disabilities (ULD) can cause Imprisoned Intelligence. Twenty people with ULD were interviewed. Each interview was detailed and focused in-depth on what it was like to grow up with this problem. Participants described how their uncomprehending teachers failed to notice their abilities. As the details unfolded, it became clear that their problems created a tapestry that wove together intelligence, creativity, ULD, and shame. This unfortunate combination created an environment of victimization for innocent people. I believe this same tapestry can describe others with learning gaps as well. It is tragic when one straddles high intelligence and serious weaknesses because destructive shame is often the result. How does this happen?

To answer this question, it is necessary to discuss shame. Shame can be helpful or toxic. Constructive shame facilitates learning. It stops people from making fools of themselves. Individuals can get the hint, pull back, and learn to behave more effectively. This is how everything from table manners to the best way to talk to the boss is learned. To learn, then, healthy doses of shame become a necessity.

However, like too much food, too much shame can stifle. Those who are subjected to shame too often, and without the opportunity for learning new information, feel enfeebled and even flawed. When there is too much shame, it is difficult to fix what is wrong because people simply withdraw. Too much shame, then, interferes with one's ability to be curious.

This sense of "flawedness" happens in smart people whose wish to learn is frustrated by invisible obstacles. However, the shame does not necessarily spring from the learning gap itself. Bright people can learn to compensate for, or get around, learning gaps in very, very effective ways. But if the obstacle is unrecognized or undiagnosed, then attempts to learn can be blocked. They do not know why, and so are ashamed.

Although those of us with learning disabilities often develop "compensations," the chances of finding effective compensations often decrease the more the problem is hidden. When people find themselves blocked over and over again by this invisible obstacle, they tend to accept blame and to perceive themselves as "stupid." Nothing else makes sense. Eventually one's self-esteem suffers, and then, it becomes difficult, indeed, to learn.

Our academic environment (teachers, parents, and peers) needs to see and accept how learning gaps can cause Imprisoned Intelligence. Then, with appropriate interventions, those properly diagnosed could have more fulfilled, dramatically enhanced lives. In short, Imprisoned Intelligence is a challenge that has and can be faced and surmounted.

This book will examine how growing up with Imprisoned Intelligence created difficulties and continues to cause problems for many individuals. It is divided into two main sections: Section I covers nine chapters and is written for the individual who struggles with Imprisoned Intelligence, his or her family, friends, supervisors, colleagues, and teachers; Section II shifts the focus and is for laypeople and clinicians alike. In order to give the reader a general overview of the book, a brief description of the individual chapters follows.

Chapter 1 will give an overview of how people with undiagnosed learning disabilities struggle and survive. Chapter 2 is an introduction to shame, an experience central to the psychological landscape of ULD sufferers. By providing some background on shame, the stories of the participants will make more sense.

Chapters 3 through 6 are the largest portion of this book. The painful problems of ULD are defined and described in depth. It is from these experiences, with their details, that an accumulated body of material can be built. When adults discover, deal with, and finally accept their learning disabilities, they walk a similar path that changes over time. It is a difficult path that begins with a bewildering sense that something is wrong and ends with reconciliation. If True Grit's (a study participant) parents, teachers, or psychologists had access to this information, his life would have been changed immeasurably!

Chapter 3 specifically highlights the chasm: the fundamental problem caused by ULD. The chasm is an experience in time. It involves excruciatingly shameful humiliation, exposure, and despair and occurs when people cannot live up to internal or external expectations. They then must struggle not only with ULD, but also with its emotional consequences. For example, a very bright boy may have poor motor coordination, and he may fail tests because he cannot write fast enough to finish them in the allotted time. He then suffers from both his own disappointment and ridicule from peers; the combination creates a huge emotional burden.

ULD itself does not cause Imprisoned Intelligence. *It is the emotional aftermath that hinders the flowering of potential.* Many people with ULD never know it and never need to know. They have created successful coping strategies. For example, a poor writer can live a fulfilling life as a truck driver, actor, or salesperson. A poor speller can use a spelling checker; however, a brilliant scientist who can answer complex questions but cannot write well will find that scholarly work is difficult (unless he or she has the money to hire a good editor). To repeat, emotional problems unfold when ULD prohibits us from meeting the demands of our world.

Chapter 4 describes how it feels to be tested. Chapter 5 discusses the painful aftereffects of learning about this problem. People grieve for what they now know they will never have.

Chapter 6 shows how people can and do triumph over this previously unrecognized learning problem. Although there is often not a lot a child can do to treat LD without help from caregivers, adults can take responsibility for nurturing themselves, and provide for their own needs. The participants in the study took action that allowed them to fulfill their potential. They showed a determination to free their intelligence in the face of frustration and despair. The book shows how they make peace with this old enemy.

Chapters 7 and 8 deal with possible solutions and explain how to help oneself and find assistance from others, while Chapter 9 highlights the necessity of academic institutions needing to face and deal with the emotional aspects of learning disabilities.

As stated earlier, Section II shifts focus. It is directed to the clinician and layperson alike. Chapter 10 explores the psychotherapeutic ramifications when working with individuals with undiagnosed learning disabilities. Chapter 11 provides an overview of the field of learning disabilities looking at the state of research and academic controversies, while Chapter 12 describes how self psychological theory provides concepts that enhance the understanding of imprisoned intelligence.

SECTION I:
WHAT EVERYONE NEEDS TO KNOW ABOUT LEARNING DISABILITIES AND IMPRISONED INTELLIGENCE

Chapter 1

Imprisoned Intelligence: How Does It Happen?

Work hard and you'll succeed.
If you don't succeed, try and try again.

Our culture assumes that success comes to those who are intelligent, motivated, and hardworking. However, for many, hard work is followed only by the frustration of the chasm.

This book is about such people. It's about Imprisoned Intelligence: adults restricted by frustrating learning gaps that can be due to undiagnosed learning disabilities (ULD). They, for the most part, are survivors who succeed despite this adversity.

They are uneven learners who accept and live in two contradictory worlds: (1) the world of success where learning is easy and fun, versus (2) the world of struggle and failure where learning is embarrassing, painful, and difficult. A girl, for example, with great verbal skills might be able to read like an adult but because of visual motor problems, may be unable to comfortably hold and manipulate a pencil. If so, she will be unable to transfer what she sees to the written page. The youngster, therefore, enters the chasm because she cannot learn to write. Her intelligence cannot be expressed in written assignments. The learning disability, in other words, interferes with and blocks her potential to achieve. These are the kinds of obstacles that create what I call Imprisoned Intelligence.

The words of the participants form the basis of this book. For the many individuals who struggle with ULD, the following stories will be an eye-opener.

TRUE GRIT

To help understand how learning disabilities have impact on real people, the reader might look to a participant in the study whom I have nicknamed "True Grit." His courage and determination in the face of overwhelming odds is a story repeated over and over by others.

True Grit, the first person interviewed, had vulnerabilities, brilliance, and a painful isolation that reflected the experiences of almost everyone in this study. He provoked an almost missionary zeal to right a serious wrong. His story needs to be told. In essence, that first interview launched this book.

When True Grit walked into the room, his charisma and commanding presence created an energy that was almost palpable. Few would ever suspect that he had learning disabilities. This articulate, good-looking, well-dressed twenty-five-year-old was successful, having started a small business that had quickly become a multinational enterprise. Clearly, he was making his way in society just fine. This had not been the case when he was in school. In fact, the differences between his current success and his school failure are startling.

In his early school years, loneliness and isolation were not yet a problem. True Grit was not aware of any differences between himself and his classmates. He felt himself to be part of the class even though he also knew that he made mistakes. At that time, he viewed them as simply a part of the learning process.

In fourth or fifth grade, his world changed dramatically. As a result of the testing that is given to all fourth graders in his state, True Grit was found to be a "poor reader" and was placed in a painfully boring "slower" reading group and was given "silly books with bigger print" to read. He hated it! Not only was he bored, but he felt separated from other intelligent students. He reports feeling demeaned and was ridiculed by both teachers and students.

> They just said, "We're going to help you improve your reading. You're going to be in reading group B, and that's it."
> They'd sit you in a big classroom, and the substitutes would be given the project to work on. . . . They'd sit at their desks, and

then reading group A would be in the back of the classroom. She'd rotate us, okay? Like inventory. . . . And, you know, this reading group B, which is the one I was in, was the worst and the lowest one. You were given silly books to read, bigger writing.

Because he felt patronized, demeaned, and ridiculed by both teachers and students, his performance continued to decline.

The teacher always treated the more intelligent students with more respect. Didn't patronize them. Didn't put them in the remedial reading group. Let them have more liberties to do what they wanted. And then while I was told to be in the remedial reading group, I was treated with what I thought was contempt, not only by the teachers, but by my peers. And I wasn't given the same privileges as everybody else was.

His performance continued to decline but he was "just promoted along" from grade to grade in deference to his well-educated, well-respected family. Grit recalls, "I just knew that school was harder for me than them [other students]."

He also felt invisible sometimes. For example, in his parochial school, True Grit was consistently passed over as a reader in chapel:

It's a big thing to be appointed to be a reader in charge, you know? Because we had school Masses. The best readers would be asked to read from the Bible or something like that. I did that once for ten seconds, and that was the end of it.

Furthermore, his motivation was consistently challenged. Teachers and principals would criticize him for not working hard enough even though he always completed his homework. Since he knew he was doing his best, his anger and frustration level was enormous.

She (my mother) helped with my algebra. The homework was done all the time, on time. Everything. I handed every assignment in. I think I missed two assignments or stuff like that, which I lost . . . and I still flunked . . . every assignment. I still got Ds and Fs and still flunked. She helped with spelling. And I memorized the entire list of spelling, and I'd still flunk.

True Grit's biggest problem was not his undiagnosed learning disabilities per se. Rather, the problem lay in the fact that no one saw them. Except for his mother (who valiantly did the best she could), no one was there to help him. This oversight created an experience of aloneness, and struggling with this alienation was extremely difficult. "Nobody had any idea of what I was going through. I was completely and totally on my own."

True Grit felt himself at the mercy of his peers when he could not live up to class expectations, particularly when tests were being passed back to the students.

> The test would be passed out around the room. You know, they'd say, "Take your test and pass it along." Okay? Well, everyone would know my grade, you know? I'd be sitting in the back of the room somewhere. . . . There would be comments made. . . . "That was the easiest test on the face of the earth. How come he couldn't do that?"

True Grit's home life was also rapidly deteriorating as a result of his school performance. He was the fourth of five children born into a family with a strong tradition of medical careers. He was expected to become a doctor. True Grit's siblings were extremely high achievers and were outstanding students in school. For example, one brother was a straight-A student and was considered a genius. His siblings began to tease him mercilessly. To make matters worse, his father felt that being tough would improve the situation. He received countless lectures.

> They were always telling me to work harder. That I was going to be a garbageman. I'd never be promoted. Grades and everything were always very important in our house. I constantly got Cs, Ds, and Fs. And every time report card time came, it was very traumatic at our house. I mean, anytime I got my report card, there was always hell to pay.

His father would bring the subject up at dinnertime in front of the rest of the family, pointing to True Grit as a model of failure and his brother as a model of success.

Although this heavy-handed treatment was difficult to swallow, the covert denigration was even worse. His siblings would repeat cruel remarks his father made about him (or he would overhear them himself), compounding his feelings of alienation, worthlessness, and shame. "I was stupid. And that was all there was to it. Very low self-esteem."

True Grit's parents sent him to several psychologists in hopes of curing his problems. But since learning disabilities were not common knowledge at that time, the psychologists attributed his problems to lack of intelligence or motivation:

> My parents decided, "We don't know what's wrong with this kid. It's time to send him to a psychologist." And that was when I hit sixth grade. I saw at least about four different kinds of learning experts—psychologists or something like that. And so I went to all these psychologists. And they couldn't find anything. They just thought I was beneath average intelligence. That's all there was to it. "The kid's a moron. Live with it." That's about all it boiled down to.

In the meantime, his father's fuse was becoming shorter and shorter, and True Grit was starting to withdraw from his family:

> I lived in a lot of fear. I separated myself from my family. I was completely autonomous. When we went on vacation, like at skiing and waterskiing, where you start very young, I would always do it on my own. I was completely separate. I would have to go outside of my family for support of things because I realized . . . I'm just totally different from everybody else, in terms of the ways I talked, my interests, everything. I was like the fifth wheel in this family.

In seventh or eighth grade, True Grit just gave up. Tired of being battered by constant accusations of not trying, yet trying his hardest and failing, he no longer had the strength to continue caring about academic success. The incongruity between his inner reality and others' perceptions was both discouraging and angering. Suffering from destructive, chronic shame, True Grit reasoned that if everyone wanted him to be dumb he would indeed act that way:

> I did not think highly of myself. I thought I was dumb. I just started agreeing with everybody else. I rolled over and died. That was it.

His life began to change in high school. For one thing, he began to realize that he had artistic talent. Since his family did not see art as a moneymaking venture, they did not respect it. He learned, however, that he had an eye for design and strong three-dimensional skills. As a sophomore, he began to visit art museums and to watch public television. "It was like a heaven in the middle of a hell."

He also taught himself to play several instruments. His family derided these behaviors as snobbish and foolish. When others outside his family discovered his activities, they were surprised that a "dummy" would be doing these kinds of things. This earned him a certain grudging respect.

Also during this time, True Grit experimented with his design talent in the landscaping business. During the summers, in his basement, he created his own landscape contracting business. He served as a wholesaler of landscaping supplies, installing and designing the jobs himself. He worked with real estate developers who would sell the building and his landscaping job together.

True Grit was able to go to college—if only to a small, mediocre liberal arts college. At college, however, he reached an important turning point. A thoughtful English teacher noticed that this bright student was flunking her class. She referred him to the director of education, who administered some intelligence tests. These tests showed that he was of above-average intelligence. However, the tests were not sophisticated enough to tell much else. They shed little light on what his real difficulties were because they could not isolate his specific learning problems; that is, they could not explain why his performance was so poor. The director told him that he had some sort of learning disability, which she was incapable of diagnosing. However, she offered to serve as a personal tutor and did so for the two years of his education there.

Although True Grit was struggling for his grades, he was also bored. Paradoxically, the institution in which he was failing was just not challenging enough for him! Recognizing this, the director lobbied on his behalf for acceptance into a more prestigious institution nearby.

Counselors at his new school encouraged him to get tested at the Center for Reading and Learning. However, he resisted during his first year at the new school until he realized that he was in danger of flunking out. Sometime in his junior year of college, True Grit finally went for testing. He discovered that he had dyslexia—not severe, but enough to hamper his learning.

After testing, he failed to deal with his dyslexia. He majored in finance and then continued to make poor choices. Upon graduating, he took a job as a clerk that involved adding up numbers with a calculator. Although this would be child's play for most finance majors, for a dyslexic who reversed numbers as he keyed them into the calculator it was a disaster. True Grit was fired. At the time, he was still living with his parents, who responded with deep disappointment.

In this instance, shame served a positive function: It "reset" True Grit. It showed him that his current approach was not working and afforded him an opportunity to rethink his strategy.

> I was afraid that this was going to like completely destroy any future hopes of me getting a job . . . and it did for about two weeks. But I got back up on the horse and went out and, you know, pursued my own business.

Remembering his high school landscaping success, True Grit decided to create his own display company. He approached hotels and restaurants and began to sell, design, and install holiday displays. Soon he landed an account with a large, successful restaurant chain. Building on this success, he began importing his supplies directly from Asia, where display items are typically manufactured.

Over time, True Grit developed savvy work habits that compensated for his learning disability. He now relies on his computer and spelling checker for any correspondence and always rewrites each letter several times. To avoid any embarrassment because of his atrocious spelling, True Grit carries an electronic pocket spelling checker. In his own words:

> It [the learning disability] is part of me, and I accept it as part of me. It's a problem I've got to deal with in the business world. . . . I cannot be a financial consultant. I cannot be an accountant. I cannot be any of those things. It has to be all qualitative. And if it involves quantitative support, it's got to be done on the computer. But I've got to be sure my entire career is not based on a financial background.

Unable to live up to school standards, True Grit found the outside world's standards more to his liking. His success became a source of pride. "This is no longer school, school is way in the background now [and] no one even cares about that." In fact, True Grit pinpoints his watershed experience—the point at which his talents were able to take off—as the time when he was finally able to "become detached from the standard."

Furthermore, as True Grit began to comprehend and reconcile his life with his dyslexia, he not only forgave himself but he also began to forgive his family. In looking back over his life True Grit is very grateful to his mother. She never lost hope. Although she had no idea he was learning disabled, she encouraged his intellect and perseverance. "My mom . . . knows that I wasn't lazy." His relationship with his dad began to heal over time; his family has been forced to recognize his success.

True Grit now realizes that Imprisoned Intelligence is not just failure to make the grade. *The by-product of these failures is alienation and loneliness, and it is these emotions that lead to Imprisoned Intelligence.* To free Imprisoned Intelligence, he says that one must confront the inevitable aloneness and alienation that can go hand in glove with ULD:

> First of all, you've got to identify it. I think that's the important thing. Aloneness is when you're not getting support for what you want. You've got to identify the aloneness to see if you're not getting it [support] from your core group of people, which is usually your family. Okay? And if you're not being supported, then you recognized that aloneness. You're alone.

Only then, after one has struggled and identified this problem of aloneness, can one consider alternatives:

> Once you've identified it, then you've got to act on it. . . . I mean no one's an island in this life. You've got to go get it from somebody else because if you don't have support, or you're completely alone, you've got to have encouragement for when those rough times come around. Because when life got rough for me . . . I had to go to turn to some of my friends and stuff like that.

To free intelligence, True Grit has these words of advice to offer parents of a learning-disabled child: "Pay attention to the things that are influencing him [or her] positively. [For example,] if the child is an artist, make sure attention is given to those strengths."

This is how True Grit achieved his own victory. He incorporated his artistic talents and people skills in the context of business. By capitalizing on his strengths, he conquered his shame about his ULD and was able to accomplish great things. His family began to express their pride in his success and to respect his abilities. Now, he has a solid sense of self-worth. He knows he is valuable. He found his place in the sun by incorporating his artistic talents and skills in a meaningful business pursuit.

WHAT SORT OF PEOPLE HAVE UNDIAGNOSED LEARNING DISABILITIES?

Throughout history, many successful people have had LD. Since testing for LD is a relatively modern phenomenon, there is no proof that the individuals discussed below had or have ULD, but the evidence strongly suggests it.

When Thomas A. Edison was diagnosed as "mentally ill" by his teacher, his angry mother withdrew him from the school and taught him at home. In his later recollections, he said that he found it impossible to learn English and arithmetic by rote. He found it necessary to "do things" or "make things" in order to learn. His interest in reading was piqued only when his mother began reading books aloud to him. His early writings display a marked difficulty with written language. And yet Edison was the brilliant mind who brought us the lightbulb, the phonograph, the motion picture camera, the ticker tape, and many other inventions.

Auguste Rodin, the famous French sculptor, had similar difficulties with reading, spelling, and arithmetic. Despite early indications of a gift for drawing, Rodin's father forbid further exploration of this talent, insisting that his son learn reading and writing to secure a better future. His father was disappointed when Auguste was expelled from two schools because he was "ineducable." Although his failure was ascribed to "poor eyesight," his later production makes this an unlikely explanation. Dyslexia historically has often been ascribed to eyesight problems.

When considering the great intellects of the modern age, Albert Einstein's name will surely come to mind. Yet he was considered slow as a boy. While excelling in mathematics and physics, he experienced great difficulty with language. He failed his first attempt at college entrance examinations, yet he formulated the theory of relativity in his mid-twenties.

Cher, a successful recording artist and actress, became aware of her LD only when her daughter, Chastity, underwent similar experiences. Throughout Cher's own schooling, teachers would remark that she seemed to have the ability, but failed to apply herself. Since she was working as hard as she could, her teachers were likely observing not a lack of effort, but the discrepancy between potential and achievement that characterizes LD. Despite her difficulty in reading and writing, Cher reports that she can often memorize a script in a single reading.

Failure in the classroom (dyslexia) pushed Olympic gold medal winner Bruce Jenner into the sports arena. There, he found he could earn a pat on the back for his hard work, instead of frustration. Eventually he was able to bring the confidence he gained in sports back into the classroom so that he could achieve there as well.

The list of successful individuals who have struggled with undiagnosed LD is enormous. I mention these examples here only to demonstrate that an intelligent mind can be imprisoned by LD; it is the individual's tenacity and inventiveness that allow him or her to exceed the expectations of others and to excel.

Once a problem is identified, solutions are always possible. A *Time* magazine article noted that Ennis Cosby, the son of entertainer Bill Cosby, grew up with an undiagnosed dyslexia. As a result of his experiences, he was working toward a graduate degree in education and helping LD students. Tragically, he was murdered before he could contribute his gifts fully. About his learning disorder, he made the following comments: "The happiest day in my life occurred when I found out I was dyslexic. . . . I believe that life is finding solutions, and the worst feeling to me is confusion" (Chuaeoan, 1997, p. 25).

UNDERSTANDING
UNDIAGNOSED LEARNING DISABILITIES

Research for this book involved finding others like Ennis Cosby: people who did not find out that they had a learning disability until adulthood. The research clearly indicates that (1) ULD constricts potential and causes Imprisoned Intelligence, and (2) creative alternatives are possible.

One serious problem, however, involves how learning disabilities are defined. Many people have a vague notion that "having a learning disability" means "having a learning problem." Perhaps the term "stupid" even comes to mind. Most people, if asked whether a person with a learning disability could have above-average intelligence, would probably answer "no."[*] This is just one of the many misunderstandings. Even if a person is deficient in certain areas, she or he may be brilliant in others. A bright, creative, literate person, for example, may have a terrible problem with math or vice versa.

To understand the emotional problems caused by undiagnosed learning disabilities (ULD), some short introductory definitions are in order. (More precise academic definitions of learning disabilities are located in Chapter 11.) According to a February 13, 1996, *New York Times* article, "learning disabilities are the unexpected failure to learn, despite adequate intelligence, motivation, and instruction; reading disorders like dyslexia are the most common" (Lewin, 1996, p. 1).

Learning disabilities, then, are disorders that, in contrast to an individual's intelligence, *interfere* with his or her ability (in one or more areas) to listen, look, think, speak, read, write, spell, or do mathematical calculations that could otherwise be done very well. Learning disabilities can disrupt normal academic or social functioning. They are presumed to result from a hardwired problem in one's brain.

An undiagnosed learning disability—the focus of this book—is one that is invisible or overlooked. It is covert. One complexity is

---

[*]There is also a literature dealing with the population of individuals with learning disabilities whose achievements range from average to low functioning. This is not the population I am describing. My work focuses upon adults with learning disabilities who possess *at least* average intelligence, and in many cases, above-average or high levels of intelligence.

this problem: How can learning disabilities remain invisible when they clearly disrupt functioning and achievement in school? Testing for learning disabilities is a relatively new procedure. (The term *learning disabilities* was not even coined until 1962.) For many individuals who discovered their learning disabilities as adults, testing was not available to them in the 1960s. Although they had the same learning disabilities as children, they did not have the benefit of testing and identification of their difficulties. From their point of view, they simply felt frustrated because they knew that their performance did not live up to their potential. They may have been average students, but they were not average thinkers. Take, for example, a student who has an outstanding grasp of mathematical concepts, but is dyslexic and cannot read or reproduce numbers accurately. Unless the disability is known, the dyslexia can prevent this person from excelling in advanced math classes.

You might ask at this juncture, "How do I know if I have ULD? What does it feel like?" It is difficult to describe the frustrating experience of wanting to learn and not being able to do so because some unknown "something" gets in the way. Interviews with adults suggest that an undiagnosed learning disability is experienced as the wish and belief to succeed without the ability to do so (an assumption and inner expectation that academic problems can be mastered). It is perceived as a permanent invisible vacuum in one's brain that creates mysterious impasses that prevent learning. Here is how some of the participants in this study defined ULD:

- Learning disabilities mean taking longer to learn.
- I can receive information but I can't put it out.

Why is ULD so difficult to identify when one is an intelligent adult? Complicating identification is the fact that bright people often learn to compensate for their deficits; however, since the problem is unidentified, they must do this, more or less, alone. They usually creatively learn to get around the problem. One person in this study who could not read well asked great questions in class because somehow she knew she had to learn by listening. She was always considered an outstanding student, and this way of acquiring knowledge worked beautifully throughout high school. In college, however, she was sunk.

Professors were not interested in her questions because there was too much material to cover.

The core of the problem is not the learning disability itself. It is the lack of diagnosis and clarification. Once a problem is identified, solutions become possible. By definition, ULD is invisible or overlooked. Because it is not identified, it is misunderstood, and the individual does not realize that help exists. The problem and the pain are magnified by impossible expectations from the world and from oneself.

INFORMATION ABOUT THE RESEARCH

All information about Imprisoned Intelligence was acquired from interviews. Being a member of the very large tribe of those who have learning disabilities was advantageous in the interviewing process. The knowledge that I was "one of us" seemed to allow the participants to feel more comfortable sharing their experiences. Because there are so many different types of learning disabilities, an objective stance could also be retained so that curiosity about the participants' own subjective experiences could unfold. My clinical training allowed me to keep the focus on experiences.

What criteria were used in selecting participants? Individuals had to be over seventeen years old before they received their learning disability diagnosis. They were self-referred, learning about my study through word of mouth or through a request that was placed in learning disability departments at local colleges.

A total of twenty participants from the ages of nineteen to sixty-one were involved in this study. A random sampling technique was not used. One was Hispanic. The others were Caucasian. There were six men and fourteen women. Their socioeconomic status ranged from poor to wealthy. Most lived in the Chicago area. Two lived outside of Chicago, one in Boston, and another in a small town in South Carolina. Twelve were in college at the time of the study, although not all for the first time. Their occupations are or were as follows: college student, social worker, artist, college professor, massage therapist, certified public accountant, meter collector/actor, contractor, secretary, and full-time mother.

Participants were recruited for this study in a variety of ways. Several students attended local universities or a community college in the Chicago area. A call for participants was placed in the boxes of all students who were working with counselors in the learning disability departments. Many were referred by other participants.

The initial interviews took place on the phone, when information was elicited to determine the participant's eligibility. Prospective participants were given the opportunity to ask questions regarding the interviewer's qualifications, educational background, and so on. Almost everyone indicated initial enthusiasm for the project.

The face-to-face interviews were usually held either in a private room in a local college or in the privacy of the participant's or researcher's home. Two exceptions were the interview in Boston, which took place in the home of a mutual friend, and the interview with the participant living in South Carolina, which was done by telephone.

Initial interviews ranged from one and one-half to three hours. As the information became redundant, however, subsequent interviews were limited to one and one-half hours. (Member checking was done by phone. Member checking is a procedure in which the researcher shares the data and findings, which are then corroborated by the participants.) These follow-up sessions took from forty-five minutes to an hour. Most face-to-face interviews were taped. Notes were substituted for the few people who were uncomfortable with being recorded. Notes were also used during member checking.

A release of information was signed by both participant and researcher. Each kept a copy. This release was in both a short and long form to help those participants who did not read well to understand its essential nature. Also, I used code names for my own identification purposes. In this way no real names were attached to the notes, thereby ensuring confidentiality.

SOME REFLECTIONS

The story of True Grit in this chapter reflects the experiences of almost everyone in this study who experienced similar contradictions in their lives. They have suffered the painful alienation and isolation that often accompanies ULD, but they also have achieved a high degree of success in their areas of strength. These discrepancies were eventually managed by learning to recognize and deal with learning gaps. Why is this important? The following are three possible reasons.

First of all, a learning gap, one that has not been understood, can interfere with the growth of potential. Picture, for example, a would-be mechanic who reads very slowly but has always been able to "get by" through high school. His love for cars and his intrinsic understanding of the inner workings of automobiles would make him a master mechanic. However, he may never achieve this goal. Because he reads slowly he may fail, as he may not have the time to understand the manuals and therefore cannot pass necessary exams. With such a problem, his first attempts in school to pass preliminary classes might end in failure. He may never get hands-on practice because either he or his teachers will quickly become discouraged.

Second, undiagnosed learning disabilities can stifle an individual's ability to compensate for overlooked handicaps. Since ULD has never been recognized, teachers or parents cannot understand the problem and then help the child figure out ways around it. The child, for example, who simply needed more time to write but had no advocates because no one knew or understood, is simply left to fend for himself.

Third, ULD can stunt the growth and enhancement of self. Without adequate self-esteem, it is difficult to stay motivated. How does this happen? When bright students have trouble learning and cannot understand why, they tend to blame themselves. Parents and educators often attribute a learning problem to lack of effort; so they may blame the student as well. Learning becomes much more difficult because excessive blame assaults one's motivation. When this cycle of blame is repeated many times, the consequences are traumatic, long-lasting, and far-reaching.

Chapter 2

A Brief Introduction to Shame

There are some people in the world one instantaneously likes. Sparkly, a college student who comes from a brilliant family, is one of them. She instantly radiates warmth and intelligence. She has such a pleasant countenance that I was not prepared for her pain.

Sparkly: You know, even now, knowing what I know, I still get so embarrassed when my learning disabilities stick out like a sore thumb. It's really terrible. I feel really embarrassed when I make a mistake reading . . . like over Christmas. You see, I was playing charades with my family. When it was my turn, I read my instructions, but I read them wrong. I read *the whole thing wrong!* So, I acted out this whole thing, and they guessed the title. But of course, the title was *not* what was written on the slip of paper I drew. They said: "This isn't it." . . . And I was so embarrassed. I made this joke, and everybody laughed, and my sister won. And I sat down, and I thought, "I wish I wouldn't have done that," you know, because I thought, "This is my family. They don't care if I can't read." I was still . . . I was overwhelmed with embarrassment. "How did I read that wrong? Why did I read that wrong?" It was very strong.

I was humiliated. And it was so . . . I mean, the perfect stage setting. There I am, standing up there by myself, doing all this crazy stuff. They guess it. (What she read but *not* what was written.) I'm standing there, and there's silence in my . . . then my cousin goes, "That's not the title. You read it wrong!" And my finale was the big joke, and then, oh, my gosh! It was awful. It was unbelievable. [silence] But that's how that went.

Sparkly's experience of shame was shared by everyone in this study. People describe the feeling of being shackled by inexplicable learning failures and how they persevered and eventually freed themselves. But, to help the reader understand the particular variety of suffering that Sparkly describes, there will be an introduction, definition, and description of something well known but which is avoided like the plague. This is shame.

Psychological literature has focused on the feelings of shame that begin in infancy and continue throughout the lifespan. This field is relatively new and has led to an explanation of human emotions called "affect theory."

Affects are innate biological responses that all humans—even six-week-old infants—have toward their environment. As people grow, their original affects evolve into complicated adult emotions. One pioneering psychologist, Michael Basch, differentiates among affects, feelings, and emotions. He says that affects experienced in infancy evolve into feelings in childhood and then into complex emotions in adults. Affects, then, are building blocks for an entire range of human emotional complexities. The phenomenon can be compared to a giant sixty-four-crayon box of Crayolas. There are only eight basic colors: red, orange, yellow, and so on. Most of the sixty-four are fancy colors, such as tangerine and raw umber, aubergine, and periwinkle. The fancy colors are simply mixtures of the original basic colors. Affects are our basic emotional colors.

Fundamental affects are never outgrown. Adults often have the same emotions as children. For example, an adult can get as excited by learning to drive, fly, or ski as a child who has taken her first steps. To understand how shame fits in, and how it can constrict learning, knowledge about affect theory will be helpful.

Psychologist Sylvan Tomkins videotaped children and infants to examine their feeling states and reactions to the world. By slowing down and observing the tapes, he discovered that every infant is born with nine instinctive "knee jerk" affects. What are these affects? Why are they important? Affect theory maintains that these "primitive" affects are, at bottom, what motivate all of us. These affects can be divided into three categories: (1) positive affects; (2) negative affects; and (3) other, or "auxiliary" affects.

The positive affects are:

1. interest that can increase to excitement;
2. enjoyment that can increase to joy; and
3. surprise that can increase to startle.

The negative affects are:

4. distress that can increase to anguish;
5. anger that can increase to rage; and
6. fear that can increase to terror.

The auxiliary affects are reactions to environmental stimuli:

7. *dissmell* (our tendency to withdraw from noxious odors);
8. *distaste* (our tendency to withdraw from unpleasant food); and
9. *shame* that can increase to *humiliation.*

The intensity of the experience will determine the power of the experience. It is similar to listening to music. If the volume is very low, we do not pay attention. If the volume is very high, it becomes painful. These are the nine basic building blocks of emotion. For an infant, this list fully describes the affective states. As children grow, they learn to think more complex thoughts, and these thoughts become integrated into the primary emotions. However, basic affects never lose their function. Obviously, adults still become startled, feel pleasure, and recoil from spoiled food. Adults and children may startle at different things, but the emotional reactions are built from the same elements.

This is particularly true of shame. Over a lifetime, shame feels pretty much the same, though as we age, we generally learn better ways to avoid it. The outward appearance of shame is lowered head and eyes and sometimes a blushing face. Inside, a person experiences intense exposure and heightened vulnerability. An individual feels cut off from other human beings and would like to "crawl into a hole."

People with ULD know all about shame. They never know when it will crop up, since it is a response to life's demands. For example, one participant who has a master's degree reads very, very slowly. She describes her exquisite embarrassment every time she eats out because she simply does not have enough time to scan the menu. When the waiter is hovering after everyone else has ordered, she experiences deep humiliation. Her way of compensating, if the restaurant is new, is simply to order the first thing she sees on the menu. If it is a familiar restaurant, she memorizes everything on the menu.

Why is shame needed? Shame is painful. To the human organism, however, pain is an important message. It prompts one to understand that something is wrong or that reacting differently to the environment is required. "The constructive intent of shame," psychologist Carl Goldberg has said, "is the realization that one does *not* know, and that which one does not know is knowable and *should* be known" (1991, p. 159).

Shame can propel learning. It can also inhibit learning. Thus, there are two types of shame: constructive and destructive. Constructive shame can help by cueing or alerting one to possible humiliating pitfalls, which can then be avoided. It is a protective device that keeps people out of trouble; it signals that something is not working, that individuals should stop and try something new.

Shame keeps people on the right track, both culturally and as individuals. Without shame, social systems would falter because the specter of shame impels their members to follow cultural rules. On the individual level, healthy shame prompts withdrawal from a potentially hurtful situation by shutting down interest. In the case of personal relationships, it alerts people to rejection—perhaps someone did not move to shake an extended hand. In this case, shame propels the withdrawal of one's hand.

Shame can also occur within oneself, without anybody else around. For example, a woman may wish to have an affair with her best friend's husband. As she experiences shame over her forbidden wishes (as opposed to her guilt over how she would hurt her friend), she stops and "resets" her desires.

Healthy shame serves another critical function: it helps people reconnect with others. When an individual is ashamed, he or she pulls back and thinks about things. Then the person reaches out and tries again. The best example of this is pulling back, reflecting, and reaching out again to say, "I'm sorry." The outward expression of this disconnect/reconnection signals others that a friend or co-worker may need help.

So, healthy shame helps us know where we go wrong and when to stop and rethink. But not all shame helps a person grow. Consider the following quote by Leon Wurmser: "Shame is the degradation that has already occurred and the enduring sense of self-contempt and unreality that ensues from such humiliation and mortification" (Wurmser, 1987, p. 67).

Destructive shame is a pattern of self-denigration. It is the outcome of this feeling experienced too intensely and too often. It occurs when healthy shame fails to do its job. When a person gets in an awkward situation and feels ashamed, yet cannot solve the problem, the shame repeats itself again and again and plunges him or her further and further into a hole.

If shame becomes too repetitive, a chronic sense of shame develops. A child who is continually shamed eventually gives up hope of reconnection. Then the child begins to attach the sense of shame not to the action or situation that triggered it, but to the self.

Shame plays a large role in children growing up with undiagnosed learning disabilities. A student will become interested in a subject and tackle it. Suddenly, the rug is pulled out from under the child when the undiagnosed learning disability hinders performance. For example, a promising elementary math student may falter on multiplication tables, when memory skills become paramount. She experiences a common shame trigger: failure. She tries and fails, over and over, and soon she develops chronic shame. Another example: an adult who is a good but slow reader begins to avoid reading to curb further feelings of shame because reading "takes too long." When help is offered, the individual may avoid it because he is still too busy fleeing additional failure/shame experiences.

Destructive shame leads to withdrawal. A person expects that a particular task will shame her. She fears even to try. She will go to great lengths to avoid whatever might lead to failure and more shame. Destructive shame, then, stifles initiative and undermines potential. This cripples intellectual pursuits.

For example, individuals who love to write, and put beautiful thoughts on paper, may lose that love after hearing too many sarcastic comments about their grammar and spelling. People with ULD learn to curtail their interests. Their intelligence takes a beating because, although they are obviously bright, they never seem to do quite well enough. When expectations are consistently dashed, shame is close behind.

Shame can also sabotage motivation. Our culture believes that hard work and adequate intelligence are a foolproof recipe for success. Individuals with ULD become confused because hard work pays off in their areas of strength. Yet, in other areas, they work and work and still fail. Their lack of achievement baffles them and those around them (Baum, Renzulli, and Herbert, 1994). Parents, teachers, and perhaps even bosses will question their motivation and accuse them of slacking. Often, people take the criticism to heart, and actually begin to consider themselves lazy. Of course, they can be hard-working and resourceful and still not able to overcome a learning disorder by force of will. This is yet another source of destructive shame.

Intellectual curiosity can also be compromised. ULD can create destructive shame by destroying one's ability to become excited about even those things that are done best. As stated previously, one of the primary affects is excitement. Like shame, excitement is crucial to development because it propels learning. Children with ULD can lose some of their ability to become excited because their victories are hollow. For instance, a child with ULD can write an excellent paper, and even get a good grade, but nevertheless find herself berated by a teacher for "sloppy" spelling mistakes that would be easily avoided if she would just "be careful" or "put in the time." Ordinarily, the student would become excited about a high grade and become even more motivated to do the work. With ULD, achievement fails to become a motivating experience because initial excitement is cut off by simultaneous unexplained failure.

Thus, children with learning disabilities develop a chronic, destructive sense of shame as they perceive their growing lack of competence. The shame itself hinders learning. They find themselves in a vicious cycle; failure leads to shame, which leads to further failure, and so on.

This book will make use of affect theory and its explanation of shame to shed light on the experiences and motivation of individuals with ULD. A discussion of shame will be interwoven with descriptions of their experiences.

Chapter 3

Something Is Wrong with Me:
A Chasm in Learning

Sparkly: Well, by the time that I found out that I had a learning disability, I was nineteen. When I was in grade school I knew there was something wrong when I read as opposed to the teacher speaking. I could understand when he or she spoke, but when I read, it was impossible. There was no mention of anything—not learning disabilities, dyslexia, nothing. I hadn't even heard of it, but I knew that I wasn't stupid. So I knew there was something that was getting in my way. At those moments when I was really frustrated, I would blame it on stupidity. And when I would rationally think about it, I knew that there was something. I didn't know what it was, but there was something that was just standing in my way, and that I wasn't stupid.

Interviewer: But that was always the struggle for you.

Sparkly: Right.

When people are faced with a gap in their intelligence that they cannot explain, they are left with the uneasy feeling that "something is wrong with me." Despite wanting to learn and believing that they can learn, actual achievement hovers out of reach. Something indefinable is missing.

I experienced that something was shamefully wrong with me. I experienced myself internally as being unusually bright, unusually capable, perceptive beyond how my peers seemed to be. But, in the concrete experience of what was happening in school, I couldn't learn the way they did.

This chapter (and my research) focuses on this frustration. It describes how people with ULD experienced a painful failure to learn, how they struggled, and how they continue to struggle to reconcile a belief in their own intelligence with their lack of success.

Bright people have high expectations for themselves and enjoy acquiring knowledge. Just as they begin to feel excited about learning something new, however, they may experience an unexpected obstacle—the undiagnosed learning disability. The result is an inexplicable failure. Since their learning disabilities are undiagnosed, they can find no reason for their lack of achievement and consequent shame. Lacking a logical explanation, they end up blaming themselves and questioning their own motivations.

The individual with ULD experiences learning failure over and over, first as a child, then as an adolescent and an adult. This quickly begins to take on a pattern with several repeating elements. Of course, no two individuals experience this in quite the same way, but the participants in the study had certain emotional experiences in common, which tended to occur in a particular order.

The diagram below summarizes the pattern of feelings that accompany a learning failure.

bewilderment → the chasm → struggle → resignation

These domains[*] of experience are laid out like a musical composition—*bewilderment* is the prelude; *the chasm* is the central theme; *struggle* and *resignation* are the postlude—all set to the overwhelming counterpoint of the repeated refrain, "What's wrong with me?"

The first domain, bewilderment, emerges when academic expectations cannot be met for reasons unknown, and confusion sets in. (Unlike the other domains, bewilderment does not reoccur later.) This is the individual's introduction to shame. Next, the chasm occurs when unpreventable and recurrent failures in school cause an individual to experience hopeless exposure and isolation.

---

[*]Daniel M. Stern (1985) employs the term "domain" to describe infant development of self in *The Interpersonal World of the Infant.*

As discussed in Chapter 2, constructive shame stops us from making fools of ourselves. We get the hint, pull back, and learn to interact with the world in a different way. Although everyone needs a healthy dose of embarrassment, too much of it can lead to a chronic condition, an attachment of shame *to the self* rather than *to the situation* that leads to failure. Since intelligence fosters interest in learning and ULD causes mysterious failure at it, this combination is a natural setup for self-destruction. In this domain, chronic shame has begun to take hold.

Third, struggle develops as individuals attempt to solve their learning problems with coping strategies or diversions of their own device. Sometimes these interventions are successful, but since they lack knowledge of the true cause of the problem (the learning disability) often the interventions are not. Resignation sets in as an uneasy acceptance of these unnamed problems is adopted as a long-term viewpoint. Here, shame becomes firmly attached to the self.

BEWILDERMENT

All my life, I knew something was wrong, but I never knew what it was.

Bewilderment occurs in a state of innocence and reflects the initial confusion that results from faltering performance. An individual who succeeds in some areas or some of the time will suddenly fail. Specifically, bewilderment results when people experience a radical departure from the expectations they build based on their perceptions of their own intelligence. Thus, failures occurring in specific subject matters or tasks are all the more poignant because they are set against the backdrop of sporadic success:

- I could understand when, you know, she spoke; but when I read, it was impossible.
- I know I'm smart, and everyone tells me I'm smart, so this doesn't make sense.
- They figured that since I was brilliant in math, I should be able to apply myself and do well enough in English.

A person experiences bewilderment when academic requirements become impossible to meet. Concepts or tasks that seem easy to others are beyond his or her grasp. Despite pedagogical advice or attention, there seem to be no intervening steps—no learning "tricks"—which can solve the problem. The individual seems unable to learn *how to learn* in this area. As a result, simple problems become confounding and embarrassing, leading to feelings of internal confusion, chaos, and shame:

- I'll never forget my father trying to teach me, when we had math problems in school, how come minus and plus become even. Both of us couldn't figure out why I couldn't get that.
- When it comes to math, I've always felt out of it—you know, out to lunch.
- I just can't concentrate.
- It's not clicking.
- Nothing makes sense.
- It's like having the information on the tip of my tongue, but not being able to write it down.
- There were these mysteries about how people learned. If the teacher says, "Go home and memorize the multiplication tables" and there's nobody to tell—how in the world are you supposed—what does that mean to *memorize* something?

Bewilderment is (primarily) a reaction to intellectual disparities. It is impossible for an individual with an undiagnosed learning disability to understand how his or her intelligence can work so effectively at times and yet seem to stop working altogether at other times. The assumption underlying the traditional educational system holds that an intelligent person can achieve academic success as long as he or she is willing to work hard. Since the child with ULD exhibits intelligence and yet experiences inexplicable academic failures, it seems to others that the child must not be working hard enough. The child experiences shame and, in seeking to find a cause for the shame, finds only the self. Parents begin to encourage the child to attach the shame to the self by calling his or her motivations into question:

- You're lazy.
- You're headstrong.
- You're only interested in your friends.
- You just don't pay attention.
- You daydream too much.
- They expected me to be smart.
- You're not interested in school because of your sports.
- My mother would tell me there was something wrong with the teachers. Then, she would say, "You can do better than this." My father would yell at me and say I was stupid and dumb. I didn't know what to think.

Educators do not seem to have the answer either. They cannot see the obstacles inhibiting learning. So, like the parents, they attribute a lack of academic success in a seemingly intelligent individual to a lack of effort. Also, like the parent, they compound the child's growing sense of self-shame:

- The principal said, "I know you can do better, so try harder."
- The teacher said, "If you had cared more and been less messy, I would have given you credit on your homework."
- "This would have been an A paper if I wouldn't have had to stop so often to correct your spelling."
- There was a tendency to see me as lazy. But at the same time, they saw me as hard-driven. So, they couldn't figure it out . . . you know, the notion of seeing me as a sloppy type of person.
- And they said, "How is it that you can get A's on papers, but you fail your tests?" I said, "Well, I like writing papers because I have time, and I don't have to work with my handwriting." And they said, "Everybody's hands get tired. That's ridiculous."

Over time, myths are created. Poised against a backdrop of success in certain areas, achievement in other areas is impossible despite effort. As the surrounding world continues to attribute poor school performance to lack of effort, the child begins to accept blame and to question his or her own perceptions. A world of chronic shame is born. Once convinced of his or her intelligence, the child now turns to stupidity and lack of motivation as feasible explanations for academic failure. Although these two explanations are in direct conflict, the lack of any other explanation binds the child in this catch-22. If children believe themselves to be smart, then they must be lazy if they fail to learn. If children believe themselves to be trying hard at learning, they must be stupid if they fail to learn.

In time, the child with an undiagnosed learning disability becomes accustomed to living with the baffling variations of doing both well and poorly. As the child is receiving internal and external messages of stupidity and academic apathy, he or she gradually incorporates self-blame into an internal belief system and accepts them as factual. Confidence and self-esteem drop while reactive feelings of chronic shame surface. As a result, it becomes increasingly difficult to learn:

- I always felt as though it was my fault because I didn't apply myself.
- Every time I lost my homework, I would tell myself it's because I was dumb.
- I would beat myself on the way home from school because I upset the teacher because my paper was so messy.
- I figured they were right: I must be lazy.

There is no longer a question that something is wrong: It has become a fact of life. These myths of stupidity and academic apathy, internally digested and externally reinforced, set the stage for two subsequent domains: chasm and struggle. These represent attempts to adapt to the now-accepted reality that something is wrong.

THE CHASM

Inside of me, there's a chasm which—that's huge. There's no way you can get from one side to the other. And that's where the learning disability goes. When there were things that I just couldn't explain when I was a kid, I just thought, "Oh, it's just going into that chasm."

As stated earlier, Imprisoned Intelligence results when the standards and goals set by academic institutions cannot be consistently met by the person with ULD. Although achievement in some areas or at some times is possible, failure is both unpredictable and inevitable. This bewildering experience can cause a temporary cognitive paralysis, the chasm, which is a feeling of being frozen. This concept is the central focus of this book. Often, this inability to proceed is seen as an unbridgeable gap.

The term "chasm" attempts to capture what it feels like during the *moment* when one expects to learn but there is a gap in learning. It is also a word that embodies the following stepwise progression of feelings that seem to connect with this momentary freeze:

> Confusion
> Helplessness
> Alienation
> Shame
> Motivational assault from self and others

The participants in this study describe this chasm as a serious obstacle in their attempts to learn. Why does the chasm occur? One explanation might be that chronic shame, triggered by a recent failure, "freezes" the individual from going forward *in order to prevent augmenting or restimulating* the shame experience. Just as individuals who have been hurt in a love relationship may fail to fall in love again, ULD children may stop themselves from proceeding into further shame once a learning crisis has evolved:

- It feels like a painful invisible emptiness inside my brain.
- Other people knew things. And I had—and I think this is accurate—that I had a "chasm" of—of no knowledge . . . but then it was just this place inside of me that, you know, was an emptiness. You know, like, if you were to draw a picture of my body, that there was this great space that other people had filled up, that I didn't.
- My brain wouldn't work.
- Suddenly, I would be dumb.
- Nothing would happen.

The chasm is not only a vacuum that precludes academic achievement, it also expresses the individual's increasing distance from the surrounding world. This cognitive freeze is characterized by a sense of being shamefully overwhelmed by time as well as by physiological signs of alienation and anxiety:

- I sat there all those hours . . . I couldn't start. I had no middle. I had no end.
- Everything stopped.
- The teacher would be talking, and I would understand her. But then, I couldn't anymore, and I knew that I would be stuck in this place of nothingness what seemed like forever—or until the bell rang.
- There was an "out-of-body" experience.
- I think I probably went numb.
- At times, it was as though I was watching myself trying to speak, watching my mouth trying to form the words.
- My brain felt like a frozen computer.
- It's like having a button, but not being able to find the buttonhole.

The person with ULD has also, by this point, established that he or she can harbor no realistic expectation that effective help will be forthcoming. Since no one has been able to understand what is wrong, solutions seem out of the question. The tools needed for accessing intelligence are unavailable. Furthermore, since there is no understanding that other tools are possible, people appear stupid to themselves and to others. Shame, which should be a signal to the individual to try another method for success, is not a help, but an intractable burden. Hope is lost, leaving the trap of Imprisoned Intelligence, where futility becomes the reality. The chasm encapsulates the experience not only of futility, but also of acute shame.

The never-ending pit of the chasm is both a source of and a symbol for shame. This cognitive gap and these painful feelings feed on each other and become intertwined in a single dance. The intellectual freeze is accompanied by feelings of exposure, fear, shame, and humiliation. One's feelings stand out in relief against the success of others, further intensifying the original feelings:

- I would stand out like a sore thumb.
- It was awful to fail and watch others learning.
- You have this totally helpless feeling that's like everyone else is getting it and you're not.
- And I would watch myself, hearing those kids, the other kids around me, sounding different, [laughs] being more fluid with what they were doing.

- I would get excited about something and ask a question, and people would look at me like I was nuts, and I realized I was feeling exposed from the inside out again.
- I hated getting my exams back because I would have to hide them from the rest of the class because the grades would be lousy.

Sometimes, a person would be able to determine that certain events or situations precipitated experiences with the chasm. When this happens, a special event might be greeted with a sense of foreboding instead of joyful anticipation. Certain school subjects or other activities could also become associated with the chasm, their occurrence and the anticipation of their occurrence filling the individual with dread:

- Passover would always make me afraid. . . . I would have to read in front of the family. . . . It was terrible.
- If I would have to go to a restaurant and read the menu, it was terrible. Then I wouldn't be able to hide from other people.
- If she announced that it was reading time, I would be in trouble.
- It was painful to read out loud; kids would snicker.
- Going to the blackboard was a nightmare because I couldn't read the letters fast enough.
- It's a horrible memory, sitting in class and then going around, each kid reading. You have a book and each kid reads a paragraph or sentence. I knew, probably after the first time I did it [laughs], that I wasn't going to be very good. And kids would just be going through it without any problem. And I'd have to read ahead, so that I'd know my sentence, and then I'd get to it, and I wouldn't know the words.

Once this lonely chasm becomes an intrinsic part of one's psychological world, an underlying mild to severe anticipation of doom follows, accompanied by fears of humiliation and exposure. There is a sense of foreboding that a chasm will unexpectedly appear and one will be shamed. Continuous fear of an unexpected shame event creates a pervasive sense of insecurity. Because there is no consistent pattern, one never knows when the deficits will be exposed or when the teacher's agenda will move into the areas of deficits. An overarching fear of shame events pervades one's life:

- I never knew when I would look stupid.
- I would have this lurking sense of doom that followed me around.
- I would never know when the chasm would hit.
- I felt as though I was skating on thin ice.
- I was always waiting for her to ask me a question.
- I'd always know it was coming [laughs]. I guess after a while, even though it was real unpleasant, I think I just got hardened to it.

This pervasive sense of shame can swallow up or contaminate even the successes experienced by a child with ULD. The individual has become so totally convinced of his or her inability to learn or succeed, because shame is attached to the self, that a success is interpreted as a fluke. Since this fluke could potentially be exposed, the child's feelings of impending doom and concealment are heightened. The undiagnosed learning disabled live in constant fear that someone will "find them out"—that even their small successes will be exposed as mistakes:

- I did well because the teachers didn't understand how dumb I was.
- I always felt that he couldn't have given me that A if he knew that I didn't know how I did it.
- I was always afraid that I wouldn't pass, and when I did pass it was because someone let me get away with it.
- I never did figure out why I got so many votes to be class president because I was terrified that I'd make it, because then I'd be given responsibilities that I couldn't deal with.

The individual with ULD now lives in a world of shame, embarrassment, pain, and insecurity. The anxiety that the chasm is looming ahead is constant. Emerging from this situation is the struggle, in which the child tries to find ways to cope with the disability and the resulting shame.

STRUGGLE: IMPASSE AND BYPASS

I would simply refuse to give up.

As time goes by, the reality of the undetected learning disability does not change: The chasm and its accompanying shame is a familiar problem. With the chasm in place, there is no longer a sense of bewilderment. The paradoxical intelligence of the ULD individual, however, causes an unquenchable desire for learning. This desire leads him or her to break the chronic tendency to avoid shame and to continue the lonely struggle to achieve. In this struggle, the ULD child employs two main strategies. The first is to continue behaving like the other children who are learning successfully, hoping that this time will be different. This strategy is called *impasse* because the result is the same repeated deadlock: a repeated strategy leading to repeated failure. The second strategy involves seeking a way to get around the difficulties the child is experiencing, creating a *bypass*. In this domain, the individual employs ingenuity and creativity to overcome an as yet undiagnosed problem.

Impasse

I was told that whatever you work for, you can get. I worked for it, and I didn't get it.

The yearning in the ULD person to put her or his intelligence to work cannot be permanently quenched. Motivation is often high, producing repeated attempts to persevere in the face of continuing defeat. With each new semester or school year, the belief resurfaces that this time hard work will produce success. Out of the seemingly illogical past of intermittent learning failure, they seek logical, consistent reasons for past failures. After all, if the failure can be attributed to a specific cause, there can be hope of correcting it. So, the individual with an undetected learning disability seeks to correct a past behavior that may be responsible for failure:

- I started each year with a new resolve.
- Each semester, I would buy fresh notebooks and come to school with new hope.

- I didn't do enough homework.
- I didn't do enough reading.
- I would stop thinking of something else when the teacher was talking.
- I would stop daydreaming.
- I would pay attention.
- I will work harder and get better grades.

The results, unfortunately, are not altered, and disappointment arises again and again. Shame accompanies each failure:

- I was very diligent . . . I would complete my homework, and I failed tests. That's how it went.
- I kept banging my head against the wall.
- I could handle myself in class. . . . You know, when she called on me, I knew what was going on because I could work out problems. But I would go home and not be able to do the assignments and hand in the work.
- I remember getting an F, and I remember my teacher taking me aside and saying he couldn't understand why I didn't get it. . . . It was almost as if I hadn't done my homework, but I was very diligent and always did my homework.
- I would say to my instructor, "How can I increase my reading scores?" He said, "I don't know. You're just too slow."

Repeatedly, the same shame events appeared to greet the individual in his or her born-again enthusiasm. For instance, time continued to pose difficulties. Many people with learning disabilities need to work at a slower pace. Despite their ability to do the homework or papers, they might therefore fail timed tests. Interwoven with time difficulties, then, is a fear of time. This anxiety can impose further burdens since fear can interfere with recall, inhibiting memory. Once again, fear of shame and shame avoidance impede performance:

- I was a good student in class, but I flunked a lot of exams because I couldn't finish them.
- Because I read so slowly, I would never get through an exam on time.

- It's not that I didn't know the stuff, I just couldn't get it down before the bell rang.
- Exams did not test me for knowledge, they tested me for speed.
- Because I knew I'd never get through, I gave up before I even got started.

Another element of the impasse is that some strategies which may have produced positive results in the past may not continue to work. For instance, if an individual was able to devote more time than others to learning in elementary and high school, the increasing academic demands of college might prevent success. The additional workload forces a ULD individual to budget time in a way that prevents him or her from achieving success:

- I never had enough time to play because of all the work.
- I was always under this time pressure to get things done quickly.
- If I knew there were a lot of things I wanted to do, I might feel just overwhelmed by what I was going to do first.

Bypass

I just knew that I could do whatever I wanted to do. It just took a lot longer time to do it in.

Bypass is the domain in which the person with undetected learning disabilities seeks a way to get around his or her cognitive problems. The individual learns to compensate, usually without any help from others, by employing ingenuity and creativity to overcome an as-yet undiagnosed problem. To express their Imprisoned Intelligence, people with learning disabilities rely on the combination of their strength, intelligence, creativity, and ability to persevere. This section discusses the roles of determination, diversion, intuition, cheating, and personal relationships in this domain.

For some participants, spending additional time and effort can create a bypass around areas of failure. Driven by positive feedback, hard work and tenacity become necessary to gain success:

- I loved getting good grades, and after a while I demanded that of myself. . . . Nothing short of perfection would do.
- My mother was so proud that I worked so much harder than the rest of my brothers and sisters.
- My grades became a source of pride for me.

Effort heightens the individual's sense of competence. So, no matter how time-consuming or difficult, he or she continues a push to learn:

- I never stopped trying.
- I would simply refuse to give up.
- I would think that I have to work ten times as hard as anyone else.
- I would put one foot in front of the other, and say to myself, "I'm gonna do it."
- It took me seven years to get through undergraduate school. I repeated a lot of classes. And I'd tape everything and listen to it over and over and over again.

Not all bypasses are of a positive nature. Some are simply shame techniques, such as creating a diversion. By rerouting conversation or distracting the audience, the person with ULD can shift the classroom focus to an area of comfort so that his or her strengths will be validated and a shame event avoided:

- I was known as the class clown, and I loved it.
- Talking was for fun and for avoidance of class work.
- Distracting teachers worked better in elementary school than in college.
- Doodling kept my mind focused.

Shame avoidance could take the form of removing oneself from class participation. Not being able to concentrate could create discomfort or boredom; therefore, daydreaming or sleeping could produce a needed escape:

- The class was so boring, so I fell asleep.
- I didn't understand a word of it.

Many students with ULD rely on cheating and lying to survive their academic experiences. They cope by mastering these tactics and employing them with discretion:

- I was the best cheater in the school. I would have never made it through elementary school and high school if it hadn't been for the cheating.
- I always knew when I could get away with lying and when I couldn't.
- I had this sixth sense as to what people would believe.
- I never got caught.
- I always thought of myself as a con artist.

For some, trusting one's intuition can become the only viable option and a way of life. An individual will often feel his or her way through an examination, guessing and relying almost exclusively on intuition. Answers seem to come out of nowhere, rather than as the result of memorization or logic. ULD often causes a sense of estrangement from one's work. Papers also seemed to emerge from nowhere and turn out to be acceptable:

- If I did well, I figured it was a lucky guess.
- I never really knew when I wrote a paper whether it would be an A or an F, but somehow, somewhere, I trusted that it was okay.
- The answers just seemed to come out of nowhere.
- It wasn't like I knew I had memorized something.
- I never knew how I got things right.
- When the paper was edited at a future time, I was surprised. I was surprised that it made sense. . . . I didn't expect that. I re-read the paper, and it wasn't really that bad . . . I guess I just had to sleep on it.

Other people also can become important resources in bridging learning gaps. Friends can provide the help necessary to circumvent learning difficulties, sometimes through swapping strengths with a ULD classmate:

- I found kids at school who were very bright. They would come over after school and help me.
- I knew from third grade that I was pretty and attractive, and I would make friends of the boys. I would be sweet and engaging, and they would do my homework.
- She would come over and fix my spelling; I would give her tennis lessons.
- She was five years older than me and tutored me on my multiplication tables. . . . I adored her.
- The teacher let us work in pairs. . . . I talked and she wrote. . . . We got good grades together.

Parents, particularly mothers, often play a crucial role in providing a bypass to success. In addition to helping with schoolwork, they can function as emotional supports by soothing the shame or counteracting others' denigration. Parents might also fulfill the crucial role of locating better instruction or learning situations for their children and often find a way to "reconnect" with their children who experience the disconnection of shame:

- She helped me with my homework every night.
- He drilled me on my multiplication tables until I finally got it. . . . It took a long time. . . . He never gave up.
- My mom would say, "It's not so bad, you did the best you could. You can do better."
- I would be so discouraged, and she would be there.
- Everyone was on my back . . . but my mom always believed in me. . . . She knew I was smart, and I knew that she knew I was smart.
- My mom was on the school board just because she knew she would have some clout about getting me a good teacher.
- My mom was a teacher, and she made it her business to go to the principal to get the best teacher for me.

Finally, tutors can also help find ways around a problem. Although not all experiences are positive, tutoring often provides an environment that a child with a learning disability finds more conducive to his or her abilities. For instance, those who are readily distracted will find less to send them "off track" in a one-to-one experience. Tutoring can have a greater effect when the student feels he or she is special, particularly because the classroom experience is providing negative feedback. The experience of having a tutor believe in him or her can counteract chronic shame and can help the student learn coping skills:

- I loved my tutor. . . . She was with me from elementary school through college, and she taught me how to get around the problem.
- The tutor made me feel like I had something, like I was worthwhile.
- Somebody else believed in me. You know, then I wanted to reach for another step and yet another step.
- It was one to one.
- I could work at my own pace.
- I had her undivided attention.
- I would have never made it through school without my tutor.
- I learned that if there is something I can't learn in a group situation, I have a better chance to understand it on a one-to-one [basis] at my own pace.

RESIGNATION

You've only got a limited number of choices, and I could only think of one. "So," I said to myself, "As long as I pass, it will be good enough. It will get me through once I get out in the world. Just don't open those grades because grades don't mean anything anyway."

The final domain, resignation, comes about when an individual comes to grips with the fact that the learning problems are here to stay. It occurs when people learn to think about, live with, and make some accommodation to their "invisible shackles." Despite the fact that they do not understand the cause, people affected by an undetected learning disability form conclusions about their "problem areas." They decide that either they will give up trying to succeed in these areas, or they must accept that certain academic pursuits will be an eternal battle with continuing shame and only sporadic victories. In either case, the individual learns to live with the pain and, with some variation, to accept the fact that one's Imprisoned Intelligence will remain unexpressed.

The individual with ULD often finds unempathic responses from important people. Although he or she feels intelligent and understands that something is wrong, the outside world continues to blame and accuse. The result is continuing shame:

- No one was interested. No one cared.
- I had the sense from my mother that she was ashamed of me and that she was thinking, "Poor dear, you can't help it and can't do any better than that." Inside, I was angry and hurt about it.

To deal with their disappointment and shame, individuals build a front. The driving force behind it is anger because the world cannot validate either their intelligence or the cause of learning failure. This protective facade can manifest itself as offensive behavior, which is used as a weapon against the world they find so frustrating:

- If somebody makes fun of you, the next time someone makes fun of you and the next time and the next, and it's all about the same stuff, you build up a front to that. And if someone's going to do it, you're going to attack eventually.
- I built a fort so no one could see, and I attacked with the intelligent comeback.
- I was sarcastic and angry.
- I was snotty and forceful.
- I was arrogant.

Sometimes, fear of retaliation could also drive the attacks underground rather than against the outside world—that is, the attacks might be expressed internally, not externally:

- And I would think, "You show me what you've got, I dare you."
- As I got older, I got sick and tired of my father saying to me, "Shape up or ship out." And I learned, very well, how to look respectful while I was imagining not nice things about him.

At this stage, people become resigned to living with what they perceive as a shameful problem. As they realize that no solutions will be forthcoming, they become disheartened and consider giving up:

- When I had it [the learning disabilities] and I wasn't aware and no one else was aware of it, it was very frustrating . . . and as a younger child growing up with it, I don't know, I probably thought it was a way of life.
- I finally decided that I was born with it.
- As I got older, I just realized that I couldn't verbally, I couldn't really get my ideas or my thoughts in a clear manner. There was nothing I could do.
- I didn't like it, but I learned to live with it. . . . What else could I do? There was a relative in the family who was mentally retarded and close to my age, and my mother would push me to play with this child. Since I had trouble in school too, I would take this to mean [that] she thinks I'm retarded too.
- I finally believed that it wasn't important to be smart. All I needed to do was to look pretty.
- My father always said to me, "If you can talk, you can write." And on some level, I always believed that, but the outcome was utterly unusable. . . . In time, I stopped trying to understand this phenomenon.

Accepting that certain areas will continue to pose difficulties, the individual begins to employ heightened tactics of shame avoidance. He or she might make a conscious decision to stay away from the problem, whether it be academic situations in general or certain subject areas. The ability to make this sort of decision differs markedly from the earlier domains in which the student continued to struggle with the learning deficiencies:

- I just wouldn't go to school.
- I stayed away from math classes because I knew I wouldn't be able to pass them.
- After some thought, even though my teacher urged me to apply for college, I decided not to do so at that time because I knew what kind of work was involved, and I would fail.
- I knew I couldn't learn this, so I wasn't going to take it.
- I would make myself invisible . . . no classes in algebra or geometry, no language classes.

Unfortunately, acceptance of the problem is often accompanied by the acceptance of the world's labels. Individuals begin to accept the conclusion that they are dumb. This is a hallmark of chronic shame:

- I figured I was pretty dumb because it always took me longer to find the page in my book.
- Something was making me have to work harder and work slower. . . . It was a fact of life. . . . I considered myself stupid.
- I usually knew the answers in my head, but I thought I was stupid because I couldn't repeat them out loud.
- I was stupid because I couldn't spell.
- Being smart and being dumb was just the way I was.

To tolerate the situation, individuals begin to develop short-term personal incentives. They rationalize to get themselves through the class, the paper, or the program. One prevalent thought is, "All I have to do is pass." Or they might build a reward/punishment schema, such as "Mom will be so happy if I pass this" and "I'm gonna get it if I screw this up":

- When I graduate, I'll never look at a book again.
- I'll never punish my kids for not passing tests the way the folks are punishing me.
- Three more months and I'll be out of this class.
- If I can pass, I'll never have to see this teacher's face again.

When these methods fail and the shame can no longer be tolerated, they may decide to give up:

- I decided it was easier for me to simply accept a failing mark than to be told I was lazy or I wasn't meeting, you know, working to my potential, or whatever the thing was. I decided that from now on I was going to design my own system which meant that I would not be judged.
- I wasn't going to be judged by the standard tests anymore, I was going to be my only judge from now on . . . period.
- I simply could not hand in inappropriate or inadequate work. It becomes somewhat of a pragmatic issue.

Resignation differs from the earlier domains in that chronic shame has taken firm hold, and the surrender to the learning disability holds a sense of permanence. In essence, hope is dead. The individual with ULD, not having the concept of a learning disability, believes that there will be no change to his or her condition—an intelligence imprisoned because it cannot be expressed adequately. While all the domains share varying degrees of shame and pain, this domain adds a dimension of sheer hopelessness.

Chapter 4

Discovery: The Diagnosis

"Brilliant" is an articulate middle-aged woman who did not find out about her learning disabilities until her forties. Here is her story.

Brilliant: The reason that I entered school again as an adult was that I came to a place in myself where the fear and trembling and the demons, as I call them, which kept me from school all these years needed to be faced. So what I did was to place myself in an untenable position. I enrolled in summer school at [a local community college] and registered for a first-year algebra class, anatomy, and a physiology class.

I remember thinking at the time, you know, that this is a matter of grit [laughs]. I wasn't sixteen years old anymore. I was a grown-up, and I had children. And I knew what it was to work hard. And, you know, my children were old enough so that I really could put my nose to the grindstone. No excuses! I could do this.

Well, it was an accelerated program because it was summer school. In other words, they were attempting to put a year's amount of learning into an eight-week course which I thought was wonderful. You know, I would just get it over with quickly.

And, you know, all I had to do is pass, except really I was thinking to myself: No, that's not true, I really need to get an A. At any rate, I went into this with a vengeance. I mean, my family didn't see me during this period of time. I just gave it my all.

In the algebra class, I very quickly discovered [laughs] that an absolutely horrible thing was happening. I mean, it was truly like a revisitation of, you know, ghosts from the nursery or something like this. I relived, in the most excruciating way, the difficulties I thought I had put behind me when I left school at sixteen. And it was terrifying. I mean, soul-wrenching, terrifying. . . .

I'll start by just trying to describe what happened. I would sit in algebra class, and the teacher would explain the algebra lesson. And, you know, I was in class with eighteen-year-olds. These were all young kids. And I had the advantage, or so I thought, and truly felt, that I had the advantage of being an adult. I wasn't having to flirt with my neighbors, or worry about how I looked, or any of these other burdensome things that these eighteen-year-olds [laughs] have to deal with.

I could concentrate on algebra. And she [the teacher] would explain to us the process and the particular algebraic problems or formulas for it. And I would take it in, and I would understand it. Instantly! I mean, really instantly! And it would be very gratifying.

Interviewer: You really enjoyed this.

Brilliant: Oh yes, first, you know, do this, and then you do that, and it's a six-part process, and, you know, you follow the format, and you'll get the answer. Right? And I understood the format.

But then, I would go to follow the format. And, I would get the wrong answer. Every time. And I would do the problem over. Gee, I've done something peculiar here, you know, I must have done something peculiar here. And I'd start at the beginning, and yes, that's the right step, step one, two, three, four, five, six—get me to the end. Hmm! Wrong answer.

Each problem was taking me a half an hour to do. And on an individual assignment, in an accelerated algebra class, there might be five pages of two-hundred problems to do. It was taking me an inordinate amount of time. And my frustration level was reaching the breaking point.

This was like my proving ground now. Right? So the grade was very important to me. I really wanted to get an A in the class and was not handing in work unless I knew that I would get a 100 percent. I would not hand it in! And I definitely got an easy mouth on me, and was participating in class. She would ask a question, I would have the answer. When she called on me, I knew what was going on.

I was handing in all my work on time, so the teacher didn't have a clue what was going on with me until she walked around one day, and saw me working out the problems. She took a look at my work and she said to me: "Oh, I see you've got the formula, but you've mixed up your signs." And then she said, "Oh, wait a minute, I see what you did: you wrote a 6 when you meant to write an X."

You know, I mean, it was like a lightbulb going off in my brain cells. My daughter had, two years earlier, gone through testing for learning disabilities. So, I had, it was still fresh in my mind, what learning disabilities was all about. And there was something about her telling me [laughs] that I had not only reversed my symbols, but that I had written a 6 when I meant to be writing an X, that went . . . that went, Bingo! You know, if this isn't a classic form of dyslexia, I'm not [name] [laughs]. And she [the teacher] said, you know, this is something to go and find out about. Because you've clearly got the mathematical ability, but there is something going screwy here. No adult, no person in my entire life had ever said that to me. You know, that there was a discrepancy between ability and function.

Eventually, many who suffer with ULD will become aware that such things as learning disabilities exist. This new knowledge, that there is a legitimate discrepancy between ability and function, can be a revelation. The period of *discovery* begins with the discovery of learning disabilities, continues through the testing experience, and ends with the person's first thoughts and feelings about the testing results.

Discovery has four domains. "Awakenings" occur when one first encounters the concept of learning disabilities. Then comes the testing experience, which itself evokes conflicting emotions as the hopelessness of the past is challenged. This process is described in "The Test: Pleasure" and "The Test: Pain." Finally, the individual receives the confirming diagnosis and experiences "The Aftermath: Making Sense" as newfound potential and future possibilities and struggles begin to come into focus.

AWAKENINGS

Awakenings begin when someone learns that he or she may have a learning disability. Once the concept of learning disabilities is introduced, the individual begins to make sense of what seemed to be chaos. Learning problems may, after all, have a valid explanation. The feeling could be epitomized as, "I might just not be crazy (or stupid or lazy) after all."

This new concept (ULD) can help many people understand the split inside themselves: feeling intelligent yet unable to do what smart people do. Once an individual understands that his or her intellectual development may have been impeded by a ULD, the old wish to make sense out of the chaos reemerges—this time, with more hope that a solution can be found.

For many, awakenings is a dramatic experience that validates past feelings. Many remember well the relief they felt when they first heard about learning disabilities:

- My professor was a very kind lady. One day in class, we were discussing something in life span development, and, all of a sudden, the topic came up . . . learning disabilities. And about ten minutes out of the class, I was hysterical in tears. . . . I went to [my professor's] office, and all I could say to her at the time was that I wondered if that was what was wrong with me. . . . She managed to get me tested.
- I met a girl who said she got special testing privileges for taking certain tests. I ran over and asked, "What do you mean, special testing privileges? What is this about?" I was like: "What is this? Tell me. Tell me." And she said, "Don't you know about the disabled student services at ＿＿＿＿ University?"

For some, this dramatic moment is not altogether heartening. It may strike an uncomfortable blow by reviving memories of shame and exposure:

- I was humiliated when my professor suggested that I get tested. He pointed out my inability to pass the tests even though I knew the material.
- When she said my performance didn't make sense, I almost died.
- My academic counselor in college suggested it [testing] after she looked at my reading score. She knew something was up. Now she even thought I was disabled.

Awakenings do not always come as a sudden jolt; sometimes they grow over time. A common scenario is for adults with ULD to find their children experiencing learning difficulties. As they learn about their children's learning disability, they realize that they too might have been affected by learning problems:

- My younger son has a learning disability. And as I was fighting the battles for him, I recognized that I had a learning disability too.
- I had the same spelling problems as my son, so this sneaking suspicion began to grow in me.
- I realized that I lost all my papers when I was a kid too.

As their parents were, the children of those with ULD are ashamed when their learning disability hinders their efforts at school. When adults observe a child's pain, sometimes they must relive their own feelings of shame that they have long tried to bury:

- I reexperienced so much of my own long-buried pain when I saw my brilliant son not being able to keep up with the class in script.
- I felt so helpless because, until the school pointed out the problem, I could only suffer with him.
- I knew how bad she was hurting because I went through the same thing. But I didn't know what to do.

The need to investigate this new idea—that their childhood difficulties may have stemmed from a learning disability—leads individuals with ULD to undergo the testing procedure.

Testing includes quite a number of tests (when I was tested, they gave fifteen tests plus an interview) and often takes several days. Some of these are standardized achievement tests similar to the ones that are given yearly to public school children. One function of these tests is to identify discrepancies in ability. For instance, a high score in math and a low score in reading comprehension might indicate a reading disorder. Subjects are also given an IQ test to pinpoint discrepancies in scores on different sections of the test, and to see if IQ scores are commensurate with achievement test scores. There are tests specifically for motor skills, reading, short-term memory, critical thinking, auditory learning, visual learning, and other areas, as the LD specialist sees fit.

You may wonder, if one is done with school and has found a career that suits one's strengths, why get tested? After all, the test is long, stressful, and most likely expensive. Yet even participants who had already finished their education chose to be tested. Some wanted to confirm that they have areas of giftedness as well as weaknesses. This consoling knowledge can boost self-esteem and clarify one's abilities. Testing was also used to satisfy the outside world, or at least to provide some ammunition for dealing with others who are critical. Many simply wanted to know the truth about themselves:

- I wanted to get more information about the fact that something was amiss.
- I wanted to have a better understanding of why I had this peculiar mix of abilities or lack thereof.
- The thought of the test as a means to give me a reason to deal with their anger was energizing.
- I had something to say to my friends when they would wonder what took me so long.

Some individuals are still completing their education and want new information to help them tackle specific problems. They hope not only for an explanation, but also help:

- People don't like to grade grammatically incorrect papers. It makes them angry. I don't like people getting angry when I cannot help it.
- I had been accepted at the University of Chicago, and I got so scared that I wouldn't make it.
- I decided to get tested because I might want to go on and get a doctorate. I wasn't sure how I would be able to do on the Graduate Record Exam.
- Maybe I can figure out how to write papers faster.
- Maybe I can get some extra time for tests.
- When I was in graduate school at [an academically prestigious school], the field of thinking about dyslexia had moved on quite a bit and lots had been accomplished in seven years. [But] I was still getting grief from my professors because I couldn't spell. And my father and I agreed that I should get tested.

THE TEST: PLEASURE

The testing experience evokes both positive and negative reactions. Individuals with ULD perform very well in some areas, poorly in others; therefore, some parts of the tests are exciting and intellectually challenging. For some, the sense of mastery achieved during the testing experience boosts self-esteem:

- It was gratifying to see that I could finish before the time was up.
- Some parts were like a good game.
- I felt like I was solving puzzles.
- It was like doing crossword puzzles—only even more fun.
- It was fun to figure out things.
- I felt like I was in grammar school again—when I felt smart because I did well on tests.

Often, for those who need more time, untimed tests are most gratifying. Freedom from the clock puts success within grasp:

- The way a lot of these tests work is that you go until you can't anymore . . . and then you've reached your level. I enjoyed this.
- I did very well on math because she said I could take as long as I wished.
- I was surprised. For once I didn't have to worry about the time—how quickly I did the test.
- I liked being able to do this as slow as I wanted to.

The person conducting the test can contribute to the feeling of accomplishment. Those tested by an empathic tester feel comfortable enough to perform well.

- I was really able to concentrate because I knew she was with me.
- I knew she was rooting for me.

THE TEST: PAIN

Testing is not invariably fun. For some people, LD testing brings back the pain of school exams. When a person runs into familiar stumbling, he or she can panic about the inability to follow very

simple instructions, solve simple problems, or make simple draw-
ings. The person may feel ashamed and defeated even before the
testing is finished:

- When we came to the part that I couldn't do, I felt very tense.
- I felt as if I would die within this space of temporary nothingness.
- My concentration was just, you know . . . I could feel my whole
  body tighten up and focus on this, and there was this kind of pit-
  in-the-stomach feeling.
- To sit there and go through the things she had me go through . . .
  I didn't know the answer. . . . Maybe the answer was that I should
  have driven a truck like my father.
- Some things I simply couldn't do. . . . I just couldn't do it.
- I felt this sense of impotency.

An individual with ULD might feel trapped or panic. In school,
some developed their own special ways to succeed in exams, such as
looking at problems and finding unorthodox solutions. For example,
simple geometry problems can be solved without knowing the formulas by drawing pictures to scale and measuring the sides. A pupil gifted
in art but bad at memorizing might get away with this for a while.
However, LD diagnostic tests are designed to prevent such loopholes
by, for instance, providing only out-of-scale diagrams and not allowing
rulers in the testing room. The test-taker's usual artillery is taken away,
and this can be scary and frustrating.

- I was used to figuring my way out of things. . . . In life, one can
  usually come at a problem from different angles. But with these
  tests, it was like coming to a dead end with no way back.
- I felt like my back was against a wall, and I could not go around it.

Some of the tests are timed. Some people feel that the time limit is
like being trapped in a box. Sometimes, a person reaches a point in the
tests where he or she cannot do any more, but time is not up yet. In
these situations, a certain time limit still has to be waited out, effectively trapping the individual with ULD in a time warp of powerlessness.

- The clock seemed never to go forward.
- I felt like the three minutes would never be up.

- I had one half hour to understand and rewrite that page, and I could not do it. . . . It was the longest period in my life.
- I hope time never gets that long again.
- Some things I just couldn't begin to do, so I had to sit there for three minutes. . . . It was one of the longest three minutes in my life.

When people feel powerless, they are subject to intense feelings of shame, exposure, and humiliation. As test-takers find themselves unable to work around obstacles, they are dumped back into the chasm of shame that they knew as children. Some were surprised that the testing situation could evoke such emotions in their adult selves:

- I felt naked.
- I had forgotten that this was the way I suffered in elementary school . . . good Lord.
- It was tortuous.
- I felt as though I was in an inescapable pit.
- No matter if I had finished the last section in record time and with minimal mistakes, when it came to drawing a face or remembering the lines I drew, I bombed it.
- I could feel the embarrassment on my skin.
- I wished I could die.
- I was surprised at how embarrassed I felt.
- I couldn't believe not doing such a simple little exercise could humiliate [me] so much.

Shame is frequently amplified because the person knows he or she is observed by another person, the tester. Some testers have been trained only in technical aspects of evaluation and have not been taught how to deal with their subjects empathically. Consequently, the testers seem cold and distant. The test-takers sense that lack of warmth; they feel uncomfortable and encounter further intellectual "cramping" while taking the tests. The test setting itself can cause alienation and isolation:

- I felt like a fly on the end of her pin.
- Having to wait out the time with her looking at me was horrible.
- It was tough because I tried so hard and couldn't make the connections; and they wouldn't even hear about my struggles to try.

- If only she could have been a little kind.
- Her face was impassive throughout the whole three days. . . . I guess that was part of the testing. . . . I felt so alone and isolated.
- Different people came in and tested me for different skills. . . . They were students, and I knew that there were supervisors watching behind that one-way mirror. . . . It didn't help my thinking process.
- When I couldn't get something. . . . I could see those two women look at each other like, "Oh, look."

THE AFTERMATH: MAKING SENSE

Sparkly: So when they told me I had dyslexia, I was almost relieved. It's like when you don't know, sometimes, it's real difficult to get through it. But when you find out, "Okay, I have dyslexia," then I could take this path to further my education. I could take this path to learn how to read, or whatever it may be. It was so reassuring. What I think it goes back to, again, is that I just . . . I just was worried. Now, there was a reason why I had such difficulty in school. It wasn't because I was stupid, or that I just couldn't understand it. Now there was a good reason!

People experience a sense of confirmation when they receive their results: "So that's what's wrong with me." Individuals with ULD can finally understand the "why" behind their lifelong struggles. For many this knowledge brings a profound sense of relief and clarity. These people feel free to finally stop blaming themselves for their performance difficulties:

- Two parts of that exam for me made sense. One was, I knew now why I get lost. And then I knew that I focus on the same thing: a small area. So, what I learned was to step back and try to observe a large picture.
- This makes sense.
- It was really good to separate out my strengths from my weaknesses.
- I always knew I couldn't help it.
- I understand now that I can't help not remembering people's faces.

Others find the results dispiriting. The knowledge they gain confirms their worst fears and simply reminds them of their shortcomings:

- I learned very little that I didn't already know.
- It only made me feel worse.
- I knew I had learning disabilities. But until I got tested, I didn't know how bad.
- I'm disabled.
- I knew I was different, but I don't like it.

But even for those who are at first depressed by their results, the new knowledge that testing provides often benefits them in the long run. They gradually begin to see the myths that they have lived with, and how these myths have fostered shame and self-blame. One day they can begin to forgive themselves for things outside of their control:

- I wasn't lazy.
- I'm not getting even.
- I'm not acting out.
- I remember coming home from the testing and telling my mother through the tears . . . that I could finally forgive my younger self. That child that I had just been so abusive to inside of myself for so long was finally, sort of, laid to rest. And I could feel infinitely kinder toward this child as a consequence of this knowledge.

An important result of testing is increased access to help: Laws have been passed mandating services for learning disabled individuals. This knowledge brings comfort to those who have ULD and can empower them to make important changes. They begin to understand that they have a right to ask for help and, in some cases, a relaxation of the rules:

- The thought that I could take my tests untimed was a wonder to me.
- [I found out that] I needed to use a typewriter if they wanted to find out what I had learned on a test. . . . Even if I wouldn't be able to do so, at least I would know that the test would be more difficult for me.
- To understand that I would need a note taker and a tape recorder gave me a new determination to try harder.

• I think what it did for me was to have this piece of paper, this document. And it gave me some other way of working and gaining the ability to get tapes from the Library of Congress. So it [the diagnosis] gave me more tools.

Discovery changes people. It creates milestones along life's path. Gaining a new understanding of self is a riveting experience, yet memories of this period seem dimmer than those from the periods directly preceding or following. Perhaps the testing experience fades in the memory because of the intensity of the period to follow. Whatever the reason, the results are clear: hope and understanding are the new tools individuals carry away with them from these discoveries. Chapter 5 shows how people integrate into their lives the knowledge gained from the LD testing.

Chapter 5

Learning to Live with It:
After the Diagnosis

Sparkly: It was the first class, or it was the second class after I got diagnosed. I looked at this man, and it was the first time I was going to be putting into practice this new "_____, the Student." You know? I said to him "Well, what does correlative imperative mean?" And I remember saying the sentence and thinking, "I don't want to do it," but I did it. He looked at me, and he laughed at me condescendingly. [He said] "It was in your book. Why don't you know?" Oh, gee! And I thought . . . I'm telling you, right there, I lost it. I almost left the room. In my mind two billion things were running, "That's it! School's out! I don't care! I'm going to get my real estate license! I don't care about this anymore! The degree's out the window!"

And, you know, that's just something that I have to learn: not to take offense. I don't have to take it so personally. I look at the man today, and I think, "Well, the guy's just condescending, and that's how he'll teach his class. And I've got four more weeks of him, so I'll get through it," and blah, blah, blah. Which is something that I'm learning how to do.

After testing, one is relieved to find a diagnosable problem. One hopes that finally a solution to long-endured learning difficulties is forthcoming. However, this relief is only the beginning of an evolving psychological process. A person who now understands that he or she has a learning disability must begin fresh attempts to resolve it. Unfortunately, despite the advantage of having a defined problem, struggling with LD is still a lot of work. There are still no simple answers. Though perhaps less harrowing than ULD, LD remains hard to treat. Furthermore, many continue to feel ashamed of their now-apparent weaknesses.

After receiving a diagnosis, one must begin to wade through the regrets, sadness, and grief that inevitably accompany learning that one has a disability. In time, grieving will give way to a healthy understanding and respect for personal strengths and limitations. The individual can then begin to take responsibility for coping with the learning disability. Armed with more information, he or she can now sift through problems, separating a "hard-wired" and often permanent disability from emotionally driven problems, such as the shame cycle. As this happens, the person may find it easier to ask for and accept help from others.

Five processes are involved here. Although they are presented in a sequence, often one experiences these domains simultaneously or vacillates between them. "Facing the Music" describes the painful struggle of confronting the learning disability and developing new ways of working around it. In "Grief: It's Here to Stay" an individual accepts the fact that the learning disability and its shame-producing ramifications are permanent. "Identifying Helpers and Hinderers" explores the uncomfortable task of seeking help from others, with varying degrees of success. In "Avoiding Pitfalls" individuals with ULD continue to treat and accept their learning disability; their they also learn to fine-tune their ability to prevent shame incidents. Last, "Taking It In" describes the attempts to reconcile, in one's mind and heart, the fact of one's learning disability with one's innermost feelings and internalized messages from the past.

FACING THE MUSIC

I can't do what I've been doing. I have to learn all over again. And I'll tell you, it's very difficult.

Facing the Music involves replacing comfortable but less-than-effective methods of achieving with unfamiliar but far more effective approaches. It can be distressing to give up familiar, comfortable methods of learning even when these techniques fail again and again. For adults, study habits are tough to change or give up; they have had many years to solidify.

Trying new ways of compensating for one's learning disability can stimulate familiar feelings of shame. As before diagnosis, the shame cycle drives people to avoid the disability and therefore fail to develop innovative ways around it, compounding the problem:

- I am adaptive. But I'll tell you—I get very tired of it.
- I now know that if I want to get A's I must start papers early. And that means that I will suffer for a longer period of time.
- It was very difficult for me to stop using my mouth and now try to listen in class.

Educational consultants (also called learning disabilities specialists) can be a tremendous help to a person with ULD. Their training gives them access to the most effective strategies for fighting LD. However, carrying out their suggestions is easier said than done. (Bringing oneself to ask for their help in the first place is another issue; this problem is discussed later in "Identifying Helpers and Hinderers.") The disability seems impossible to surmount and may even prevent the individual from absorbing the new ways of learning that the consultant is trying to teach:

- No matter how much help I get, nothing is going to stop me from getting sleepy when I read.
- I can't remember what my tutor told me.
- Since I'm so disorganized, I can't keep my notes straight.

The hope engendered during testing is tempered by the difficult reality of finding appropriate tools with which to learn and work. Slowly reality sinks in: no magic formula will fix a learning disability.

- I do it [compensate], but I hate doing it.
- I need to research every damn thing that comes up . . . nothing stays in my head.
- I can't break down things into steps.
- I resent having to work so hard.
- How can I write papers when I can't think in a clear, organized fashion?

Time, a familiar enemy, returns. Both teachers and bosses value the ability to work quickly. However, many of the necessary steps suggested by educational consultants involve restraining oneself, taking more steps, or repetition. The techniques slow down the ULD person when they may already feel "too slow." These new, time-consuming steps generate frustration. The slow pace of work in the area of disability contrasts painfully with quick success in other areas:

- I'm a hard worker and I love school . . . no matter how badly I do. I do my best, but why does it have to take so long?
- Sure, good for her [the tutor]—she can casually say, "Tape the class and then listen to the tape and take notes from the tape." But this is only one of our four classes, and it takes forever. Not only that, I have to listen three or four times before it clicks in.
- Every time I look at an article or a book, I first look at how thick it is. . . . The longer the article, the more hours and hours of painful work ahead of me.
- My brain works in slow motion. . . . Two hours from now, something will kick in.
- I can't read something, digest it in a reasonable period of time, and give it back in an appropriate way.
- She wants me to spend at least a day in the library just finding the books, and then it will take me forever to read them. . . . I'm used to writing a paper in one day.

Seeking ways to work around a learning disability may again raise the specter of the chasm. As an individual tackles old problem areas once again, the familiar paralysis and isolation of shame may hinder the effort. These feelings must be overcome to bring success within reach:

- It's so painful to know that the first four or five times I try to memorize something, absolutely nothing—nothing—will stay in my head.
- I hate putting up with that place of nothingness in my head until something finally clicks.
- In the meantime, until I master the assignment, I have to put up with this "nothing" feeling.

- It's as though I were back in first grade again being asked to read with the bluebirds.
- I feel I'm up against a brick wall. . . . There is no place to go.
- It's embarrassing.
- It's like the belts [being whipped] all over again every time I try to retrieve information.
- I feel degraded. . . . Why should I have to have it so special? Why can't I do it normally?

In summary, soon after diagnosis, ULD people must replace familiar ways of achieving with what at first seem to be harder, inefficient, and confusing methods. Confronting the familiar areas of difficulty can again evoke the feelings of the chasm. The shame instinct to stop, coupled with the educational consultant's instructions to proceed doggedly forward, can make the learning experience almost unbearable. As the enormity of the task of compensating for a disability becomes clear, the grieving experience begins.

GRIEF: IT'S HERE TO STAY

It's always there. I knew it in my head, but then I knew it in my heart.

People go through a grieving process not only when a loved one dies, but when anything dear to them is lost. This can include a cherished dream, a valued relationship, or an idealized picture of who they are and how they fit into the world. One step in any grieving process is accepting the loss as permanent. In the case of ULD, an individual comes to a sobering realization: after years of fighting learning difficulties, then years of not really dealing with them, the individual finally must face the fact that he or she can do certain things, if at all, only slowly and deliberately. This will not change. Although there are tools and tricks for dealing with a learning disability, they cannot make the disability itself go away:

- No matter how much therapy I have, I'll always need to tape things and then have to slow down the tapes. I think that's a problem that's just there and that I have to learn to live with it.

- I was born this way.
- It's never going to go away. So as long as I live, it will be there.

Part of the grieving process also involves regrets. An individual with ULD regrets lost opportunities and unnecessary suffering:

- So much that could have been learned has been lost.
- Because I was labeled a behavior problem, I never had the opportunity to learn from and like other bright kids.
- I have to go back to school to do art now, and I'm twenty-nine years old.
- You can't erase all the trauma I've had because nobody knew why I wasn't learning.

Regret can also take the form of jealousy. Comparing oneself to others often leaves the individual feeling isolated and unfortunate. This experience echoes earlier feelings of "Why me?":

- I couldn't stand it when it took me hours to learn what a child would learn in five minutes.
- Why do I have to start my papers early in the semester when people in my dorm have lots of time to do other things together and then finish their papers anywhere from one night to, at most, a week?
- It's not fair that I work so much longer and harder than other people and they get better grades.
- This guy frustrates me because he looks at something one time and he knows it. . . . It's not right that I should have to work so hard.

Once the individual really accepts the disability and grief has run its course, the person can begin to seek help.

IDENTIFYING HELPERS AND HINDERERS

Following diagnosis, an individual with ULD will often decide that it is necessary to seek help. Apart from making use of the help once it is received, asking for help in the first place runs counter to the strain of independence that has helped a person with ULD survive thus far. In the past, working around these invisible problems was a lonely endeavor. Success depended on an individual's own ingenuity, creativity, and initiative. These self-governed strengths, therefore, enhanced early self-esteem. Now, asking help from the world evokes feelings of exposure and is understandably difficult:

- I figured out how to get by myself.
- I've always stood on my own two feet.
- Sometimes it hurts even though there is a need.
- I don't like putting myself on the line like that.

Since the diagnosis—perhaps even the knowledge of learning disabilities—is new, a person may be unsure whether it is appropriate to seek help. The ensuing feeling of dependence can become even more humiliating. It seems as though one is asking for help one does not deserve:

- Maybe I was asking for something special. I really didn't know.
- I was told I had the right to ask for this, but it felt as though I was taking advantage of the situation. . . . Now I know better, but at the time it was difficult.

Of course, once the person with learning disabilities overcomes these roadblocks and seeks help, he or she does not necessarily meet with success. The two main sources of help are LD specialists, who give one-on-one consultations, and educational institutions or teachers, who have the power to grant special privileges. It is generally easier to ask for help from the former than from the latter. For one thing, since it is their job to be well-informed about LD, specialists rarely fail to understand and cooperate, while schools and teachers might have little information or experience. Also, seeing a specialist does not feel like asking for a favor, but seeking help from a school often has that meaning, even though such assistance is a legal right. Consulting a specialist, therefore, might be a somewhat less daunting task—although not all specialists are consistently supportive:

- Asking for someone to be my note taker is embarrassing. I feel like an idiot.
- I hate asking the professor for more time.

Hinderers are those who meet requests for help with annoyance, misunderstanding, and accusations. Some who are asked for help intensify the discomfort of the person with ULD by reacting with insensitivity or ignorance. In this case, asking for help can be disconcerting. When attempts to communicate a need for assistance fail, the paralysis and despair of the chasm reemerge:

- I told one instructor I had dyslexia, and she said I should go to an optometrist for new glasses.
- She [the professor] accused me of manipulating her and demanding extra attention no one else gets.
- He [the professor] said, "This is college, you know."
- The first time I did it [asked a question], I knew I wasn't making much sense to him because his eyes glazed over. I could see it, and I sort of gave up.

Eventually, many persons with learning disabilities become quite adept at seeking and receiving aid. In some instances, however, this process can somehow still feel dishonest and deceitful, requiring furtive behavior:

- I say, "I've heard that you know this stuff. What should I look for?" And they won't tell me what I should look for; they'll tell me the answer. . . . I've always thought of this as cheating.
- I have been able to use people, but I feel guilty about doing so.
- If I need something to read or something checked over, I know how to finagle people to get what I need out of them. . . . Not that I'm doing this in a deceitful, mean way. It's just called survival.
- The better I make them feel, the more complete their answer is to me.

Receiving needed assistance engenders a new set of feelings. First, the person with ULD can feel validated: another human being listened and accepted his or her disability. It may be that the solution is simple; a slight bending of the rules will suffice. Most important, the door of achievement is finally opened. The person may find success in subject areas that had previously caused tremendous pain and difficulty. The Imprisoned Intelligence begins to experience its first taste of freedom:

- If someone can understand the difficulty—even if they won't change the date due, for example—it helps so much.
- He can see my artistry and my disability, both.
- If I'm heard, I can switch to another way of learning. I can move to another direction and find the way through.
- If somebody can take the time to very slowly say things to me, I can then read better.
- I don't need sympathy. I just need a place where I can type my exams.
- All I needed was another hour for my exams.

Some individuals can also have their own semisuccessful coping methods validated when competent professionals and understanding educators show them how to build onto these approaches:

- She started where I was at. She never had me do things the way others had to do things.
- Since the normal ways didn't work, I felt like she and I were working together to figure out creative ways to free my intelligence.
- She always waited to see how I did it first.
- I could be a computer operator because I did not learn from the books. . . . I walked into the lab and said, "Show me." And they showed me, and I graduated.
- She started with what I had and then helped me learn a better way to organize.

As individuals with ULD begin to ask for help, they encounter both hinderers and helpers. In the former case, they may re-experience the shame and paralysis of the chasm. In the latter case, they begin to experience personal validation and learning success. Over time, an individual will try to limit experiences with hinderers by developing proactive strategies.

AVOIDING PITFALLS

> I was at Passover, and they wanted me to read a portion. . . .
> Now, I can't even read regular English words, let alone He-
> brew translations. And I went up to somebody and said, "Do
> you know what that word is?" They said, "You don't know
> how to read?" It felt like I was back in third grade again. It
> took me longer [to read], people started blurting words out,
> and I was nervous. If I go to a Passover reading, I will not read
> in front of the group unless I have rehearsed it. But I will not
> go point blank. I won't do it.

The above incident illustrates an embarrassing situation that exposed a learning disability. It also illustrates an individual with ULD
drawing the line—he has decided that a certain task is not worth the
grief and will not let himself be pushed. By avoiding such pitfalls,
one protects oneself from recurring painful experiences.

One important pitfall individuals often face is prejudice against
learning disabilities. They come to realize that, while some people
can be approached as helpers, information about the disability is
often best kept secret. Not only could knowledge of the disability
result in a loss of respect from colleagues, teachers, supervisors, and
friends, it could compromise future career and academic success:

- I've never said I have a learning disability at work because I
  wouldn't have gotten to where I've gotten if they knew.
- If I told someone, I would be thinking, "Oh, they're going to
  see a weakness here, and it's not going to be good."
- I didn't tell anyone I had learning disabilities because I had
  tried that once over there [at a major university] and it was a
  big flop. . . . So I learned to be very careful and disguise it.
- When I told the dean of students because I was behind in papers, she was just fine. But this is not the air we're breathing in.
  There aren't many learning disability people out of the closet.
  They may not even know they are in the closet.
- I need a reference from that lady. . . . Do you think I want to
  give her a reason not to think highly of me?

TAKING IT IN

> Even knowing what I know, I can't help it. Blaming myself is like a habit I can't break.

After testing, an individual has the information that the learning disability is most likely physiologically based. This intellectual knowledge is often accompanied by a nagging inner voice: *It's your fault. You're lazy and stupid. You're not fooling anyone with these excuses about LD.* Because these childhood voices are powerful, individuals must struggle to integrate what they know to be the truth with what they *feel* to be the truth.

From testing, people understand that parts of their intellectual functioning differ from the norm. They struggle between blaming themselves and accepting the learning disability as a product of physiology and/or development:

- I still think the conventional way—that I should be able to pick up a book and read it.
- I still think that there's something wrong with me and I must be stupid.
- I can get it, but I feel humiliated because it took me too long.
- Sometimes I think I'm failing because I'm lazy and sometimes I know that I'm stuck and need help. . . . It's hard to know which is which.

Most realize that they are having a hard time integrating their knowledge, as these quotes show. In some cases, however, blaming the self has become so ingrained that it is difficult to stop. They continue to place blame on personal behavior or traits rather than on the disability:

> Part of knowing that I'm LD now is not good because of wanting to use that as an excuse—and like, not working hard or something. But maybe if I worked a little harder at it, I might get it. But because I know I'm LD in that area, it's kind of like, why do it if it's not going to work? So part of that— part of me wishes I hadn't found out. Maybe I would try harder. But part of me is glad that I did because I stopped beating myself up for not getting certain things.

The acceptance of the physiological nature of the problem can be enhanced when individuals with ULD realize that others in their families probably suffer from similar disabilities:

- My brother suffers from the same problems, but he never did anything about it.
- My father is just like me. It takes one to know one.
- My daughter has exactly the same problem.
- My mother said she couldn't read because she didn't know English. But now I know she can't read in Spanish either.
- I wonder about people like my parents who can't read. . . . I used to think it was the language; now I know they just can't read. I wonder, is it a learning disability?

Suspicions about the genetic basis of the learning disability can be bolstered by similar diagnoses in the family:

- My sister was diagnosed before I was, and she was younger.
- When my daughter was diagnosed, I knew I suffered some of the same problems.

The individual learns to confront the learning disability, grieve over what cannot be changed, find appropriate ways of seeking help and avoiding hinderers, and begins to integrate the knowledge into the ingrained message he or she had previously accepted.

Chapter 6

New Reflections:
A Different Mirror

"Scholar" is a successful academician who discovered his learning disability in late adolescence.

Interviewer: Has learning about your learning disabilities been helpful in understanding your own development?

Scholar: Oh yes. You have a lot more flexibility in dealing with the educational world. At the earlier levels, I didn't have a mechanism for dealing with the teachers who wanted to see me as stupid, who found me frustrating, who reacted very negatively to my inability to spell and to write well. And to be honest, I think there are an awful lot of anal compulsive people out there who see their job to get Johnny to *spell it right* but they don't have a particular model on how to help kids learn to *think*. So it would have been very useful [for] me and my parents to have this rhetoric to deal with these teachers.

Interviewer: Has it helped you now, in your day-to-day living, to know about your LD?

Scholar: Oh sure. Absolutely. The more you know, the more you can make sense out of it, the better off you are. I'm in a profession now where the whole question of how bright you are and how good a scholar you are is endemic; I mean, this is a professional liability. No one in a top research university doesn't spend a certain amount of energy worrying about just how good their work is; and having an understanding of my history as dyslexic means that it's helpful in dealing with these problems. The initial response [in academia] is to evaluate people according to volume; how much they publish. But on the other hand, I think over the long term, people look at the quality and the impact the piece of work has. [For example,] the guy who just got the Nobel prize in economics, he only published twelve articles in his life. Period. They were just twelve great articles [laughter]. Enormous impact. If you look at his life, the lack of the number of articles published must have caused him a lot of grief. But if you look at the *quality* of what he did, it resulted in his getting the Nobel Prize.

Interviewer: So, in this sense, one's learning disability gives one time to think more creatively. Why do you think this is so?

Scholar: Well, it's like the experiments with rats about how you get feedback. If you want to make the rat most persistent, you give him intermittent feedback. If it's just regular [feedback] they do reasonably well, and if it's not regular, they won't perform at all. But, if it's random, you get the most positive behavior on their part. They will be the most aggressive at pursuing something.

Well, if you look at my life, sometimes [I] got lots of positive feedback and sometimes [I] got negative. It was random and this keeps one tenacious.

Coming to terms with a newly diagnosed learning disability requires a great deal of psychological and practical effort. One has to work both to change oneself, by reconstructing learning skills, and to accept oneself, by realizing that the disability is a physical fact and not a malleable character flaw:

> I've accepted my learning disability in my heart and in my mind now . . . I'm smart. I'm gifted. I'm talented. And even though the learning disability frustrates me, I just have to accept it.

Chapter 5 explored the struggles involved in learning to live with LD. This chapter will discuss what happens when the struggle is reconciled.

Reconciliation has four domains. These domains will overlap, and an individual may oscillate between them. In the first, *personal definitions* evolve for the individual. Then *acceptance* slowly emerges. The painful events of the past are resurrected and resolved as *personal history is reinterpreted.* The world's standards lose their awesome power to define the individual, and *personal perspectives* can be developed.

PERSONAL DEFINITIONS

One part of reconciliation is developing a personal definition of learning disabilities. This is quite different from parroting an expert's technical or legal definition. Creating a personal definition involves encapsulating and articulating a lifetime's worth of learning experiences and therefore requires considerable insight and self-knowledge. Some of the following definitions are deceptively simple. Their elegance resides in their capacity to transform what was once ineffable and mysterious into an explicit and comprehensible problem:

- Learning disabilities are like a short in the system.
- [Having] learning disabilities means taking longer to learn.
- [Having] learning disabilities is like watching TV and you're blind.
- I hear the word, but I can't match it to an experience or a feeling. Maybe that's what learning disabilities are all about: no matching.
- Imprisoned Intelligence is the sense of myself as being intelligent, but outward expression becomes excruciatingly difficult.
- Imprisoned Intelligence is being able to hear better than I can see, but having to learn by reading.
- Imprisoned Intelligence is feeling trapped.
- Imprisoned Intelligence is the opposite of the goodness of fit.

If evolving a personal definition answers the question "What?" then accumulating a knowledge base about one's LD answers the question "Why?" Knowing and accepting the causes of one's constrained learning can be a great source of comfort:

- Now when I hit the "chasm," at least I have a "because."
- I have an auditory processing problem, so sometimes I can't retain what people are saying.
- Now I know why I couldn't read a book no matter how much I wanted the information in it.
- My brain works in slow motion, but I know that two hours from now something will kick in.

ACCEPTANCE

There is no one moment when an individual "accepts" her or his disability. Acceptance develops only with time and experience. It grows out of day-to-day involvement: dealing with frustrations as they come up, and gradually learning what one can and cannot do. Acceptance allows one to set realistic goals and standards for oneself:

- I'm not a whole, perfect person, and I've got some missing parts, so that feels bad. And then I say, "But you've got all these other talents and skills, and a lot of people have missing parts." . . . I say to myself, "You know, you're not going to ruin your life over this. You just can't."
- I finally became detached from the standard of the school.
- I don't think I'll feel fully comfortable in school because it's just not my element.
- I'm trying to get through school the best I can.
- I'll always carry this extra baggage when I learn, and I have gotten used to it.

The emotions connected to the learning disability may never disappear, but they do become bearable and under control. Painful feelings are not as overwhelming as they were in prediagnosis days:

- It's like dipping into the pool of pain and pulling up a bucket as opposed to falling into the pool and being drowned.
- I've done so much to make myself not feel so bad that, when I talk about it more at this level, it makes me understand why I feel so bad about this learning disability.
- The feeling never gets so overwhelming that I really fall into a deep depression like I used to.

LD sufferers learn to tolerate their own imperfections. Like every other human being, they are flawed and will sometimes fail. This no longer seems like an unforgivable sin:

- I'm handicapped here, vulnerable here. And I need some help.
- I could finally forgive the younger self in me that I had been so abusive to.
- Now I could finally lay it [the learning problem] to rest and feel infinitely kinder toward that self as a consequence of this knowledge.

Because their disability can now be separated from their intelligence, these people are free to examine their intelligence objectively. Without the distortion of ULD, they can know and appreciate their strengths. They begin to take pride in their gifts, talents, and accomplishments. Indeed, acknowledging the disability enhances self-esteem, as they recognize the tenacity and resourcefulness that it took to survive all those years:

- My dyslexia forced me to learn to think for myself.
- My strong suit had been tenacity, and that usually pulled me through.
- I did not take the advice I was receiving from the rest of the world, and I'm glad I didn't because I'd be sitting in a mental institution if I had done that. I just kept on fighting.

Individuals can now use their intelligence and talents with confidence. A newfound feeling of empowerment allows them to seek out appropriate alternatives and to make good choices for themselves. They take charge of their own learning environment:

- I am learning things about myself. And I can say, "I don't learn that way; this is the way I learn."
- I can choose the necessary tools to help me learn another way.
- I will decide when I want to take tests untimed and when I don't.
- I don't need to tape all my classes, just a few of them.

Another indication of acceptance is the ability to joke about one's disability. Previously, the learning disability was too painful to be humorous. With acceptance comes an ability to make light of the situation:

- I don't need sleeping pills; I just need a book.
- I just pick up a boring book, look at a page, and I'm sleeping.
- Every time I give my wife a paper to read, she begins groaning.

PERSONAL HISTORY REINTERPRETED

Armed with new information, individuals can look at their past and make new sense of it. They can reinterpret events that their confused younger selves did not understand, and can now debunk old myths:

- I can look back with some sense of hindsight. I mean, it really was like, you know, having my life as a jigsaw puzzle with two-thirds of it missing.
- I wasn't lazy.
- I don't hate my mother.
- I'm not getting even.
- I'm not acting out.
- I alternately had what I now see is an inflated grandiose sense of myself—of my intelligence—versus the exact opposite of that—a kind of retardation. And it was very difficult to find a balance between the grandiosity and the terrible self-esteem. And you know, ego damage was done.
- I was always an ambitious and driven kid. And when I was in junior high, I had a headmaster who was fully convinced that I wasn't very smart and that I was an overachiever [laughter]. Unfortunately he passed away, because I always wanted to go back and tell him about myself.

Grief and despair over what might have been evolve into a more benign wistfulness. The note of anger and desperation fades:

- I feel I wish I could have done this a long time ago.
- If I had known, if they had known, if there had been help, what if?
- I saw a Montessori school program recently, and I thought to myself, "Geez, I wish I had that."
- I wanted to be an architect, but, you see, nobody ever taught me anything.

One reexamines past relationships. Realizing that no one knew about LD then, the individual is able to accept the ineffectual attempts of parents and others to help as well-meaning. After all, how could anyone offer much assistance when they didn't understand the problem? One can forgive former nemeses:

- I guess it mainly all goes back to that people aren't aware, people that are in contact with you and would be able to help you if they knew about it.
- When my mom found out I had learning disabilities, she was the one that came out to apologize to me.
- My mother has been very hard on herself now for what she said to me then. We fought a lot.
- No one apologized to me. And I guess, maybe I expected them to, but then later on I thought to myself, "Look, your parents aren't people that hate you. They tried to help you."
- I know now that my father was trying to motivate me into being a better person. It didn't work, but now I can forgive him.
- I have the sense that people who reacted negatively to me were either professors who gave up hope and thought I couldn't learn or maybe, I don't know, people who have undiagnosed learning disabilities themselves.

PERSONAL PERSPECTIVES

Many individuals with ULD are especially interested in scrutinizing the practices of the schools they attended, since the classroom was where they experienced their first learning failures and consequent shame. With the knowledge they now have, they can identify specific practices that stopped learning in its tracks:

- After I found out about my learning disability, I thought, "How dare you have such a title as Reading Instructor when you don't know anything about learning disabilities?"
- Sometimes, it wasn't the teacher's fault, it was the system.
- In kindergarten I learned to read quite well using phonics, but then we transferred to another school where they taught reading using sight. And being a dyslexic, I was dead, right there.
- When she spoke, I learned everything easily, but when I had to read, I failed.
- When I was in high school, I was the world's worst French student and a lot of that had to do with the fact that French was taught in an almost exclusively auditory way and I just couldn't process it. And this was in contrast to my being one of the very best Latin students in school. In Latin you had to read and translate.
- I failed the test because I couldn't write it. But when he asked me all the questions, I knew every answer.
- I spent a semester at [University #2]. It was so enormously different than [University #1]. It really pretty much blew me away. The emphasis [at University #2] was so much on neatness, getting it right, having it said correctly, so on and so forth. I did very well at [University #1], Phi Beta Kappa and honors and all sorts of things. And, I have to tell you, I didn't work too hard. I had a good time. And it was really clear to me that if I had gone to [University #2] on a permanent basis, which I think is not nearly as good a school, I would have done much worse.

Out of this reevaluation of school standards comes a concern for others with ULD who might still be at the mercy of an unyielding educational system. Many emerged from their experience with a feeling of group solidarity and an interest in LD as a social issue:

- I think teachers should be aware of learning disabilities or shouldn't be in a position where they can't help students.
- I think about all the kids who never get a chance to use their brains.

- I think about these other people, and I guess that they're not so tough or not so strong.
- I guess they just gave up . . . it's so sad.

In fact, many of the individuals who participated in this study did so to reach out to others who might be suffering in ignorance:

- I think this is very valuable research. It's information that is not really easy to get at and that's not well reported.
- This message needs to be spread.
- I'm only doing this so you will teach others about this when you finish.

Reconciliation is the final acceptance of living with an undiagnosed learning disability. Over time, one develops new perspectives and views of the self that provide some degree of meaning and comfort. Reconciliation, however, is ongoing, a process that will continue for the rest of one's life. By and large, the individual grows increasingly comfortable with the disability as time goes on. Even so, this comfort never overlooks the fact that early diagnosis could have mitigated the pain of growing up and vastly improved one's academic and intellectual careers.

Chapter 7

Fulfilling Potential: Bootstrapping

Interviewer: Since this problem was unknown, others could not be there for you in the most effective way. Can we talk about how you helped yourself?

Scholar: Well, first of all, my dyslexia has developed analytic skills for me for what we might call independent thinking, though I don't want to use that in a cliched sort of way. You know, when the old grid or patterns don't work, the mind has the capacity to think of new creative ways of being; and that's kind of nice in a way. My dyslexia interfered with these "normal" grids or patterns and forced me to learn to think for myself. I don't mean that in the jargonistic way that we typically say that; but rather, a lot of people solve problems by having people *teach* them to solve problems. [Because of my dyslexia] I couldn't be taught in the usual way and, I think, would go off and find my *own* solutions, which is exemplified by my scholarly work.

My reputation is a person who produces very high [-quality] work but not fast. People complain about the fact that I don't produce fast enough. Well, I know something about why I don't produce fast enough: it takes me a lot longer for me to craft the paper into a top work than it does for most people and it has to do with the dyslexia. When I write papers it's easier because I understand why I have this problem, and so I have to work harder to compensate for it. And to think about that problem as being dyslexic as opposed to "you're stupid" is a lot easier.

When I write a paper, I get my wife to go through it, I get the secretary at work to go through it, I mean I find other kinds of compensating mechanisms now. When I go to the university, I'll say, look, I need a secretary that doesn't have to do a lot of work, but she has to be brilliant in spelling and grammar, because that's what I need. The world out there sees me as extremely well organized, extremely proactive. I tend to keep a fairly rigid calendar. When you go into my office, there's a spot for everything. I'm very big on lists and am always asking, "What do we have to do today?" I tend to always have things in on time, but I must!

Scholar has, obviously, over time, figured out ways to help himself succeed. This is what *bootstrapping* is about: the ability to figure out what's wrong and how to fix it. How do people do this? How does this process begin? Let's begin with a story:

Upon the death of his father, a prince returns home after many years of education in foreign lands. He is now king. He returns to a country split into two dangerous factions: the Achievers and the Nonachievers. The Achievers are aware of being smart and quick and efficient. They are also somewhat arrogant and impatient. They run the country and pride themselves on their efficiency and competence. Their lives are comfortable and the country runs smoothly. The achievers don't think much about the nonachievers. The nonachievers are simply an unfortunate extraneous footnote in their lives—nothing to pay attention to.

The Nonachievers are aware of being different. They are not smart, quick, or efficient. They spend their time wishing to be, and comparing themselves to the Achievers. They feel shamefully shortchanged. Because their focus is always on competent others, they never learn about themselves.

Now this liberal-minded young monarch knows two things: (1) a well-functioning country must help *all* its citizens find a productive niche and (2) his country will not be a world leader and will be torn apart unless these two factions can understand and negotiate with each other. The Achievers must control their impatience. The Nonachievers must overcome their hopelessness. He knows that a bridge needs to be created between these two disparate factions. An edict, therefore, is issued for a summit conference with the following goals: the Achievers must learn to recognize and understand the alienation of the Nonachievers. This will, at least, begin a dialogue between the two groups.

Because this king is wise, he knows that dialogue will be impossible if one party is suffering from intense feelings of exposure and humiliation. He needs to find a way to disrupt the Nonachievers' shame cycle. Therefore, another edict is issued: everyone must learn to recognize feelings of shame. Then the Nonachievers *experiencing* the shame can point this out to the achievers *causing* the shame. Different interactions could then possibly ensue. In other words, the king is creating a détente between the two factions to help them communicate.

Clearly, the thinking process of intelligent adults with ULD, is divided like the country in the story. Some parts are fruitful and function like the Achievers. Other areas function like the Nonachievers. And, if ULD is problematic, there's not much connection between the two.

When the demands of the world are easily met (as a bright math student does in a math class) one assumes that learning will be relatively quick and painless. And it is. But when the demands of the world cannot be met (the same math student does poorly English class) the same assumption, that learning is easy, makes it more difficult to succeed in these areas. In other words, the part of one's mind that learns easily is impatient when learning is not comfortable. At the same time, the nonachieving part that learns with difficulty is painfully ashamed, because in difficult areas, it's not only hard to learn, but there is exposure in the face of inner critical impatience.

What can be done about inhibiting internal criticism? Becoming aware of this "voice" (as opposed to simply reacting) can develop and nurture a benevolent "monarch" inside one's own mind. This inner mediator can attempt to look at all sides of the problem and can negotiate between the Achievers and the Nonachievers.

A person suffering with ULD, however, might declare, "I cannot simply create a benevolent monarch inside myself out of the blue;

how am I supposed to do this?" Well, it will be neither simple nor out of the blue, but this problem *will* respond to intuition, curiosity, and introspection.

Becoming aware and respectful of discrepancies in cognitive functioning allows for compassionate self-exploration. Individuals can then wonder about when, where, why, and how they feel accomplished or incompetent. Understanding their deficits nonjudgmentally helps people learn to view their learning disabilities from a responsible, yet nurturing, perspective. By taking responsibility for both strengths and weaknesses, one's strengths can be used to *help* weaknesses.

Taking personal responsibility is the overarching message behind this chapter. It will suggest four ways to begin to fulfill potential: (1) facing the problem; (2) facing the chasm; (3) finding support; and (4) finding appropriate professional help.

Facing the problem involves two strategies: (1) identifying strengths and weaknesses; and then (2) finding appropriate compensations.

FACING THE PROBLEM

Identifying Strengths and Weaknesses

People with ULD know themselves best. Not all learning disabilities are problematic. Let me be clear about this: *ULD matters only if it interferes with fulfillment.* Many people have created comfortable niches where their intellect is challenged and their learning disabilities bypassed. The brilliant computer programmer, for example, does not have to worry about spelling because of spelling checker programs. But, if a person's intellect is drying up or his or her world changes, it might be very important to know about this hidden dimension in how one learns. For example: (1) previously successful people who have been laid off from a comfortable job find it difficult to learn under different circumstances; (2) previously successful students inexplicably cannot learn from one teacher; or (3) friendly people who have always lived in the same place cannot seem to make friends after moving. If goals are waylaid by unknown factors, ULD is a possible problem.

However, before getting help (and in order to get help) it is very important to honestly evaluate strengths, because then motivation for further investigation will be enhanced. This will help determine whether to proceed. This sounds easy. It is not.

Most smart people are proud of their intelligence. Pride takes a beating when one admits that in some areas, learning does not happen. Recognizing one's weaknesses is painful and individuals try to create a world in which they feel wholly competent. The problem is that this comfortable world is a fiction that cannot be maintained. Sooner or later, school or work will make demands that call upon areas of weakness, and people are rudely and painfully shocked. This shock, and the subsequent descent into the chasm, can be prevented if there is an awareness of weakness that then can be addressed and treated. An internal bridge is needed to bring strengths and weaknesses into contact.

One factor that prevents this bridge from developing is prolonged shame. Sporadic but chronic feelings of stupidity can cause individuals to be caught in a cycle of destructive shame (see Chapter 2). Once it starts, shame is difficult to stop. It becomes almost impossible to keep from berating ourselves or to remember our intelligence. This may sound like a catch-22: If people do not understand their weaknesses, they become acutely ashamed, and if they are acutely ashamed, they will not be able to understand their weaknesses. This is why ULD is neither easy nor simple to treat. However, gradual awareness of the shame cycle will help curtail its effects. This chapter will suggest ways that foster such self-awareness, as well as other methods for straddling strengths and weaknesses.

One of the participants in this study learned that the reason she cannot read maps or easily find her way in new situations is because of visual-spatial learning problems. After diagnosis she could more readily understand her husband's frustration when she was lost and late so often. She could also be more self-forgiving because she knew this was not her fault.

Without a diagnosis, however, analysis of one's strengths and weaknesses is complicated and requires self-observation over time. It helps to focus on taking a broad enough view to *encompass* both intellect and deficits. This keeps us from falling into the shame/ blame cycle. Then when strengths and weaknesses become more familiar, it can be helpful to seek out more technical information about learning disabilities and about your particular diagnosis. (For further reading, see the Bibliography.)

Learning disorders are idiosyncratic; they occur in a wide variety. Unless an individual is that rarest of creatures, the "textbook case," a list of learning disabilities will not be specific enough. *One's own perception of learning discrepancies, on the other hand, will tell a great deal.* The fundamental question is: Are individuals very good at some things and very bad at others? For all intents and purposes, this is a defining characteristic of learning disabilities. The goal of diagnostic tests is to find such discrepancies. In essence, a discrepancy between ability and function is one very strong clue indicating a possible learning disability.

Two other broad questions may be helpful. First, how did the person do in school? Second, how is she or he functioning now?

School

A history of repetitive difficult experiences at school can be an indicator of learning disabilities. Of course, there can be other reasons why people have trouble in school, but if there seems to be a pattern, learning disabilities can be a possibility to consider. Individuals, for example, who were labeled overachievers may have been compensating to hide the fact that it took longer to study or finish assignments. The following are other questions to consider.

Was the person an overachiever who never had time to play with other kids because of diligently *always* working on homework? Did he or she excel but somehow think and/or feel like a cheater? Was the person considered an underachiever? Was there trouble getting started? Did the person get A's in some classes and fail or nearly fail in others? Was there boredom in school but fascination elsewhere? Could the student learn from some teachers but, independent of effort, fail to learn from others?

Current Functioning

The following may serve as markers for possible undiagnosed learning disabilities. Some people may be:

- Competent at some things and hopeless at others.
- Good at math and bad at English or vice versa.*
- Sloppy.
- Consistently late.
- Fond of reading but bored listening to lectures or vice versa.
- Delighted to watch the educational channel and bored reading a book.

Other possibilities, in terms of current functioning, might include:

- Feeling the frustration of sporadic failures in the face of high achievement at work.
- Feeling that one's weaknesses and not strengths are being exposed. (Sometimes this is manifested by high achievers who think they are fooling everyone.)
- Struggle with variation in performance: some days people can function like greased lightning, while on other days they function like a car with a flat tire.

Conditions at home can also be problematic:

- Organizational problems may create a messy household.
- Tardiness may prevail.
- Being unable to help one's children with seemingly simple homework may provoke frustration.

Are there other explanations for these discrepancies? Functioning can suffer, for example, if people are worried about losing their jobs, are suffering from depression, and are grieving in particular. It is difficult to know. It is important to foster an inquiring attitude.

One's intuition is important. In certain areas, does it feel almost impossible to learn or achieve, no matter how hard the attempt? Some people keep persevering no matter how many times they fail but never achieve their goals. (One participant, for example, wanted to be an

---

*There is an argument about this. Some people feel that learning discrepancies such as this are really simply learning differences. Perhaps this is so, but if it is, schools still need to radically alter their curricula so that they do not prevent students from learning in their areas of "difference." Teachers must expand their teaching methods and find alternative educational materials that address a multiplicity of learning styles.

engineer but eventually realized he could not conquer the mandated math courses.) One marker is consistency and time. If these problems have always been present, it is more likely that the problem may be an undiagnosed learning disability rather than a reaction to stressful situations. If there is current stress such as a breakup, an accident, or a depression in one's life, the ability to use one's brain effectively can temporarily diminish. In other words, it may be ULD or it may be something psychological. By paying attention to *both* possibilities a person will benefit. Essentially, the most important clue is that irrespective of intelligence, there is a sense that something is permanently wrong.

Finding Appropriate Compensations

Compensations help avoid exposure and embarrassment. Individuals will go to great lengths to avoid feeling embarrassed. It is amazing how children can figure out how to hide or modulate their deficits even when teachers and parents do not understand the problem. However, a child's capacity to strategize or get around unrecognized learning problems muddies the waters considerably because identification becomes more difficult.

For example, take the class clown. In many cases, class clowns are inordinately clever underachievers who entertain their peers and drive their teachers crazy. This role can be a form of compensation for students with ULD. For example, a smart boy with ULD becomes embarrassed when he cannot excel, and he hates to think of himself as dumb. The class clown does not put his head on the desk and cry because he cannot achieve. He compensates for his inability to learn by deflecting attention to his clever antics. Even though he may not be able to do academic work, he can still show his peers he is smart—even if he irritates the teacher in the process. The reasons underlying his lack of achievement are concealed by his seemingly psychologically based misbehavior.

The participants in this study compensated in very creative ways to subvert the invisible "something" that kept getting in their way. Some could talk their way out of any situation and managed to do quite well until the written work in college overwhelmed them. Others who could not listen or articulate comfortably would find themselves doing a great deal of written extra credit. It is interesting that, for the most part, the "writers" had an easier time in college than the "talkers."

The capacity to compensate can enhance growth and development. It creates pride in one's creativity and independence. Children with ULD have their feet to the fire. Because no one understands their problem, they have to figure out how to get around the "something" that keeps them from learning. Consider, for example, the participant who asked questions that got teachers to talk at length because she could not learn by reading.

However, compensations present their own problems. Children are left to rely on their own devices, and the techniques they employ may compromise their sense of self; the class clown is a case in point. Although idiosyncratic strategies may allow a child to function adequately, treatment could provide more effective methods and increase mastery and self-esteem.

To further complicate matters, compensations can fail when one's psychological world is in jeopardy. Those who can hide their deficits live fairly comfortable lives until something in the environment throws a curve ball. For example, adults with hidden dyslexia have learned that *q*s are really *g*s. So, when they read they convert the *q* into a *g*. This extra step is a part of their coping in normal times. But, when they become extremely emotionally distraught, fatigued, or ill, this extra step may not be possible.

This can be very confusing. How are individuals to know when (1) they are just being lazy and not trying hard enough, (2) they cannot excel because of ULD, or (3) their compensations for ULD fail? Here is where responsibility enters the picture. It is necessary to determine whether one is struggling with motivational problems or whether new ways of compensating need to be learned. Fundamentally, each individual person knows best what *feels* psychological and what *feels* innate.

A boss is picking on an employee because expectations are not being met and the employee is not working up to snuff. If the inability to produce is emotional (for example, the employee hates the boss) then the problem is psychological in origin. But if the employee (1) truly cannot figure out what the supervisor wants and

(2) has the feeling that something invisible, permanent, and immovable is getting in the way, the problem could be ULD.

Curiosity about the problem can be effective if people take a moment to wonder whether their intelligence is imprisoned. Is there some block to explain why performance is under par? ("I can't get organized"; "I'm always losing things"; "I really can't read directions fast enough"; "There's too much commotion around me and I can't concentrate"; and so forth.) Questions such as these can then help people figure out if there is any creative way to get around the problem.

Sometimes compromises have to be made that are not pleasant. Individuals may have to acknowledge problems such as this:

> OK, I'm different. Even though everyone else can finish their work during office hours, I cannot. So, even though I resent it, I guess I'll have to take work home with me.

Some of those interviewed said that they had trouble, at first, asking for help without feeling that they were compromising their pride and independence. It is difficult to admit deficits. They also had learned that, at times, confiding to others was *not* to their advantage. It is only sensible to hide your deficits if people will think less of you.

FACING THE CHASM:
THE BIGGEST CHALLENGE

Facing the chasm is the hardest part. It is difficult but necessary because recognition creates possibilities for change. The chasm, as explained earlier, is the place of nothingness; a horrible freeze where all thinking stops. Experiencing shameful failure when a person expects more success causes withdrawal. A person who cannot learn becomes humiliated, and the humiliation stops thought. People will do anything to avoid these nonfunctioning moments. The chasm makes people afraid to try to learn. But after testing, and armed with different strategies for learning, they have better tools for confronting this fear. However, facing the frozen parts of ourselves is inevitably difficult.

Although it is difficult, one can stop running, turn around, and look at what makes one's mind freeze up. For some it might be math, for others spelling, and so on. This can be very painful. The chances of experiencing self-shame in one's own critical eye will be very high. This is where the "internal negotiator" comes in, talking to the self like a good parent. For example:

- It's OK, the shame will pass.
- Others can help.
- This is a treatable problem.
- I'm transposing numbers—it's not my fault.
- Do something for ten minutes and then come back and try again.
- How can I make this better?

In the chasm, individuals view learning failures with an unforgiving eye. Optimally, the chasm is trying to give us a message: "Get out of the situation now. Wait until later to think and regroup." But when there is *only* an inner dialogue of judgment and contempt, the chasm is prolonged and takes on a life of its own. Those who break this cycle do so by cultivating empathy for themselves.

Reacting to and *not* recognizing shame is what a person is doing (and doing far too much) while in the chasm. In the chasm one feels frozen and controlled by shame. In fact, an individual is trying so hard *not* to feel shame that he or she cannot think about it or learn from it. Recognition is the key. Allowing oneself to experience shame can help identify its cause and allow for new possible alternatives.

One man, a learning disability teacher, evokes miracles in children with serious learning disabilities. He, however, cannot read aloud. One day, while attending an in-service training, the facilitator asked the participants to read from the material. This gifted instructor almost died from the anticipated embarrassment of having to expose his learning disabilities in front of uncomprehending people. "After all, I am the learning disability teacher. Surely, I should know how to read." Because he knew that reading out loud only leads to his chasm he excused himself before it was his turn and went to the bathroom. It worked!

It is sobering when people face their undiagnosed learning disabilities, and this knowledge can cause both anxiety and depression that further contributes to Imprisoned Intelligence.* The feelings diminish in intensity as people learn to get help and live with this. Over time, with help, the feelings will fade.

FINDING SUPPORT

The next two sections of this chapter deal with finding mentors and friends who can help. Each serves a different purpose.

Finding a Mentor

Mentors are people of wisdom who can eventually be trusted to respect both an individual's strengths and weaknesses. Usually they are successful in the areas of the learner's potential. The best are ethical human beings who have excelled in their fields of expertise. Learning from them can be most rewarding because no matter what mistakes are made, they can keep the potential of the learner in mind. Within this framework, the learner feels free to share what is unknown or what feels impossible to accomplish. One can learn without the hovering presence of shame and fear of being patronized. Finding mentors, then, becomes vital for people with LD and ULD.

Mentors can see potential, accept weaknesses, and foster growth. While good college professors are famous for this, mentors can be found in all walks of life. Many participants in this study said that finding mentors made all the difference in their efforts to overcome difficulties. They began with areas of interest and found individuals who excelled. Students, for example, who loved writing found professors who became enthusiastic about their papers. One vital criterion is the need to look up to one's mentor. Admiration becomes a key

---

*This is why learning disability specialists cannot do it all. Learning disability specialists can automatically cause anxiety because their primary focus and training involves confronting the learning disability itself. Having a psychotherapist to help with emotional issues frees the learning disability specialist to do his or her job more effectively.

ingredient that allows one to tolerate the internal shame that can occur when learning is difficult.

Finding people who can understand deficits without disregarding potential is essential. One can send out feelers to rule out intellectual snobs. One participant was careful to protect herself against her department chair for precisely this reason. Instead, she found someone in another department who was glad to be of help.

Finding mentors can be frustrating, but they are out there. Often people who are successful like to help others get their start; they may have had a mentor themselves and want to give something back. A good mentor gets a thrill out of someone else's growth. Although the mentor may tell you things you do not want to hear, it is with the goal of propelling learning.

In the process of finding a mentor, however, protecting oneself from the judgments of people who do not understand LD is paramount. One young man talked about a teacher who was excited and interested in his discussions in class. After the student turned in his first paper, however, organizational problems were obvious and the professor's disappointment became quite clear.

Protecting oneself does not mean dropping the class. It means realizing that some people do not know how to accept both strengths and disabilities. Looking for clues early on is helpful. Some people, despite their success, may shoot down others to boost their own self-esteem. Supervisors or professors who become impatient easily or are excessively critical may indeed be wonderful teachers and have much knowledge, but trusting them with one's vulnerabilities could subject an individual to unnecessary shame and humiliation.

Pragmatically speaking, sometimes it is necessary to put up with impatient people who make subtle or unsubtle fun of others. A supervisor, teaching someone new computer skills, may be annoyed by the way that person learns. It is difficult to face such judgment but when push comes to shove, the supervisor has the skills necessary for the learner's advancement. Criticism can be tolerated if it's time-limited and the rewards are meaningful. (One participant remembers getting barely passing grades on papers he struggled to complete and saying to himself, "After three more months, professor, you're out of my life.")

Furthermore, well-intended people sometimes truly believe that their denigration is helpful: "I'm doing this for your own good." Their intent may be honorable (or perhaps not) but one needs to accept that learning from them will be more difficult. In other words, expectations need modification. Learning from some people will be easy and from others difficult. But finding mentors that can teach what an individual is yearning to learn is indeed an exhilarating experience.

Finding Supportive Friends

Friends are not mentors. They are trustworthy people who can make significant connections with others. Friends, in the context of this book, are the people one turns to when shame imprisons intelligence or when Imprisoned Intelligence creates shame. Family members can also serve this function. The antidote to shame is reconnection with others. Individuals with ULD need friends who have the potential for understanding their plight. They will be there when a person is struggling to learn. They can, for example, be called when one feels discouraged, and they have the capacity to inspire in the face of defeat. Friends do not teach, nor do they necessarily make suggestions. But they must be willing to listen.

Even though many participants reported having serious trouble in school, their friends were very bright and academically successful. During the interview as people reflected on this, they realized that their friends recognized their intelligence, and were often more than willing to offer practical aid. One participant, for example, who was a superb tennis player spoke of how she gave a friend tennis lessons in exchange for help with her math.

This benefit can hold true at work as well. People do find friends on the job. Deals can be made. In fact, making deals is one way to acknowledge both strengths and weaknesses. For example, a worker with first-rate math skills can help a trusted math-deficient co-worker who has good organizational skills. The thinking process might be: "She'll make sure I understand directions and I'll check her math." In school, someone who cannot take notes but understands concepts through listening might find a good note-taker who needs tutoring with concepts before exams.

FINDING APPROPRIATE PROFESSIONAL HELP

ULD and Psychotherapy

This study clearly indicates that ULD creates a world of anxiety and emotional distress. ULD is traumatic because expectations about the ability to succeed are frustrated by factors beyond one's control. Motivation, then, can be attacked as parents, teachers, or bosses conclude, "You didn't try hard enough." *Attacks on well-intended motivation sabotage self-esteem.* By the time people are adults they have learned to compensate, but the specter of shame lurks. This is one reason why the learning disorder and psychological problems are intertwined like a tightly knit fabric.

This idea of an orchestra with all the instruments representing different aspects of one's self is a good analogy. ULD is the horn section and the rest of the instruments are psychological factors. Each section has its own properties, and when combined, the results can range from delicate music to unbearable noise. If the horns are too loud, they will block out the most sophisticated aria of the flute.

Instruments in orchestras can be separated from one another. ULD and the psychological consequences of shame are not quite so easily separable. That is why psychotherapy can be very helpful in unraveling innate learning disabilities from psychological factors. A psychotherapist who understands the emotional consequences of ULD will not try to change a client's personality or disregard his or her learning disabilities. The therapeutic focus here is understanding the influence of one on the other.

Finding a Therapist

People with ULD are caught between two disciplines: psychology and learning disabilities. The field of learning disabilities is part of education, and its focus is on academic achievement. The field of psychology focuses mainly on motivation and behavior. Falling between the cracks, a person with ULD needs a psychotherapist who is aware of how learning disabilities influence emotions or a learning disability specialist who is psychologically attuned.

In a perfect world, psychotherapists and learning disability specialists consult. Schools training psychotherapists, however, do not generally provide courses on how LD influences psychological development. In time, this interface will happen more and more, but for now the field is too new.

The person with ULD is really the expert, although this may sound incredible. No one knows more about these experiences than the survivor. There are therapists who are eager to learn from their clients. These therapists can then use their expertise to help the clients gain a new understanding of how ULD affects on one's emotional life.

Finding a therapist who can suspend his or her beliefs in order to learn about ULD is a necessity. There may be disagreements but *the client's point of view must be respected.* For example, sometimes people find themselves saying "uh huh," thinking how smart the therapist is, when nothing is really making sense. Although the client looks interested, confusion and stupidity reign. In essence, the client is in the chasm and this experience needs to be discussed. Without this input, the therapist is in the dark. Alternatively, discussion about the chasm may then open the door to understanding more about ULD. Therapists who become patronizing in the face of the chasm need to be confronted. Lack of change in the therapist would indicate the necessity for a different clinician.

For example, a therapist was treating a client with "New Age beliefs." LD testing found that undiagnosed learning disabilities had caused great discrepancies between the client's intellect and his achievements. The metaphysical differences in philosophy between the two people were quite apparent, but the client was willing to teach the therapist about his worldview. The client believed energy was entering his body from outside sources. He and the therapist could work with this belief system, and the client eventually came to understand how his ULD interfered with this free flow of energy and blocked his wishes for success. From his perspective, recognizing his ULD allowed him to understand how the energies in the world interfaced with his ability to learn.

Is testing beneficial? If so, when? First of all, there is no need to hurry. If problems mostly involve emotional adjustment, putting off testing and finding a psychotherapist might be the first priority. Much can be understood from memories about how one learned and did not learn. In fact, many people have more than adequately compensated. Help in understanding how this hidden dimension of ULD affected on emotional life may lead to the conclusion: "If it ain't broke, don't fix it."

A therapist, however, may feel undiagnosed learning disabilities may be constricting potential and testing could be beneficial because testing:

- corroborates intelligence, which can give self-esteem a much-needed boost;
- isolates and defines strengths and weaknesses, which can give one a handle in working on more readily understood problems; and
- allows a person to develop a more understanding and forgiving view of him or herself.

If testing is indicated, a qualified specialist who understands adult LD testing will be needed. People who test for LD are either educational psychologists or learning disability specialists. Interviewing the person with the following questions in mind can be helpful:

- Is the tester empathic?
- Has this person tested adults? If so, how many? Can she or he understand and verbalize the difference between testing adults and children?
- Does he or she know how to test for learning disabilities as opposed to psychological problems?

These questions help deal with the gaps within each discipline. For example, the field of learning disabilities provides a great deal of training for testing. Most of the training, however, focuses on children. Information on how to test adults is scant. The training, furthermore, focuses more on testing procedures than on the emotional consequences of being tested.

The psychologist, on the other hand, may not have specialized knowledge about LD. She or he might not have the ability or inclination to provide the extensive tests necessary to tease out complicated learning disabilities. Educational psychologists (EdDs) are an option, because they are often trained to test for LD.

People with ULD have had the picture of their intelligence obscured by some overall *average* score. When scores are averaged, strengths and weaknesses are combined into a total score. This means nothing. This final score is useless because intelligent, uneven learners need to understand the *difference* between strengths and weaknesses. Then, once it is determined where one's intellectual strengths lie, creative strategies can be employed to deal with newly understood weaknesses.

Chapter 8

Psychotherapy: A Lantern for the Darkness

Interviewer: So you couldn't stay in college and had to leave. OK? You came home.

Brilliant: Yes. My mother took me to see a therapist known for his interest in learning disabilities. He was the first person I talked to. She had no suspicion of any learning disability. She had no real definite answers as to what was going on. And, in fact, she probably thought it was her fault as a parent. So she sent me to somebody she respected, a social worker or somebody, and he brought it up.

He brought up an outside reason the [LD] for why I was having troubles in college. Before this, I just accepted that life was difficult because I had so much trouble learning and because I felt so stupid (even though I didn't always get bad grades). Sometimes I felt stupid, or didn't know what was wrong. So to think that he had an answer. . . .

The therapist recommended that Brilliant get tested for LD.

Brilliant: Those tests did show I had high intelligence. And I never knew that I did. I thought I was smart, that I worked hard, and that I was smart enough. But I didn't know that I was *very* smart. And in the fact that I compensated in the way I did showed that I was *very, very* smart. It validated my brain. My head swelled [laughter]. Really, you know, I had really good feelings.

Interviewer: Once you knew about the testing, did you continue in psychotherapy?

Brilliant: Oh yes. I would always come back to . . . I never quite believed it was true. . . . Just because it was such an unreality. It wasn't part of my life experience or understanding of myself for . . . years. And then, suddenly, there's this new information about LD given to me. Suddenly. And it had to be integrated. I found a way to dialogue about this, and psychotherapy allowed me to process parts of my past in a new way. Memories from my past would come up about, "Oh. So this was happening because of the LD," and this gave me a new understanding of how I went about and grew. And then also to understand my emotional self. That was a whole other [thing] I had never done before.

Going to a therapist was something I might have done anyway, but doing it with this information [about the LD] was different. I had a place to talk about feeling like I had "missing parts." Now, the feeling about my having "missing parts" is a little bit better controlled. It doesn't become disintegrated. The feeling never gets so overwhelming that I really fall into a deep depression. And it probably used to all the time. I can have perspective on it. The feeling doesn't get all out of hand.

IS PSYCHOTHERAPY NECESSARY?

Determining how psychotherapy might be helpful to those with Imprisoned Intelligence requires an adequate definition of the word "psychotherapy." One would think that with all the books on the subject, this question would be easy to answer. It is not. Conventional definitions of psychotherapy are often limiting and misleading. *Webster's New Collegiate Dictionary,* 1981, for instance, says psychotherapy is "treatment of mental or emotional disorders or related bodily ills by psychological means." This definition is based on a medical model and focuses on pathology. Psychotherapy can, of course, be used to treat psychopathology, but it is also used by: (1) people who are in pain, for whatever reason, and (2) people who wish to understand or change their lives to a degree that they have not been able to on their own. The cultural stereotype that psychotherapy is only for the insane or hopelessly neurotic is unfortunate indeed. Rather than considering therapy as visiting a doctor for a cure, one can think of it as voluntary schooling. It is like a night class taken purely for one's own benefit. Therapy is part of a person's education.

Psychotherapy is difficult to describe because it can affect nearly any aspect of life: relationships, intellect, passion, creativity, sexuality, spirituality. My definition is this: psychotherapy is interactive learning about yourself and your relationships with others. This interaction involves verbal and nonverbal communication about one's emotional life with a trusted professional. It involves understanding how life's evolving patterns help and hinder daily functioning. Psychotherapy can be helpful for those with ULD because psychotherapeutic goals can include bridging strengths and weaknesses. It allows individuals to view themselves in a more realistic and hopeful light while going through the painful and difficult task of facing vulnerabilities. This process is manageable when seen in light of potential and resiliency.

Psychotherapy is not always necessary for adults with undiagnosed learning disabilities. Many people have learned on their own to compensate more than adequately. Their sense of self is intact and they lead fulfilling lives. Others have found that assistance from a learning disability specialist is what they need to proceed successfully.

But when survivors suffer from Imprisoned Intelligence, appropriate psychotherapy can indeed be beneficial. Imprisoned Intelligence leads to frustration. When frustrated, people tend to blame themselves and self-esteem plummets. Appropriate psychotherapeutic experiences, over time, can curtail this cycle and reverse damage to self.

The following questions may help the therapist decide whether a person is suffering from Imprisoned Intelligence and needs psychotherapy.

- Does a person suffer from the chasm: the seemingly endless and painful place of nonlearning?
- When one is trying to learn does the person feel roboticized or stunned?
- Is time a problem? Does it take longer to finish?
- Is the individual afraid to act on his or her initiative or be spontaneous?
- Is he or she afraid to speak up?

- Is there a perception that one's efforts are negatively judged by others?
- Is feeling lazy, dumb, or just not caring prevalent?
- Are there feelings of spaciness and/or getting lost easily?
- Does the person know the right hand from the left?
- Does the person concentrate intensely on one thing but in the process manage to neglect other critical responsibilities?
- Are stopgap measures used to avoid embarrassment?
- Does the person know they are smart but feel stupid?
- Does the person consider himself or herself an underachiever?
- Are there real differences between intelligence and achievements at school or at work?
- Even though intelligence is apparent, are faux pas often made?
- Do people unknowingly embarrass themselves in social situations and find out only when told by someone else?
- Are difficult subjects in school avoided even though intelligence tests show potential?
- Is reading or math hated?
- Do individuals automatically think about how long it will take to read a book? Is reading boring?
- Was the individual considered an underachiever in school? Was this a source of embarrassment?
- Is daydreaming a problem?
- Are job changes occurring because one's temper cannot be controlled?
- Does an obviously smart person appear not to be working up to potential?
- Does it take successful people longer than others to complete projects?
- Is one's life partitioned into segments: sometimes excelling and sometimes failing?

Many of these questions can also apply to people who suffer from problems other than ULD, but they have particular importance for uneven learners *because of the emotional residue ULD can leave.* Effective psychotherapy, then, is complicated and may touch upon myriad of aspects of the self. The following parable elaborates:

Once upon a time there was a respected artist who created many fine pieces of tapestry, which were hanging in several art galleries in town. He was considered a success. But inside, he felt frustrated. A tapestry he had envisioned for most of his creative life was eluding him.

This inner picture had haunted him since childhood. It involved a hodgepodge of material with many different colors and textures: threads of silk, metal, and cotton, yarns with vastly different sizes, textures, and materials. In essence, this work represented his life.

Even when he was a child this image was in his mind and as his artistic talents developed, he would play with its design and start the project over and over again. However, it never came to fruition because the knots that would maintain the structure and lock in the pattern would not hold. Obviously, critical knots were missing.

Seeing this image but being unable to create it drove him crazy. He decided to take a couple of years off just to work on this project. He tried one technique after another. Sometimes, he couldn't even get started because it wouldn't come together. Sometimes, he felt satisfied because the work seemed to be solid and hold its structure. But, over time, again, it softened and became distorted, losing its shape and definition. Different techniques were tried over and over again. Experts were consulted. They told him to forget it, to move on to another project. But he knew this tapestry needed to be created and wouldn't give it up.

After many months, he become more and more discouraged. One day, he heard of a magical weaver in a far-off land. He decided to go to her. After arduous travel through dangerous forests and deserts, he came upon an oasis. There she was, sitting under a beautiful palm tree near a rippling brook, weaving what seemed to be a very simple fabric. Her smile created hope and peace in his heart. He respectfully approached and, through an interpreter, asked, "Please, can you help me?"

She reached for his unfinished tapestry, looked very curious, and smiled. She was obviously both puzzled and intrigued. She stared at his undefined work for many days. He painstakingly showed her how he tried to create his patterns, demonstrating all the knots he used in his attempt to lock the patterns in place. She kept asking more and more questions. He got tired of teaching and wondered if the trip had been a mistake.

Finally, she said she had learned what was wrong. The knots he knew and used to lock in colors and patterns would not work because the creation was too complicated and dense. That was why some knots, over time, began to loosen. He learned that he needed to expand his repertoire of knots.

He was very discouraged. He had spent a lifetime learning how to tie different knots. In fact, he was known as a knot expert and it was a source of pride. It was a jolt to learn that crucial knots were missing. He now understood that his knowledge, up to that point, was not enough to allow him to bring his vision to life.

The interpreter asked if he wanted to learn from her. Despite his disappointment, he nodded. After all, he came this far.

He learned that his right-handedness obstructed his capacity to create knots that would hold the patterns in place—that he needed to use both hands equally. In other words, he had to become ambidextrous. This would allow him to create new knots and give him the freedom to choose alternatives that never occurred to him before. In other words, she freed him from a right-handed bias.

He went home knowing that his work was cut out for him. It would not be easy to train his brain to depend on his left hand as easily as his right. But hope had returned. Although mastering these new techniques would be time-consuming and difficult, he knew he had reached a decisive road, torturous as it was, that would lead him to the creation of his vision.

The lives of people with ULD are like this tapestry. The threads are the self and all that has been learned. The patterns woven and knotted from those threads are the course one's life takes. The knots are the tactics used and the choices individuals make to direct their lives.

This story suggests that psychotherapy can teach new ways to go about living a meaningful life and can keep hope for a better life strong. By attempting to understand the patterns of anxiety and depression that accompany learning failures, individuals can learn how to interfere with those patterns. This is what therapy can do for people with Imprisoned Intelligence.

Many adults who suffer from Imprisoned Intelligence could benefit from psychotherapy because they instinctively know they have vulnerable spots in their tapestries. They know that, under certain circumstances, knots can loosen and the pattern in the tapestry can lose its shape and definition. For example, a bright and creative but disorganized person can function very well under a boss who is focused on outcome, not process. In other words, the boss does not care how the employee does something as long as it gets done. No one cares if the employee makes a mess as long as the outcome is satisfactory. But if this old boss is replaced by a detail-oriented person (who expects process to be as perfect as outcome), then the employee might be in trouble. Demanding neatness from smart but disorganized people can evoke intense anxiety. Too much anxiety will keep us from thinking and performing effectively.

Psychotherapeutic knowledge is power. First of all, because of the focus on feelings, psychotherapists can help people examine their vulnerabilities in a safe, empathic environment. Anxiety can be kept within tolerable limits. Only within a trusting and respectful relationship can an individual freely express his or her true feelings; if there is worry about ridicule or a cold response, the person will not feel safe enough to start the exploration process. Safety is especially crucial for those who suffer from chronic shame, since the trauma originated in unsympathetic learning environments. However, once one finds a safe environment to explore one's weaknesses, an amazing flowering takes place. It is a great relief to talk without fear of reprisal, and a new learning process can begin.

Second, psychotherapy can help uneven learners recognize the emotional complications that cause the problems in their tapestry: For example, some necessary threads may be missing, and new skills may need to be learned. Someone who has avoided math because he cannot copy numbers accurately may have to bite the bullet and learn some math. A therapist can provide necessary emotional support through this difficult time. Then chances of learning enough math to complete a college degree are greater.

New knots, or techniques for coping with LD-related weaknesses, can be learned. In these situations, it is the learning disability itself that interferes with the unfolding of potential. For example, an uneven learner whose brain automatically reverses letters may be a superb writer who cannot get started because he will never overcome his inability to spell or master grammar. He becomes afraid to try again after so many failures. A therapist who recognizes the dyslexia can encourage this individual to use a computer with a spelling checker, or have a friend edit his work. The computer or editor then becomes a "bypass" that frees his intelligence by getting around the learning disability. Then it becomes easier for him to express himself and use his gifts.

Some hidden threads may need to be highlighted or clarified. Therapy can provide a platform to unearth strengths that have been invisible. Sometimes, potential can be overlooked. For example, a young gang member who dropped out of school because he could not read may assume that his keen understanding of automobiles and guns is no big deal. But if a therapist had been called in to attend to his behavior problems, picked up on the learning difficulties, and given attention to his reading problems, this young man might have become an engineer.

Many times, people deal with fear through avoidance. For example, many intelligent people avoid attempting to obtain graduate degrees because they fear research and mathematics (particularly statistics). Psychotherapy gives us the opportunity to uncover and deal with these fears and helps us figure out how to meet our goals.

One's life tapestry has to be cohesive enough to withstand outside scrutiny. For some, psychotherapy is a necessary preparation for LD testing or consultation with an LD specialist. Both of these procedures, by their very nature, focus on exposing disabilities. Being exposed in this way may be too painful for someone whose self-esteem has been damaged by years of chronic shame. A psychotherapist can help mitigate such painful feelings. Just sharing one's pain often serves to reduce it, and gaining insight into causes may help even more. Also, a therapist can offer support while one undergoes the sessions, which makes them much more bearable.

A few more words on psychotherapy and LD specialists: Interventions from LD specialists can be essential to ULD sufferers. But if shame/blame patterns have been internalized, then learning disability specialists have to deal with emotional consequences that fall outside their area of expertise. If individuals believe they are stupid, it makes the LD specialist's job much more difficult. In a nutshell, without some expectation of success, learning anything becomes difficult to impossible. An understanding psychotherapist can intervene and address this pattern of discouragement. Psychotherapists have been trained to understand and disrupt downward spirals of low self-esteem. Therefore, working with a learning disability specialist will be more effective if psychological patterns can first be understood.

In summary, going to a psychotherapist is like consulting a master weaver about a tapestry with patterns that one does not quite understand. Examining developmental and current patterns is vital, because only an understanding of the tapestry's overall design can allow an individual to alter it to properly reflect his or her ambitions and goals.

WHAT CAN BE EXPECTED FROM PSYCHOTHERAPY?

When seeking psychotherapy, certain rights are inalienable and self-evident. Essential for everyone, but especially for people with ULD, is mutual respect between client and therapist. Uneven learners become embarrassed when their vulnerabilities are exposed by an overly critical world. They do not need therapists who perpetuate this cycle: who, for example, are sarcastic and make them cringe. Respect involves:

- *Safety.* Feeling safe enough to talk about vulnerabilities and safe enough to show deficits without feeling "pathologized" contributes to feelings of self-cohesion. For example, people who have trouble expressing themselves verbally need to find therapists who can help modulate their embarrassment.

- *The client's agenda.* People intrinsically know what troubles them. Therapists can lead individuals into other areas that might be interesting but irrelevant. For example, a therapist can ask for a life history, but if the individual has a recall problem this particular modality will not be helpful. The platform for therapy needs to focus on the person's perceptions of his or her problems. The therapist's job is to facilitate the creation of that platform. The client's input is vital. Otherwise, old school patterns can be repeated in which the agenda is set by the teacher. Therapists are not teachers. At school, it is appropriate for the teacher to set the agenda. In therapy, it is appropriate for the individual to set the agenda.
- *Timing.* Many people with ULD could achieve beautifully if only they were given enough time. Being forced to finish at school or work before one is actually done is incredibly frustrating and stress-producing. This is one reenactment that should not occur in treatment. If time constraints are a problem, the last thing needed is a therapist who pushes people to speak before they are ready. Effective psychotherapy can best occur within a milieu of comfort. Feeling rushed makes this impossible.
- *The client's point of view.* Therapists need to understand the client's point of view. They may, however, respectfully offer alternative perspectives that expand knowledge.
- *Therapy will not work if clients become passive and compliant. Buying what the therapist says, hook, line, and sinker, even when it really doesn't make sense, will only further repeat an unpleasant pattern from the past.* Uneven learners know all about the experience of pretending to understand when they do not, to avoid embarrassment.

Fighting against one's passivity is difficult but necessary. Compliance sabotages learning. Good therapists are aware of this problem and are trained to understand how their clients perceive life. In other words, therapy usually is not learning new things out of the blue but *adding to what is known.* To add to what is known, one must *begin* with what is known. So, if a person feels like a bug under a microscope in the therapist's office, something is wrong.

How can this problem be addressed?

- *Talk about it.* Feelings of exposure and loss of self will be a jumping-off point for further learning. If the therapist does not understand and, after several tries, cannot be educated, find someone else!
- *Putting oneself first.* Therapists are trained and paid to listen to others. That is their job. Worry about hurting the therapists' feelings should not be a priority.
- *Validating the need for connection.* One overall goal of psychotherapy is to provide a sense of connection. This does not mean that disconnections never occur. But, when one feels safe enough, then issues of anger or discouragement can be worked through. In safety, all feelings can be talked about, which allows learning. That is the beauty of psychotherapy.
- *Struggle with the chasm.* One pitfall in treatment is the reemergence of the chasm. Rest assured, there will be times when an individual will feel disappointed because he or she is "not getting it." The first impulse may be to suffer silently, but therapy is intended for talking about painful feelings. Getting beyond the painful feelings involves talking about them first.

It is important to underscore here that the chasm is not bad. It is a message that a new approach is needed. When the chasm hits in treatment, it can be used as a springboard to talk about how and where the disconnections occurred. Many times, therapists make some kind of leap that cannot be followed. The chasm then becomes a marker or sign that indicates that there is a gap in understanding and steps need to be filled in.

Let me give an example. If a new client comes into the office, and the therapist falls into lecturing while the client's head keeps nodding, the discussion might unfold in the following way:

Therapist: Am I making sense here?

Client: Well, I'm not sure I understand.

Therapist: It must be hard to sit there trying to understand while I go rambling on.

Client: [nods]

Therapist: Can you tell me what that feels like?

Client: Well, I feel stupid.

Therapist: When you feel stupid, that's a signal that we've gotten off base or I'm not on the money. So, we want to respect that feeling because it helps us get back on track. Would it be possible for you to let me know when this happens in the future?

It can be difficult not to buy into a therapist's logic, because it sounds reasonable. Logic is only helpful if it resonates with good common sense. If this is not happening, the client needs to let the therapist know about this "glitch." In this way both people are creating new patterns and knots. The tapestry will be stronger in the future.

THINGS LEARNED IN THERAPY

- If one finds a therapist disappointing, it is not the end of the world. Discussing disappointment with an empathic therapist reveals valuable knowledge about how one interacts with others, and the renewed connection with the therapist will be even stronger.
- When feelings are put into words, different perspectives and alternatives can be acquired.
- Learning how a person feels about learning will free the individual to learn more.
- If getting a diagnosis is important, the therapist should scout around and find empathic testers aware of issues with adults. In my opinion, LD specialists who only work with children are not qualified to diagnose adults. Some issues for adults are different. Appropriate tests can help people find out:
  —How to get help from others.
  —How to interact better with others.
  —How to recognize the chasm, and how to help oneself through it.
  —How an individual compensates, and how to capitalize on it.
  —How to find a clearer identity. Testing should underscore a stronger sense of "who you are": one's strengths, weaknesses, and goals. These issues then will no longer seem so troubling and bewildering.

To summarize, this chapter shows how psychotherapy is helpful to adult survivors of ULD. Therapy can help consolidate our emotional and intellectual lives. By unraveling the emotional consequences of ULD, people will have more options for dealing with the problem. Life takes on new meanings when the emotional consequences of our patterns of learning are understood.

Chapter 9

Conclusions

Growing up with ULD shapes individuals in myriad ways. It can foster an individual's determination, creativity, and unique talents. It can also make school a painful experience, block achievement, and erode self-esteem and relationships with others. The negative emotional consequences of ULD can be prevented, or at least modified. As educators, parents, psychotherapists, and concerned citizens we can work to give people with LD better opportunities.

Educators, especially, are in the position to profoundly influence young lives. Consider Sparkly's school experience:

> **Sparkly:** I remember coming home from school and being exhausted. I'd always have to be a step ahead of them [the teachers] so that they wouldn't ask *those* questions: "Where's your homework? Why didn't you do it?" I wouldn't know what to tell them. I didn't know why I didn't do it. I'd sit down and I wouldn't see anything. It was frustrating. I wanted the information everybody else was getting, and I wanted to get it the *way* they were getting it. And it was also more frustrating when some teachers reacted with that ignorance. I mean, as each class went on, not only didn't they care, but they were almost rude and condescending about it like, "Nice excuse. Why don't you do your work?" At that point I was ready to quit.

Sparkly's experience of judgmental teachers was a common one for the participants in this study. I feel obliged to comment on our educational system and the way children with ULD are taught.

National Public Radio station WBEZ commented in 1996, "Leonardo was a genius, but without the proper tools, he could have ended up finger-painting." Without necessary skills, intelligence dies on the vine. Children who grow up without skills, learning disabled or not, have many of the same problems. Similarly, people who cannot read suffer, whether because of constitutional deficit or environmental neglect. All citizens in this country need the skills necessary for a fulfilling life.

Academic standards, of course, cannot be compromised. Standards in skill-building must remain high, but the methods used to achieve those standards need to be flexible (Gardner, 1983). A student who is not a visual learner may be able to learn necessary skills through the sense of touch. Copying from the board is not the only way to learn to write. Some people may learn more easily if they can feel three-dimensional letters. For some students, to avoid the chasm and consequential Imprisoned Intelligence, learning computer skills may keep their intelligence mobilized. Inflexible teaching methods can contribute to Imprisoned Intelligence with all of its emotional underpinnings and aftermath.

Another serious impediment to learning is the inability of many educators to deal constructively with the chasm. Teachers must be able to identify and understand this phenomenon. The chasm is not bad. It is a pragmatic clue that another approach is necessary because the current one is not working. It is not the chasm that causes constriction of intelligence; it is the shame and withdrawal that follow. For example, if a student could say to a teacher, "I'm in the chasm," perhaps the teacher would more readily understand that motivation is not necessarily the issue. The teacher could then help the student clarify the problem and offer different teaching tools.

Emotions preclude and follow learning, and teachers need to learn how to integrate emotional reactions into their lexicon of teaching strategies. It is easier to learn when one likes the teacher and is excited about the topic.

Academics and clinicians must focus their energies on this problem if substantial change is to take place. This book is based on a study of subjective experiences of adults who discovered their ULD. More studies, both subjective and empirical, must be done. It is striking that such a variety of people have had similar experiences that evolve into a similar developmental process. I hope that this book will add another diagnostic and treatment dimension for psychotherapists and educational personnel who see people with ULD, but far more research needs to be done. There are already many dedicated professionals who are concerning themselves with this problem, and I believe that the field will continue to grow.

Imprisoned intelligence is a social problem that concerns not only educators and clinicians, but everyone. Like other previously "hidden" issues, such as sexual abuse, workplace discrimination, and homophobia, it requires public awareness to spur social change. Concerned citizens can participate in their local school boards, join LD organizations, and let the government know that they support LD programs and research. Members of the media can ensure that the issue gets adequate coverage.

Many of my interviewees were able to persevere, survive, and thrive in the face of their LD, but what about those who cannot? ULD hits the economically disadvantaged especially hard: remedies such as psychotherapy, tutors, and LD testing are prohibitively expensive. It is difficult for many to get a basic LD remediation, let alone help for the emotional aftermath of LD. Change may come slowly, but it has the potential to drastically improve the quality of life for many. When LD and its emotional consequences are understood and treated in this country, we will be significantly closer to providing a truly public education.

I would like to end this section of the book by making a final comment on the enormous difficulties faced on a daily basis by those with LD. I have a sense of awe and respect for their attempts, no matter how successful, to deal with these difficulties. No word can really capture the profound achievements of those with LD, who most often fail to get any recognition for their labors. If this book has helped even a tiny bit to encourage others with LD, it was entirely worth the effort.

SECTION II:
PSYCHOTHERAPEUTIC, HISTORICAL, AND THEORETICAL PERSPECTIVES

Chapter 10

Treatment:
A Chapter for Therapists
and Interested People

Therapist: Even with all your success, do the learning disabilities still cause problems in your life?

Scholar: Well, when the world gets chaotic, it gets very difficult for me. You know, simple things like when I'm involved at work, and my wife starts to talk to me on the phone, I want to kill her. When she does that my head really spins. It's enormously disorganizing. And knowing that, I can sit down and talk to her about it and we can understand that you can't do that with me [because of my inability to take in information easily through my ears] as opposed to putting blame on her or on me, like I'm so cranky, or why should I be so sensitive that I can't have her talking to me on the phone at the same time?

INTRODUCTION

This chapter is written for therapists and for interested and potential clients. Although some things may appear repetitious, looking at therapeutic issues from the therapist's perspective may prove enlightening. The attempt here is to show how psychotherapy enhances the lives of adults who are unaware, or have recently become aware, of a learning disability.

It is important to understand why the recognition and treatment of learning problems is critical. After all, people are not born cognitively equal, and each individual possesses strengths and weaknesses. The discrepancies, however, between strengths and weaknesses in bright ULD sufferers are especially pronounced. Such individuals are caught in a particular dilemma; they have not learned to expect and allow for uneven achievement. They will never achieve as well in their areas of weakness as in their areas of strength, and *ULD sufferers do not know this because their deficits are not clarified.* Therefore, no matter how successful they are, because they fail to meet their own expectations, they are left feeling incomprehensibly flawed. This "flawedness" is a secondary reaction to the primary problem of ULD and is clearly a psychotherapeutic issue.

For example, the following is an excerpt from Ann Landers, advice columnist, in the *Chicago Tribune* (Landers, 1976b).

No Clue When It Comes to Faces

Dear Ann Landers:

I just finished reading your column about people who have no sense of direction. Please make your readers aware of another, even more embarrassing, glitch in some people's neurons. It is the inability to recognize people.

I have suffered from this curse ever since I was a child. When I was in college, I used to be humiliated because I could not recognize my professors on campus, just hours after I had been in one of their classes. Even today, if I were to bump into my next door neighbors while in another city, I would not recognize them until I heard their voices or saw their beat up car. Just this morning a neighbor from down the block spoke to me, and I thought he was the furnace repairman until he mentioned something about my lawn.

Since misery loves company, I was delighted when I heard others have this problem too. I was comforted when I read that novelist T. S. Stribling couldn't recognize his next door neighbors either. Soon after he won the Pulitzer Prize, he was seated next to Eleanor Roosevelt at a dinner. He had no idea who she was and kept wondering why so many people kept coming over to speak to her.

I always try to look for clues, either by listening to people's voices or letting them do most of the talking, hoping for a clue from the dialogue. I'm sure some people think I'm a snob or extremely unfriendly, but the truth is, I have this problem that is impossible to explain, so I have stopped trying. Please print my letter so people will be more understanding.

Finger Lakes, NY

Dear FL, NY:

Your letter illustrates yet another example of faulty cranial wiring. Your problem is probably a second cousin to dyslexia—which few people knew about until fairly recently. Children with dyslexia were thought to be stupid until research proved otherwise, and in fact, they are often brighter than average.

Thanks for a letter that is sure to make a lot of people feel better. (Permission granted by Ann Landers/Creators Syndicate.)

A letter such as this shows how cognitive endowment can have a major impact on emotional development. Without a clear conception of the problem and guidelines to address it, very bright people can suffer from secondary painful emotional reactions such as shame.

Many uneven learners, no matter how successful they are, complain of feeling estranged or not comfortably fitting in. This feeling is the result of having to figure out creative ways around their invisible and unidentified problems. People knew they could not learn through the teaching techniques used in school. Poor handwriting does not lend itself to brilliant "board work"; it lends itself to fear of exposure. Because there were no effective teaching tools, uneven learners' strategies were idiosyncratic and often stopgap. They had to rely on their own ingenuity. Independence was enhanced but so was loneliness and isolation.

How can psychotherapy help? The goal of psychotherapy for people who have suffered from this problem is to strengthen self-cohesion. The following interventions can be used:

- *Explanation of the problem.* Therapists need to be alert to the possibility of ULD in undiagnosed clients, and if indicated, explain the emotional ramifications in an appropriate and empathic manner.

- *Integration of ULD into the client's life history.* Therapists can provide a safe, appropriate environment in which the client can learn how past experiences of both learning failures and successes affect current living.
- *Enhancement of potential.* Therapists can encourage the expansion of the client's options once old cognitive and emotional patterns regarding ULD are understood.

The clinician's chief concern is establishing an empathic relationship with the individual with ULD so that his or her deficits can be understood without undue shame (Galatzer-Levy, 1993).

Therapists can help ULD adults understand and alleviate their emotional pain. This chapter is divided into three sections: Recognition: Helping People Become Aware, Integration, and Conclusions.

RECOGNITION:
HELPING PEOPLE BECOME AWARE

Recognizing ULD in intelligent adults who seek treatment for other problems such as depression or anxiety can be difficult. The learning problem itself interacts and interfaces with a broader self-structure (Kohut, 1971, 1977, 1984). What makes diagnosis so difficult is: (1) the problems indeed may be psychologically based; (2) even if there is a learning disability, people may have compensated adequately and their problems may truly lie elsewhere; and (3) people may be so ashamed of their inability to achieve in their areas of weakness that an untimely discussion of the problem could cause them to drop out of treatment. Gensler (1993) reiterates this caution. He says:

> An evaluation of an adult patient specifically for a learning disability should not overemphasize the influence of learning disability on personality development. It should aim at integrating whatever is found regarding a learning disability into a more general picture of functioning. (p. 685)

When contemplating a diagnosis, respect for the client's feelings should always be the foremost consideration. Clearly the interface between constitutional and environmental factors is inextricably intertwined. Although in many cases pinpointing a learning problem is inordinately helpful, the issues are complicated because of the emotional implications.

It is important that clinicians not immediately assume that the learning disability is the only root of the problem and that diagnosis and treatment of the disability will alleviate the person's pain. Diagnosis and treatment are vital but may not help the client with concomitant emotional problems. In other words, with this population, a therapist must avoid being "a bull in a china shop" from the patient's perspective.

We will begin looking at this concept of recognition by discussing the implications and ramifications of: (1) how to recognize ULD, (2) how to introduce the concept of ULD to the client, and (3) how to introduce the concept of the chasm to the client. A judicious introduction is more important than a formal diagnosis because the problem may cause a strong emotional reaction in the client.

How to Recognize ULD

Living with an undiagnosed learning disability is not easy. People seek psychotherapy because they suffer from inexplicable emotional pain. The relationship of ULD to the presenting emotional problems may be unclear. Buchholz (1987) comments on how intangible this problem feels when first encountering a patient with ULD:

> These analysands, uncertain of both their strengths and deficits, accept that help is required, but often do not know what needs fixing. At the start, neither patient nor analyst sees the learning difficulties as core material to be analyzed. (p. 432)

Early in the therapy, under most circumstances the therapist must protect and enhance whatever sense of self-worth the client can muster. People do not carry their learning disabilities on their sleeves. It is embarrassing for bright people to feel stupid.

Furthermore, as described in previous chapters, people with ULD have learned to compensate more or less, and compensations mask or camouflage deficits that could cause feelings of exposure and embarrassment. It takes time and trust to expose what is painful. Therefore, in the beginning, it is difficult or impossible to isolate the disability. Take, for example, the student comedian who hides his deficits by shifting the therapeutic focus to his clever sense of humor. This may protect him from the devastating shame of learning that "My suspicions are true, something is really wrong with me."

If ULD is so elusive, how can therapists recognize it in people who come in for other reasons? Let us begin with the obvious. It is vital to take a school history. In the patient's retelling of school experiences, clues about ULD become evident. For example, people talk of loving some classes and hating others. However, not everyone who did badly in school has a learning disability.

Another obvious sign is the therapist's observation of cognitive processing problems in the session. Because ULD is so multifaceted, it would be difficult to give a comprehensive list of all possible processing problems. The following provisional list might give a sense of what to look for. For organizational purposes, I will expand on Scheiber and Talpers' (1987) concepts of how the brain uses information. They use categories of intake, storage, retrieval, and output. Hopefully, as more is learned about the clinical issues of ULD, more comprehensive categories will evolve.

Intake

- Cannot read the therapist's face
- Vocal nuances get no reaction
- Does not seem to listen well
- Hates to talk on the phone (auditory dyslexia)
- Does not pick up on tonal inflections
- Cannot sit still and focus on the subject at hand
- Cannot look at the therapist
- Cannot comprehend what the therapist is saying

Storage

- Easily engaged but internal processes not occurring
- Does not appear thoughtful
- The hour never gets beyond light conversation

- Client appears superficial
- Information is "interesting" but never makes an impact
- Client fears being "found out" that he or she is intellectually flawed
- Nothing seems to change

Retrieval

- Cannot remember discussions from week to week
- Cannot remember names, faces
- Remembers but it takes too long and the client loses out in conversation
- Clients constantly test themselves to see if they remember—becomes an issue
- Complains of not being able to think
- Whenever time or date of session is changed, sessions are missed
- Clumsy—bumps into things in the therapist's office

Output

- Issues of performance become highlighted
- Complains of being tongue-tied, stutters
- Handwriting will deteriorate
- Sense of animation is inhibited
- Physical constriction—body seems to freeze
- Verbal constriction—cannot talk
- Organizational problems: tardiness, poor handwriting, sloppy physical appearance

The above list is fairly straightforward and while sometimes ULD can be obvious, that is rare. More often, ferreting out ULD variables in current psychotherapeutic interactions requires recognition of subtle cues. Three markers or clues point to the possibility that ULD is affecting a patient's emotional life:

1. Complaints about deprivation
2. Discrepancies between apparent abilities and achievements
3. Use of characteristic strategies to compensate for a cognitive weakness

Deprivation

Patients may complain of feeling deprived or that something is missing from their lives. They may feel their potential eludes them. They might talk about the sense of emptiness in their lives and their lack of self-esteem. They may complain about their lack of motivation, their jobs, or their unhappy relationships. Their lives seem to lack meaning or excitement. Not infrequently, they talk about a sense of boredom.

For many, this sense that something is missing reflects inhibitions that lie outside of their awareness. For example, boredom at work may be the result of being afraid to try for a more interesting job. On some level, they are afraid their deficits will be revealed. One example of such inhibition of potential is seen in the significant number of social workers I have talked with who never pursue a PhD because they are afraid of math and statistics courses. In any event, the therapist's empathic sense of the client's vulnerabilities and propensity for shame is mandatory if these inhibitions are to be overcome.

Discrepancies

Very early in the treatment (in fact many times in the first session) it becomes fairly clear that there are curious discrepancies that feel confusing to the therapist. It is common to see people who appear quite mature and "together" yet are dissatisfied with their functioning. Of course, these discrepancies may not be the result of ULD, yet they are illuminating nonetheless. Kaplan and Shachter (1991, p. 195) list the following indicators:

- Significant discrepancies between apparent intellectual ability and school and/or work performance
- Significant poverty of social judgment in intelligent adults from apparently normal families
- Cognitive distortions and distorted perceptions of life events in the face of good intelligence, reasonable rearing, and adequate reality testing
- Specific avoidance of selected tasks incongruent with apparent ability in other areas
- Hatred of reading when intelligence is adequate

- Problematic school history without evidence of poor intellectual ability or rearing
- Impulsivity, explosiveness, poor frustration tolerance, and concentration problems in an adult with good intelligence and reasonable rearing. This may include a pattern of frequent job changes and difficulty relating to authority.
- Poor self-esteem and confused self-concept, particularly in school and work performance
- A pervasive sense of badness, particularly in childhood recollections, despite good intelligence and reasonable rearing
- Feelings of intellectual inferiority despite adequate educational test performance

Compensatory Strategies

In working with the recognition phase in treatment, therapists can begin to discern strategies people use to get around areas of shame. One strategy is avoidance, especially the fear of trying. Wurmser (1987) cogently confirms such inhibitions by defining what he calls shame anxiety. Shame anxiety creates inhibitions that keep people from experiencing destructive shame. A case in point is individuals who refuse to try something new for fear of experiencing the chasm. The chasm, the experience of stupidity, is a humiliation that people avoid at almost any cost. Smart people with ULD hate to look stupid. For example, bright and capable students will avoid math or other courses for fear of failing. In this manner, they shift the environment. One participant who could not write would engage teachers in dialogues to learn the material and make the time pass so that the classroom written assignments would be overlooked.

Another strategy is perseverance. This self-enhancing strategy usually promotes success. Intelligent people with ULD realize they need to work much harder and longer. They know how to hang in there. They persevere for two reasons: (1) they have experienced the joy of learning, and (2) they are afraid of the chasm and feel that if they work hard enough they can avoid it. Psychotherapeutically, this strategy enhances the chances of successful treatment.

Last, and most important to achievement, are the creative strategies people use to get around the chasm of deficits. These strategies are idiosyncratic; people have learned to rely on their own ingenuity.

Whatever the strategies people with ULD employ, they can vary from quite successful to less than optimal. For example, when a mathematician who cannot recall information quickly is given time to process, he accesses more than enough information for the tasks at hand. If asked a question, he can compensate by saying, "I'll think about it and call you back." This gives him the time he needs but causes delays that interfere with his work. Even though his achievements are outstanding, he has always felt like a cheater because he cannot access information as other people do.

Some uneven learners find others to help them. A successful student who has trouble categorizing may request help from librarians to access information. Even though she now knows better, she still has to fight feeling as though she is cheating because she cannot do it herself. If a client is critical of his or her own learning strategies, this may indicate ULD.

How to Introduce the Concept of ULD to the Client

As noted in the section on recognition, identifying ULD markers can be difficult. Introducing ULD can also be quite tricky. In uncomplicated situations, early diagnosis may be necessary to a client's well-being. A quick referral to a competent learning disabilities specialist can make a real difference for a failing college student or a person who is about to lose a job. The client may eagerly embrace suggestions for circumventing the problem. The emotional implications of ULD make a great deal of sense because the diagnosis provides the language necessary to move out of a confusing process and into a dialogue about feelings. As a rule of thumb, if the learning disability is interfering with daily functioning, an early formal diagnosis is indicated. Gensler (1993) states:

> An adult's decision to undergo a psychological evaluation for a learning disability is not an easy one. A patient may be more likely to accept the recommendation to seek evaluation if the learning disability is seen as interfering with activities that are vital to current income or education. (p. 685)

If the client's functioning is not significantly affected, then making ULD a topic of therapy is much more difficult. At this juncture, it is necessary to issue a caveat to clinicians. Helping clients to understand that they have ULD runs a serious risk; it is not easy for proud, independent, smart people to entertain the notion that their troubles might stem from an undiscovered learning disability. The suggestion may make them angry or devastated. Adults with ULD have worked long and hard throughout their development to compensate for their problems. Since most of them had to learn to compensate on their own, they are fiercely independent and understandably proud of their achievements. Their independence and pride are instrumental in maintaining their self-cohesion. Careful thought and enough time to build a relationship must precede a recommendation for testing.

How does a therapist broach the topic of ULD in an appropriate, timely fashion? One way is for the clinician to be curious about the person's experiences in school. (As mentioned in the section Recognition: Helping People Become Aware, this is also an excellent way to detect a learning disability.) If a therapist says, "Tell me about school" and the person replies, "I hated school," further exploration might lead the client to discuss relevant constitutional deficits. For example, perhaps this person hated gym because she has motor-coordination problems. Maybe she dreaded the first class of the day because she had problems keeping track of time and was continually late to school. Creating a more empathic history for such a client is one of the goals of therapy. If the suggestion of LD makes sense to the client in this context, windows of opportunity are comfortably opened for further exploration.

The following is a brief vignette showing the interface between current functioning and personal history:

> A creative, high-functioning woman in an executive position is suffering from anxiety because she has a new boss. In the past, this woman has been respected for her capacity to make creative leaps and come up with novel solutions to seemingly impossible problems. Her secretary handled all the details. However, there was a change in administration and within a short period of time, this woman lost her secretary and got a new boss who was oriented toward detail and demanded speed in administrative duties.

Historical inquiry about her school experiences found that this extremely intelligent woman, who was captain of her chess team, read very slowly. She always "got by" because her work was so creative and interesting that teachers were captivated by her originality and did not pay attention to the fact that the numbers of references in her papers were minimal.

She painfully confessed that while dealing with legal aspects of her job, she did not read contracts before signing them and instead relied on her assistants, who unknowingly provided her with summaries. Her chasm was her absolute inability to meet the standards of her new boss. This left her feeling painfully anxious.

If a careful school history had not been taken, treatment might have proceeded quite differently. For example, it may have been assumed that a conflict or an unmet need caused her inability to achieve with her new boss. Her inability to read at an optimal level would never change with psychological interpretations. This line of inquiry might have led the therapist to look at underlying motivations involving her fear of her boss, which might have lead to issues involving family conflicts or an expression of self-depletion resulting from a lack of nurturing in her childhood. These factors, of course, can be important in any treatment situation, but without a proper recognition of her cognitive deficits, this woman could end up believing that her Oedipus complex or her cold mother was the principal cause of her problem. *The inability to read quickly is usually not a motivational problem and therefore will never disappear. In this case, emphasis on intent or motivation would cloud the issue and cause this woman to feel responsible for a deficit that is not her fault.*

Explaining Compliance

Another pitfall in the early stages of treatment is overlooking the possibility of compliance. Patients may "comply" with what they perceive to be the therapist's agenda and fail to bring up the issues that are important to them. They protect themselves from feeling stupid by sticking with topics that are of interest to the therapist. Unfortunately, the therapist may think everything is right on target and overlook the client's real concerns. Gensler (1993) elaborates on countertransference and compliance, quoting Poznanski (1979):

... [the therapist] is likely to be threatened by his own feelings of helplessness in the situation. As a result, the interview with the patient can be distorted in several ways. One way this can happen is for the therapist, who is not in touch with his own feelings, to gloss over the degree and extent of the handicapping situation (the therapist does not clearly ascertain what the handicapped person is and is not able to do). In order to be effective, it is absolutely necessary for the therapist to recognize the environment and constraints that act upon the patient. Nonetheless, the handicapped patient often enters into a conspiracy of silence with the therapist by not volunteering practical information about the extent of the disability. . . . Rather than avoiding discussion of the patient's disabilities, the therapist and patient may unconsciously focus on narrow, concrete, and somewhat isolated areas of the patient's ability to function while avoiding the central issues of total adaptation. This too, serves a defensive function for both the patient and the therapist and helps avoid the anxiety associated with the handicap. (Gensler, 1993, p. 677)

Poznanski is writing about children with obvious handicaps. Issues of overlooking a disability become even more complicated when the adult patient is not even aware of the problem.

When starting psychotherapy, patients often feel as though they are in school again and the therapist is the teacher. ("If I do good work for my therapist, he will approve of me and I will succeed.") Even in the best of treatments, it takes time for patients to understand that inquiry into their emotions takes precedence over pleasing the therapist.

The chasm adds still another wrinkle to the early stages of treatment. Initially, since uneven learners with ULD will do anything to avoid feeling stupid, the therapist's attempts to facilitate learning will be undone whenever the chasm erupts. Under normal circumstances, when people cannot learn, they feel frustrated, experience some shame, and use that shame to regroup and try another approach. When a child fails an exam, he may figure out which steps in the ladder of learning were missing. When those steps are understood, he realizes he has to study harder or differently so he can do better.

But, when dealing with a patient with ULD who is drowning in the chasm, there are no steps on the ladder to further learning. In fact, there is no ladder! For example, a client who has deficits in time management may be consistently late to sessions. The more the unsuspecting therapist tries to find out what is wrong with the client's motivation (i.e., why the client is late all the time), the more embarrassing and "chasm-like" the hour becomes. It is not that uneven learners cannot cope with "why" questions. It is that, in the past, when they were asked such questions, (for instance, "Why do you fail spelling when you are such a good reader?") they did not know. Their inability to answer evoked tremendous anxiety because they felt stupid. The therapist must be aware that "why" questions can evoke old patterns of fear of exposure. It is fear that keeps people from being able to think.

Silence can be still another pitfall. Although people need enough time to think, if silences are too prolonged, they take on a life of their own. If patients are silent for a very long time, scrambling for words, do not know what to say, or seem to be rambling, it is possible that they may desperately be trying to find a way out of the "hot seat" because they cannot access the information in a timely fashion. Learning then becomes impossible because clients are drowning in the chasm.

How does this "drowning process" occur? It involves the following progression: First of all, early in psychotherapy, people may feel their attempts to investigate and learn are scrutinized and judged by the therapist. (In many cases they are correct.) Then they feel isolated and alienated, and cognition freezes. They are not able to think. Furthermore, since there is no way to remove themselves from a one-on-one therapeutic encounter, people become embarrassed and are vulnerable to a pattern of internal ridicule which lowers self-esteem. Then, since these feelings are too difficult to bear, they cut off all feelings in the therapeutic experience. They may quit treatment prematurely.

Thus, if the therapist asks questions that make an uneven learner feel stupid (such as a simple "Why do you think you feel that way?") and the individual truly does not know, a desperate attempt at some kind of answer will ensue. Countertransference may emerge: the therapist may feel that something is missing, and this vague feeling is often translated into a sense of boredom. Discussing the feeling that "something is missing" with the client can sometimes lead to a discussion about previous learning gaps, which then gives meaning to previously unrecognized problems.

This section ends as it began. It is of utmost importance that therapists see undiagnosed and diagnosed learning disabilities in the context of the client's total experience of self. ULD is one of many threads that run through the fabric of one's self-structure. To ignore this thread leaves the individual feeling that something essential is missing; to isolate the thread of ULD outside of the client's total personality is to pathologize a common deviation that needs integration, acceptance, and understanding.

INTEGRATION

In the previous section, special emphasis was placed on the recognition of ULD. This section focuses on integration; more specifically, it focuses on empathically integrating the invisible threads of ULD into the fabric of the patient's awareness. The question posed here will be: How can a therapist facilitate this integration in a way that has meaning and contributes to the client's overall emotional growth?

Essentially, integration is psychotherapeutic learning. It is adding to or combining what is known so that people can progress from experiences of fragmentation or feeling in pieces to cohesion and coherence,[*] in which the various aspects of the self are experienced as interrelated. Furthermore, integration entails knowledge about the difference between the causes and consequences of emotional pain. This inquiry seeks to examine and question the assumptions that govern our understanding of emotional life. However, little is clear-cut.

For example, as psychodynamic psychotherapy developed, clinicians have learned to wear various theoretical hats regarding "what causes what." In the beginning Freud thought trauma was the basis for emotional pain. He later changed his mind and concluded that internal conflict was the culprit. Recently, trauma has been brought back into the picture. In addition, over the years psychological theorists have added other ideas that also alter our assumptions or our theoretical postures. For example, chemical imbalance is a possibility many therapists consider; so is the quality of caregiving a client received as an infant and young child.

---

[*]See Palombo (1991) for a thoughtful discussion of these concepts.

Though clinicians have become adept at wearing different theoretical hats, and although certain cases require unusual approaches, some of our assumptions remain constant. For example, development is seen as an important lens through which to view the client's pain. Therapists ask questions such as: How it is that this person has come to experience so much distress? What is the history of the distress? How has it changed over time? It is not unusual to consider the possibility that development has been blocked by environmental factors. In other words, something happened, either once or habitually, that compromised this individual's development. Moreover, it also is generally assumed that when developmental needs are empathically addressed and understood, emotional growth will remobilize and potential will flower.

When treating adults with ULD, the therapist must constantly question and reevaluate his or her stance. Certain questions must remain in the foreground. The question "What causes what?" is of central importance to ULD adults' treatment. For instance, one may assume that if the patient is a survivor of trauma or neglect, the facts will unfold naturally within a therapeutic milieu. Ordinarily, this is a fair assumption. However, because uneven learners have learned to hide their deficits by compensating, ULD seldom comes to light on its own in treatment. As explained in the previous section, how a hidden cognitive deficit is handled will massively influence the outcome of therapy. Furthermore, the cultural truism that intelligent people can always succeed if they try hard enough is rarely questioned. This oversight can mask ULD as a primary cause of emotional pain (Rothstein, 1998; Kafka, 1984). Therefore, when people suffer from Imprisoned Intelligence, the relationship of ULD to emotional pain must hover over psychotherapeutic inquiry. One question is this: Do deficits affect relationships or do relationships affect deficits?

This question is very difficult to answer because the interaction or interface between LD and emotions (between constitutional and environmental factors) is complex. Yet addressing this question is crucial because, depending on what is primary, one will form different conclusions. For example, does Johnny not read because he gets beaten up at home, or does Johnny not read because he is dyslexic and his failure to read angers his caretakers, who then beat him up? Which comes first, his failure to perform at school or the fact that he is physically abused?

To make things still more difficult, Johnny may be an invisible dyslexic who, by compensating, has somehow learned to read. But because his father beats him up, his compensations fail him, he "regresses," and he can no longer read. Diagnostic confusion reigns as the complexity of the situation manifests itself. What looks like a regression may be a reemergence of an invisible, constitutionally based learning disability minus the individual's compensatory mechanisms.

Paradoxically, if ULD is a factor in treatment, the therapist's ability to live with a state of diagnostic confusion provides an important step toward integration. It is vital not to jump to conclusions too early. When it comes to ULD, no one theory can explain everything. I am suggesting that you, as the therapist, depending on the needs of the client, may need to wear different theoretical hats within each session.

Furthermore, it is important to differentiate obvious primary reactions (such as deep shame) from secondary reactions (subtle self-denigration). It is easier for bright people to call themselves lazy than to recognize and integrate permanent cognitive deficits. This process of separating reactions can only occur against the backdrop of a strong therapeutic alliance. The client can only expose shame and pain over being "stupid" in a trusting environment.

At this juncture, let me demonstrate how this process works in a session.

Presentation of a Case

Robert is a composite of several patients, and the details are disguised to protect his privacy. He represents the kind of highly successful person who struggles with language processing difficulties.

Robert is an engineer who successfully teaches and supervises workers who, in the past, have not been able to master necessary computer skills. Although a highly respected and very well-paid employee, he suffers from depression and self-depletion. Even with extensive help from LD consultants, if he is under stress, spelling and spontaneous speech become very difficult. Robert discovered his problem while in college and now, because he understands this problem, he compensates by carefully preparing for each presentation he makes. Then, because he knows what is coming, his performance is consistently outstanding. He is considered extremely successful and, in fact, his presentations have become a model for others in the company.

Robert walked into a session very angry because a good friend backed out of a planned vacation that was to have taken place within the next few days. His first impulse was to completely end the relationship.

Robert: He was blowing me off.

Therapist: That doesn't fit. Didn't you just say that he was willing to spend the week with you doing something else? He just didn't want to go to Washington.

Robert: Yeah, that's true.

Therapist: So do you have any idea why you might be feeling this way?

Robert: I always come back to this. This is why I have trouble with friends and dating girls. I think it's a fear of intimacy.

Therapist: How do you mean?

Robert: Well, I cut them off before they do it to me. This way I don't get hurt.

Therapist: It sounds like you need to protect yourself.

Robert: You bet. I can't stand being blown off.

Therapist: So you do it first. Can you tell me more? What's so hard about being blown off?

Robert: It's terrible. Even though I had some friends in high school, I always felt like I was one of those guys who was the person looking in from the outside at people who fit together. I was never one of the "in group." Those guys could have such a good time shooting the bull with one another. All I could do was listen because I knew if I opened my mouth they would look at me like I was out of it. They let me hang around because I was the quiet one that admired their intellect and laughed at their jokes. Now that I know about how hard it is for me to talk easily, I probably was out of it.

Therapist: It sounds like you felt like a misfit, never fitting in.

Robert: [Excited] Yeah, that's it. I did feel like a misfit.

Therapist: It sounds like you're haunted by this.

Robert: [Nods. We go from his anger to his reason for the anger: feeling blown off (cognition) and feeling like a misfit (feeling).]

Therapist: Good Lord, what a burden. You know, it's interesting. You don't feel that way at work, do you?

Robert: No, I feel fine at work. I know what I'm doing and most people respect me for it. I can joke around and have a great time.

Therapist: That must feel great.

Robert: Yeah. When I'm at work, I feel like I'm all together.

Therapist: It's so interesting. At work, your intellect and strength have a place to go and you feel like a whole, integrated human being who can connect with your co-workers. So, I wonder, how come this stuff about feeling like a misfit comes up with other friends and with the possibility of dating?

Robert: Well, this old stuff just gets kicked off. I can't help it. I just start beating up on myself.

Therapist: What do you say to yourself?

Robert: "Oh, he's just blowing me off because I'm stupid, I'm boring, I'm not interesting, I'm no fun" . . . stuff like that.

Therapist: So you start judging yourself.

Robert: Well, yeah, but it's better for me to do it to myself than have other people do it to me.

Therapist: Really. How come?

Robert: Listen, I grew up never knowing when the ax was falling. I'd open my mouth and people would look at each other and then there would be silence. How do you think that felt? It was awful. I figured I was just stupid because other people didn't have this problem. Now I know better . . . [silence]. Gee, it would have been so nice if I had known that it just takes me more time for words to get from my brain to my mouth. Maybe I could have stopped beating up on myself so badly . . . if I had only known.

Therapist: [Softly] Yeah. That would have helped a lot. [Silence]

Robert: It's still terrible. The other day we had a training session. People had to go to the board. I almost didn't go because I couldn't see making a fool out of myself with spelling errors. But I thought I'd give it a try and if I got into hot water, I'd get a headache or something and leave. Well, it turned out okay. In fact [laughs] some people were much worse spellers than me. They sort of laughed about it. We all sort of laughed about it together.

Therapist: How lovely. You had a different conversation in your mind. So the voice you use to comfort your trainees could be used for yourself. Not bad, Robert.

Robert: Well, even though I'm always complaining about how much you cost, I guess I'm getting something out of this. [Laughter]

Therapist: You know, I think we can tease out two very important threads here. Okay?

Robert: Sure.

Therapist: Correct me if I'm wrong. If someone in the real world disappoints you, it kicks off a kind of negative internal conversation in you that causes a downward spiral. You start out feeling disappointed about something real in the world but then you believe the reason for the disappointment is because you're essentially flawed.

Robert: [Nods.]

Therapist: Then, that makes you feel worse and then you do a real job of beating up on yourself, which makes you even more discouraged and more angry.

Robert: Yeah, so what?

Therapist: Well, we have to, if you want, stop this cycle of shame by figuring out what you do to yourself versus what someone else is doing to you.

Robert: Well, I can't help it.

Therapist: Of course you can't help it. When it came to talking, growing up was a nightmare. You had no answers. There was no one to help because no one understood. So you assumed you were stupid. What other choices did you have? None! [Long silence]

Therapist: So how about if we try to figure out what kicks this off in you? What starts it and what stops it? Wouldn't that be nice to know?

Robert: Well . . . yeah. [Silence; he appears angry.]

Therapist: So how do you think this started? You weren't born this way.

Robert: Yes, I was. I've always had a problem talking.

Therapist: That's true. You do have a learning disability and it can take you longer to process what you hear and what you want to say. But why should you cut people off and beat up on yourself when you become sort of tongue-tied? [Long silence— he's deep in thought.]

Robert: When I'm working with computers, I know what I'm doing. I don't have to think about myself, and besides I don't really care how I talk because I know that I know what I'm doing. If I make mistakes I can fix them and I can help others fix theirs. That's why people like me at work.

Therapist: Right. So when you're in your area of strength, all the work you've done with your LD specialists kicks in. You can compensate just fine.

Robert: [Nods]

Therapist: So, we have to figure out what sabotages your ability to compensate. I've got some ideas. Do you want to hear them?

Robert: Yeah.

Therapist: Well, first of all we know you have a permanent disability when it comes to speech and that you've worked very hard to compensate for this. Most of the time your compensations work just fine. But once in a while, like in that in-service training, you get scared that your LD will be exposed and you imagine how humiliated you will feel. In the past, before you knew what the problem was, that would stop you. What's different now, because you know and have some tools, is that you can talk to yourself in a different kind of voice and hang in there.

Robert: Most of the time, yeah.

Therapist: So the first part is your disability. That's clear. The second part is more complicated. You don't beat up on yourself because of your disability. You beat up on yourself because you think you're dumb. Isn't that right?

Robert: Yeah, that's right. I believe I'm really stupid when I get in that place.

Therapist: So, beating up on yourself is the emotional consequence of living with your disability. It's not the disability itself. It's the emotional consequence. Now, Robert, we can't change your LD, but we can change the emotional consequences of your LD.

Robert: That's what you think. I can't stand sticking out like a sore thumb.

Therapist: Of course not. It's terrible to feel isolated and humiliated because you can't do what everyone else can. It makes us feel painfully ashamed and vulnerable. Nobody likes that. But, Robert, there's a big difference between being shamed by others and shaming ourselves. You and I can work on helping you cut way down on this self-shame.

This vignette captures a therapeutic process that involves helping the client differentiate between an immediate emotional reaction that is primary (a gut reaction to someone else) versus an emotional reaction that is secondary (a gut reaction to his own expectations and assumptions). Robert was truly disappointed and angry because he was looking forward to this trip. This was a clear primary reaction. However, his anger was complicated by the fact that he felt rejected. When we were able to tease out the fact that the friend was not rejecting him (because his friend wanted to spend the week with him and was even willing to take the same trip in a few months), then Robert could look inside himself and discover a secondary reaction, and some bedrock assumptions: in this case, feeling humiliated and like a misfit because he felt rejected.

These bedrock assumptions develop in childhood and adolescence, when there are no other explanations for why one learns unevenly and cannot function as others do. Once people believe it to be true, they are haunted by it. They never know when the feeling of stupidity will hit. That is why these are "bedrock" assumptions.

However, once Robert and I were able to empathically discern a more accurate picture of his friend's intentions, we were able to see the difference between (1) what was going on between Robert and his friend, and (2) his internal emotional reaction that surfaced because of his negative assumptions and judgments about himself. This differentiating process involves active participation from both therapist and patient.

Each participant has a somewhat different role to play. The patient must commit to a process of learning and self-exploration. The therapist must use his or her knowledge to promote the patient's curiosity in an empathic, respectful, and sincere milieu.

Therapists might ask themselves the following questions to devise starting points for particular clients:

- Why is potential constricted in an obviously bright, functioning person?
- Is there evidence of learning disabilities?
- If so, are the disabilities the *cause* of emotional distress or the *consequence* of emotional distress?
- How did/does the disability affect the client's emotional world?
- Is the client aware of both strengths and disabilities and can he or she use strengths to compensate for these disabilities?

To work productively with these questions, the focus will be upon therapeutic interactions and interventions. The rest of this section will be divided into two broad parts: Setting the Stage: Creating the Therapeutic Environment, and Facing the Challenge: Dealing with Confusion, the Chasm, and Grief.

Setting the Stage:
Creating the Therapeutic Environment

Therapists set the stage for successful treatment by providing a milieu of trust. A patient needs a backdrop of feeling safe, comfortable, special, and connected with the therapist in order to experience and work through the painful feelings that emerge in treatment. The following are general guidelines for creating an emotional "safety net" to help vulnerable clients feel comfortable in therapy.

Empathic Investigation

A therapist must inquire and investigate in an empathic manner. Empathy involves understanding the other person's point of view. For many uneven learners, understanding was sorely lacking in their early experiences; they were constantly bumping into others with impossible expectations and judgmental stances. Because clients are still haunted by the feeling that "no one understands," they may be prone to feeling misunderstood in therapy. Talking about these frustrating, shameful experiences is very helpful because patients will feel less alone, more understood, and more comfortable in the session. Also, when the time to do interpretive work comes, the therapist and client will have a shared knowledge base from which to work. Painful feelings will become familiar phenomena that are empathically experienced by therapist and patient alike.

Differentiating Strengths and Weaknesses

Therapists differentiate patients' strengths and potential from their deficits. When people come into treatment these factors are confounded and impossible to distinguish. Careful examination allows us to begin to make sense of the confusion. First of all, therapists must be very careful not to assume that intelligence can correct deficits. For example, a bright student is verbally sophisticated but fails his tests because he cannot access his memory through handwriting. Do not say, "It's wonderful how bright you are. Too bad you can't use that to pass your tests." This kind of dialogue creates a painful reenactment. People have heard these judgments all their lives. It only causes them to withdraw. Mirroring a patient's potential is vital to develop a positive therapeutic experience. Uneven learners desperately need someone to become excited about their strengths and their ambitions. Affirming questions such as: "What gives you pleasure?" or "What did you like to do as a child?" interfere with the sense of disconnection that goes along with Imprisoned Intelligence.

Avoiding Pitfalls

Avoiding treatment pitfalls also enhances the safety net. What are some pitfalls a therapist might stumble across during the integration phase of treatment? One treatment pitfall involves therapists confusing their own expectations with the patient's ability. Although bright clients may appear to function extremely well, they may have hidden deficits. Clients will take expectations of their ability to perform very seriously. Encouraging high expectations for performance can boomerang if an invisible disability interferes with the therapist's recommendations. The therapist must be careful about falling into this performance trap. For example, a patient may complain about an impossible supervisor. Obvious suggestions about changing jobs or departments might backfire if, in the new situation, the same complaints appear again. Furthermore, the person may be fired because the undiagnosed learning disabilities (that the old supervisor put up with) are seriously interfering with the new job performance. To make matters worse, the patient may also feel he or she let the therapist down. Optimally, therapy validates both strengths and weaknesses. Then patients can be free to make their own decisions.

Facing the Therapist's Feelings

Therapists need to be aware of the feelings of helplessness and hopelessness that uneven learners can engender. Because people with ULD can provoke these feelings, often therapists find themselves wanting to tell the patients what to do, in order to alleviate their own feelings of chaos and disequilibrium. Instead, if realistic interventions are necessary, it can be more helpful to suggest that the individual consult with a learning disability specialist. Such specialists know how to tell uneven learners what to do and will come up with all kinds of strategies to circumvent learning disabilities. Your job is to promote self-esteem and one vital way to do this is to provide your client with experiences of safety, validation, and partnership.

Facing the Challenge: Dealing with Confusion, the Chasm, and Grief

Why is treating people with ULD such a challenge? One factor is the complicated interface between learning disabilities and emotions. Therapists must consider ULD an important factor in the totality of the patient's experience, and a possible cause of emotional pain. But flexibility is vital.

Think of ULD as a few steps in a complicated dance. Each of the steps are interesting, but the dance does not come alive until the steps are done together. Imagine dancers changing from ballet slippers to tap shoes to bare feet on a moment's notice, never knowing which shoes will be demanded next. Working with people with ULD can be similar to that. The shoes are like different assumptions, and the assumptions create the questions asked. If therapists believe environment is at the root of the problem they ask: What happened? Who did what to whom? How did it affect the individual's emotional growth? If LD is suspected, questions follow, such as: How did the deficit affect relationships? How did the individual compensate for the deficit? Would the patient benefit from testing? No one pair of shoes will suffice.

Flexibility entails giving the patient empathic but evenly hovering attention, that is, listening without being too quick to reach a conclusion. This allows the patient to express what is important at the moment.

Another challenge is to help uneven learners move from a state of fragmentation to a state of cohesion in which their vitality enhances their potential. What is a cohesive self?

The self is made up of ambitions, skills, goals, and ideals, the relationships among them, and the actions that they dictate. With ULD individuals, it is precisely these components—their skills, goals, and ambitions—that become clouded, blocked, or frustrated by the hidden disability. Therefore, the self-cohesion of a ULD sufferer is constantly being jeopardized by the very nature of the disability.

How do ULD patients find and maintain a sense of cohesion in therapy? Verbalization contributes greatly to cohesion. Putting inner feelings and thoughts into words can help people reassess and reorder their inner world and understand their ambitions, skills, goals, and ideals in a new way.

Imprisoned Intelligence and the inability to verbalize go hand in glove. Yet, for uneven learners to understand the consequences of

ULD, talking is required. One of the main challenges of therapy with ULD individuals is finding ways to facilitate verbal communication. This section discusses how to create a language that makes sense to the patient and explains his or her pain. Some of the obstacles to developing a lexicon for exploring ULD are: (1) confusion, (2) the chasm, and (3) grief.

Dealing with Confusion

A therapist starts to see someone who is obviously successful and bright but seriously depressed. To make sense of the client's depression, the therapist will wonder about environmental inputs, such as a loss or a trauma, that might have contributed to it. The therapist may also wonder if a chemical imbalance contributes to the person's emotional pain. These questions will usually lead to clarification: trauma, neglect, or chemical imbalance may emerge as the primary problem. For example, if early childhood sexual abuse is discovered, this knowledge can foster the profound changes that occur in psychotherapy. Often, the client's understanding of his or her world profoundly shifts as the abuse is addressed in treatment. Although still a grueling process, there is a sense of cause and effect.

However, if ULD is a precipitating factor in depression, confusion will increase rather than decrease. Why does this happen? It is difficult to know "what causes what" because environmental input and constitutional deficits are inextricably intertwined. There are no easy answers here.

The first rule in treating people with ULD is that the therapist and the client must form a partnership amid the diagnostic confusion.* Both must learn to respect the patient's ideas about "stupidity." Confusion in the treatment setting is vital, because prior to therapy, the individual will have suffered with inner confusion alone. The new partnership becomes a decisive intervention. If the therapist can tolerate the confusion that goes along with ULD, he or she will interfere with a reenactment that plagues ULD sufferers. In the past, confusion and isolation were the order of the day. In other words, the individual's confusion is part of the material that is reenacted in the therapist's

---

*Arnold Goldberg, MD, presented an interesting case that involved tolerating confusion titled "The End of Inquiry" at the meeting of the Chicago Psychoanalytic Society on September 27, 1994.

office, but this time he or she will not have to tolerate it alone. The therapist will explore it with him or her.

Another source of confusion is the individual's disavowal of the learning disability.[*] While taking a school history, the therapist may find clues that an invisible learning disability affected the client's performance. However, when questioned, the client may minimize its importance. For example, she might say, "Yeah, I was lousy in math, but no one is good at every subject" or "I get along just fine." Disavowal is a defense that contributes greatly to confusion.

At times, tolerating confusion can be extremely difficult for the therapist. Material presented in session can be viewed from either the perspective of a learning disability or the perspective of defective environmental input. For example, a former patient was sexually abused as a child. She sometimes wondered whether the abuse caused or significantly contributed to her ULD. Did she merely have ULD or did the abuse exacerbate a problem for which she could have compensated more easily? There is no exact answer, but a therapeutic milieu validated her struggle to find answers to such questions. The threads of ULD and environmental input will never be teased out in a clear or concise way. What is important, however, is to keep an open mind so that the person in treatment over time can consider all the pertinent points of view that have meaning. In other words, the confusion needs validation.

What further muddies the water is that whatever you look for in the patient you will probably find (Goldberg, 1990). If you ask an environmental question, you will probably get an environmental answer, and that answer will carry some truth:

Therapist: Why didn't you like school?

John: No one liked me.

Therapist: Why not?

John: Everyone picked on me because I was poor and my clothes didn't fit.

Therapist: That must have been so difficult.

---

*For a comprehensive examination of disavowal I refer the reader to Michael Basch's work *Doing Psychotherapy* (1980).

If the therapist has her or his environmental cap on, this answer will suffice. It certainly makes sense. When kids look and feel different, problems with peers can certainly arise. Furthermore, as this story is being told, it is important to validate what the person is feeling.

The same question can have a ULD slant:

> **Therapist:** Why didn't you like school?
>
> **John:** No one liked me.
>
> **Therapist:** Why not?
>
> **John:** Everyone picked on me because I was poor and my clothes didn't fit.
>
> **Therapist:** Were there other kids who were poor and looked it?
>
> **John:** Yes.
>
> **Therapist:** So why you?
>
> **John:** Well, they weren't stupid.
>
> **Therapist:** You felt stupid? How come?

Again, what is most important is staying empathically attuned. When treating someone, it is usually beneficial to make his or her agenda center stage. If the patient is curious about "stupidity" it could be helpful to keep a ULD hat on and continue the exploration. If the patient is absorbed in alienation and embarrassment, exploration might only heighten the pain because he or she feels like a specimen.

Separating a patient's ULD from environmental influences is a process that never stops. The treatment goal becomes not merely understanding what happened (although this is a vital component), but also to teach uneven learners how to take responsibility for the complex sorting-out process. One caveat: clients cannot blame their parents for invisible learning disabilities although they may well be responsible for not addressing the problem. Most often, the parents were also in the dark.

The Chasm

As described earlier in this chapter, the chasm is a chronic hyper-awareness of a futile attempt to learn coupled with shame. It is a traumatic reaction to disappointed expectations with far-reaching

emotional consequences. Individuals experience the chasm as endur-
ingly shameful, and as a place over which they have virtually no
control. It occurs when no matter how hard they try, they cannot
fulfill the standards or expectations set by their inner or outer world.

*It is very important to underscore here that in the chasm, it is not
the LD itself that causes traumatic shaming but the dashed expectations.* It is also crucial to remember that the chasm, in itself, is not
bad. Essentially, it is healthy. Shame is a disconnection from others
because current tactics are not working and it is necessary to regroup.
Nevertheless, if, instead of being an occasional painful feeling, the
chasm occurs too often without apparent rhyme or reason, it can
become toxic and fixed within our repertoire of painful feelings.

Why does the repetition of the chasm become traumatic? First of
all, one is unable to predict when it will occur, and this uncertainty
increases learning failures because fear of cognitive freezing makes
people afraid to try. No one likes to feel embarrassed by failing to
"keep up with the class"; furthermore, if people fear they will look
stupid in the near future, this contaminates initiative. Without initiative learning dies a painful death.

Second, people with recurrent chasm-shame experiences feel
judged. Patients report that the chasm becomes fixed when they feel
judged too often, and when they have no way to remedy the situation.
Others' disapproval can be a subtle but potent force. Disapproval can
be conveyed through: outright verbal expressions; tone of voice (irritated, patronizing, sarcastic, full of contempt, etc.); gaze (rolling one's
eyes, closing one's eyes in despair, looking away with impatience,
etc.); or body language (tapping one's feet or hands in an impatient
way). Patients may misperceive the body language, tone of voice,
and so on of the therapist because they have come to expect it. When
this happens, clarification of the therapist's intent is mandatory. If
patients feel silently judged, they will withdraw.[*]

Third, the chasm becomes traumatically fixed when one cannot
meet the demands of the clock. In our culture the concept "slow" is

---

[*]If you're interested in more material on nonverbal communication, see Chapter 5
of Fred Levin's book *Mapping the Mind* (1991). It contains an interesting discussion
on the psychological ramifications of nonverbal communication.

nearly always equated with being "dull . . . mentally dull; stupid; naturally inert or sluggish; lacking in readiness" (*Webster's New Collegiate Dictionary,* 1981). In contrast, "quick" is equated with intelligence. A teacher who says a child is quick is, in essence, imputing something about that child's intelligence.

Learning involves first being able to tolerate not knowing. What most people without learning disabilities find is that not knowing leads to knowing. People with ULD experience, in their areas of deficits, that not knowing leads to more not knowing. Uneven learners know how to work hard. But mere hard work is not enough if their intelligence is imprisoned by ULD. As not knowing becomes more and more associated with humiliation and exposure, people become afraid to try. Giving up may then affect other areas of learning not obviously related to the area of concern. For example, the inability to spell correctly or copy from the board in a timely fashion can impede learning how to write. In many cases, therapists may have to slow down to accommodate their sense of timing to the patient. Some patients need a great deal of time to think and respond. Others respond very quickly. Sometimes, in fact, some patients become irritated when the therapist is slow to respond. This too becomes a therapeutic issue for further discussion.

The next section focuses on remediation. How does the chasm manifest itself within a psychotherapy session? How does the therapist know the chasm is being reenacted in the hour? What is helpful? The following are some indications that the client may be entering into a chasm state:

- There may be bodily changes: flushing, an avoidant shift, looking away, a painful silence that lasts too long, a vacant stare, a rigid stance. Meaningful interactions deteriorate; the patient seems to be grasping at straws. At this point it is crucial to restore emotional contact and to avoid actions that interfere with connection.
- Some people defend themselves from the pain of the chasm by a subtle withdrawal, which is quickly replaced by a secondary defense such as anger or disavowal.
- Patients attack their own motivations. Perpetual self-denigration may permeate the therapeutic hour. People often refer to

themselves as stupid or lazy. Many uneven learners have long histories of being called lazy, thoughtless, uninvested, careless, or worse. After hearing insults often enough, an individual internalizes them. Reciting this litany of alleged faults can indicate that the client is sliding into the chasm.

- The therapist's feelings can alert him or her to the chasm. There is a sense of "running into a wall," a feeling of abrupt confusion coupled with a sense that all connection with the patient has been lost. Something should be said to clarify the situation, but there is absolutely nothing to say. The therapist may begin to feel bodily discomfort such as a creepy feeling on his or her skin (Bollas, 1983).

- Another clue is the appearance of fluctuating compensatory strategies. Patients who seem "all together" at one session may inexplicably "fall apart" at the next. Intelligent uneven learners are extraordinarily resilient; however, when under sufficient stress, their compensatory capacities unravel because compensations rapidly ebb and flow. It is difficult for clinicians to know whether people look "regressed" because they are defending against painful emotional material or whether the regression reflects a temporary loss of compensatory strategies. For example, one dyslexic patient knows that when she is fatigued and stressed, her handwriting deteriorates. As she says jokingly, "It's not a good time to write a check." Another patient who normally is quite verbal will suddenly become tongue-tied.

Assuming that the clinician has a good idea when the client is in the chasm, what should he or she expect next? The chasm is not an enemy to be fought, but a potential therapeutic tool. If the chasm can be understood in a way that is meaningful to patients, they will be much closer to calmly experiencing their problems. Then the learning process can begin.

If a chasm experience is incorrectly labeled as defensive and motivationally based, rather than secondary to loss of adaptive capacities and strategies, then the cycle of blaming motivations is reenacted. Telling patients that they are regressing or defensive is akin to telling them that they are not learning because they do not try hard enough. This is a crucial distinction that clinicians need to think about.

Another subtle but important distinction must be made: the therapist needs to differentiate between the chasm itself (as primary) and the feelings that protect against the chasm (but are secondary). There is a big difference between the primary gut-wrenching response of the chasm and the secondary protective emotional reactions that people use to protect themselves from the chasm.

Again, the issue of theoretical "hats" and how assumptions affect the course of treatment is vital. More specifically, are the patient's problems and pain a reflection of the following:

- Underlying environmental trauma such as abuse?
- Underlying developmental delays such as self-depletion?
- Cognitive, constitutional deficits such as ULD?
- A secondary defensive reaction that protects against the chasm?
- A secondary defensive reaction that protects against overwhelming recollections of abuse?
- A secondary defensive reaction that protects against fragmentation?
- An indication of the unraveling of usually firm (or fragile) capacities to compensate?

At this point, the therapist may be thinking:

> How am I to determine whether symptoms are the result of psychological pain that needs further exploration or the result of cognitive deficits that are permanent, need validation, and require compensatory strategies?

Struggling with symptomatology that could be either motivationally based or constitutionally based is indeed difficult. Furthermore, if the problem is ULD based, the client's ability to compensate will vary, often to extremes.

Therapist: [gently] Why did you cut class today?

Teenager: I don't know, I just didn't want to get up.

Therapist: Something must have been bothering you.

Teenager: [annoyed and feeling stupid] No, I just didn't want to go. [The chasm hits because he doesn't know how to answer. Silence.]

Therapist: You're so quiet. Maybe you're quiet because you're afraid to talk or maybe something is making you mad. [This interpretation assumes an emotionally based problem.]

Teenager: Yeah, I'm mad because I'm so stupid. [The patient stops talking and starts looking at the clock, then bolts out of the room as soon as the hour is up.]

How can one approach the treatment of this client? First of all, if this client had known about the chasm, he might have been able to identify and talk about his isolation, embarrassment, humiliation, and exposure. The silent chasm-shame cycle might have been interrupted earlier. *In other words, a discussion of the chasm as both phenomenon and experience becomes a decisive therapeutic intervention.*

Of course, it is paramount that any investigation of the chasm be done empathically so that the client's feelings of isolation can be managed. Within a safe milieu, a different understanding of past and present functioning can evolve. As a consequence, the individual will no longer feel as alone. Then there may also be less vulnerability to internal and external ridicule.

Living with confusion is the name of the game for therapist and client. The chasm (which is the epitome of nothingness) gradually becomes more defined once it is identified. Awareness of this non-learning, frozen, empty place is useful as a marker. To put this in the patient's language, the question becomes: "Am I shamefully frozen because I can't learn or am I shamefully frozen because I'm afraid to look at something?"

Irrespective of the cause, the therapist works with the patient until the patient has the resources to discern the source of discomfort. It is the patient who, over time, can determine whether the chasm points to innate deficits that require careful strategy building and remediation or to psychological deficits that require psychological investigation and interpretations.

Thus the awareness and understanding of obstacles becomes the window of opportunity for therapeutic interventions. The chasm is not easy to see in vivo because it is too shameful and is quickly replaced by some protective device. Nevertheless, the therapist can recognize the chasm when it manifests in treatment. As noted above, the chasm can be seen as a signal that withdrawal is occurring. Withdrawal followed by consideration of new or different strategies becomes crucial in helping the client reestablish conditions that allow learning.

How does the therapist help the patient identify and reconstruct this problem? Feeling cognitively frozen, stupid, and exposed is a nonverbal experience that needs to be put into words. When this happens, the chasm gains a context, and can be recognized by the patient. The sharing lessens the client's sense of isolated exposure.

Once a shameful cognitive freeze is identified and dealt with, expectations begin to change. It becomes all right to feel stupid because this feeling is merely a tip-off to important information. Linking curiosity to the feeling of "not getting it" becomes a decisive tool for further therapeutic growth. Moreover, it is easier to figure out appropriate strategies to circumvent the chasm-shame cycle in the future when shame is no longer a major obstacle. To enhance the possibility of sharing material such as the chasm, certain ground rules are helpful:

1. The patient sets the agenda (not the therapist).
2. Early on, the therapist explains that feeling stupid is to be expected in therapy. Prior to therapy, not knowing makes people with ULD feel defective. This experience will probably be reenacted in the session involving the explanation of such ground rules, but this explanation creates a bridge for further understanding.
3. Because the chasm is a reaction to disappointed expectations, therapists assume that they inadvertently have been or will be the cause of clients' shame. They explain this to clients. Then, hopefully, clients can be less inhibited in sharing what caused them to feel stupid. Then, client and therapist together can trace how the chasm evolved in any particular session. The burden of shame shifts from the patient to the therapist. Almost always, if one observes empathically, there is a viewpoint from which the patient is right. In other words, there is an advantage in at least temporarily assuming that in some way or other, the therapist made a judgment that evoked the chasm.

When the chasm manifests itself in treatment, the goal is to modulate its intensity. Figuring out how to soothe someone who is drowning in the chasm can be very difficult, particularly in the beginning of treatment. Whatever is said may exacerbate the feelings of exposure; on the other hand, silence can be golden, but can also make people feel further trapped in the chasm.

In the beginning of treatment, ascribing motivational causes to the chasm can be disastrous because people are feeling raw and exposed. *Any comment that makes individuals feel minutely observed by the therapist will generally not help because the feelings of exposure are so pronounced.* One patient started to blush and turn his eyes away from the therapist, who said, "You look so embarrassed. What's up?" He walked out of the room. Later, he said he could not talk and the assumption that he should say something when he could not gave him no choice but to leave.

There are times when metaphors can be extremely helpful, because this form of communication allows the patient to withdraw from the chasm by focusing elsewhere (Levin, 1991). Sharing a personal experience with the client may alleviate the intensity. At other times, the sound of one's voice is more soothing than the words. Patients may leave favorite books with the therapist, and at times it is helpful to read them a pertinent section. Within the confines of appropriate boundaries, sharing affection for the patient can be helpful. Occasionally, the therapist may hum favorite tunes. One client would draw the way she felt. Another started to write. What is important to remember is that when the chasm hits, verbalization leaves. Furthermore, if people know that once or twice a week they can be with a therapist who understands the shame they experience, they will be able to better endure painful experiences and learn how to soothe themselves. In time, this process can be explained to the client as a developmental necessity. The clients will learn to respect rather than attack their frustrated feelings and wishes.

When treating uneven learners with ULD, one goal is to engage in the mutual process of struggle: to pull out the clues that facilitate a better understanding of how cognition and emotions connect. When this happens, the person in treatment begins to consider new learning options and eventually creates a sturdier sense of self.

Grief

Uneven learners mourn when they discover their ULD. Feelings of loss and deprivation manifest themselves when people begin to realize either that no one understood the problem, that no one was interested or cared, or that their shame over unexplained failures stifled their curiosity and desire to learn.

It is a psychotherapeutic challenge to allow these experiences to unfold in a timely way. The duration and intensity of a patient's grief will depend on circumstances. People such as college students who struggle with their deficits daily will be dramatically confronted with their feelings. Others who, for example, are understanding how ULD has contributed to depression will grieve more sporadically but just as intensely.

This process is not unlike the mourning process described in psychoanalytic literature (Freud, 1917; Kaplan and Sadock, 1991; Pollock, 1961; Moore and Fine, 1990; Krystal, 1988). This grief is a watershed that allows people to come to grips with their deficits. Surely, it is easier to think of oneself as competent but lazy than to accept that one is *not* lazy, but disabled.

Deaf people also go through this mourning process. Although they know they are deaf, in therapy they mourn for a hearing world they will never know (Stein, Mindel, Jaboley, 1981; Levin, 1981). The same process holds true for ULD sufferers. Over time, the grieving process allows them to reintegrate what they have learned about themselves and what they must give up.

The losses such clients experience have three different components. People grieve: (1) for what might have been, (2) for what will never be, and (3) for what they have to face.

Grief for what might have been. These days, parents with ULD are gratified to see that their learning disabled children receive help in school. However, it is painful for them to think about what might have been if their caregivers had only known about LD. They think about the educational opportunities that are forever closed to them. Choices about ambitions, colleges, vocations, and even friends might have been very different. Furthermore, when adults with ULD acquire new learning strategies, they become painfully aware of what was missing during their school years. If the problem had been diagnosed earlier, and if appropriate supportive assistance had been available, much of the emotional pain could have been avoided. The example of intelligence tests is instructive. Deficits and strengths can cancel each other out so that people end up looking average. That may have meant average classes, average colleges, average friends. There is much to grieve for.

Grief for what will never be. Living with ULD makes people ingenious. They learn to get around their disabilities in one way or another. This evokes a sense of pride. True Grit in Chapter 1 is an example of this. However, when newly diagnosed individuals have to rely on others and learn new ways of compensating, their independence and ingenuity are challenged.

Self-esteem temporarily plummets as they realize they can no longer live by the creed: "I can do anything I want if I work hard enough." Psychotherapy provides a milieu in which their feelings of loss can be explained as part of the mourning process.

This leads to another loss: the loss of self-pride.[*] Many adults with ULD have very high standards and goals for their own achievement. They expect themselves to do very well, and in areas of strength, they do. When testing forces them to reassess their goals as untenable, they may feel great loss. Their internal self-structure is temporarily challenged. In the past if they did not enjoy the success they expected, they could criticize themselves for not trying hard enough and continue to believe in their own perfectibility. When they learn of their ULD, they are forced to realize they can never achieve certain goals, no matter how hard they work. They also compare themselves to others who achieve quickly and easily in their areas of weakness. These comparisons highlight their loss and, until other compensatory structures develop, they struggle with a sense of despair. People have to change their "internal picture" of themselves as highly intelligent but "not working hard enough" to seeing themselves as intelligent and unintelligent in certain areas. This is a jolt. Mourning creates a bridge for connecting the intelligent and unintelligent parts of the mind. Psychotherapy validates grief and validates the individual's strengths and weaknesses. This validation modulates the grieving process so that, over time, one can integrate both strengths and weaknesses into a cohesive sense of self.

Grief for what must be faced. Learning how to compensate for a learning disability may be the hardest job individuals ever face. If they

---

*Shane, 1984. Shane's explanation of primitive grandiosity in children with learning disabilities is applicable here.

hope to make any progress, they must think about and carry out tasks that they may have avoided for years. For instance, a dyslexic sociologist who hates math may have to: (1) realize that he has avoided math completely, and (2) decide that he will never achieve his goals (say, to carry out a sociological study with statistical significance) unless he both learns as much math as he can and asks for help from his colleagues. This individual now has to confess his weakness to colleagues and spend hours poring over elementary statistics, at which he is painfully slow and inaccurate. As he studies, he may be subject to chasm experiences. In times of stressful new learning, the chasm will probably reappear. He may wonder if he should go back to doing small qualitative studies that do not reflect the scope and significance of his ideas. Fortunately, it will get easier. Especially with the help of a good psychotherapist, he can adapt to a new reality. He can alter his self-structure to include his disability, and he can begin to feel pride in his newfound compensations. When he can finally complete his study (and knows that he can do more in the future), he will feel a peace and satisfaction that eluded him in the past.

Clearly, psychotherapy can help people through the necessary experiences of grief and mourning. Psychotherapy can interfere with the disappointment and hopelessness that accompany diagnosis. It is imperative that the therapist maintain empathy in the face of possible unreasonable assaults that might occur defensively when a client tries to avoid facing these issues. Learning how to help patients modulate their massive disappointments without shaming them is one of the more difficult "basic problems" of psychotherapy.

Treatment also includes helping people adapt by encouraging the growth of compensatory structures. The therapist helps the patient discover ways around the learning gaps through effective use of appropriate others. This is where the fields of learning disabilities and psychotherapy intersect. Each field contributes to a knowledge base that can help people who struggle with Imprisoned Intelligence.

The resilience and courage people show when they struggle with newly discovered seemingly insurmountable problems is to be admired. They have a flexible sense of independence. They know how to keep going when the going gets rough. They do not give up.

Some Final Comments

This discussion of integration will conclude by reiterating that the chasm/shame/exposure experience is the end result of years of unattended cognitive deficits. This chasm, the cognitive freeze, the frozen inability to think or perform, all lead to emotional pain and contribute to the constriction of learning. It evolves in the following manner:

1. Learning frustration (when one wishes to learn and cannot figure out how to do so) leads to feeling lost and exposed.
2. Tragedy occurs in the form of a learning failure. People blame themselves and their motivations because no explanations are forthcoming (at least, none that protect the self). Erroneous assumptions about not trying hard enough cause people to despair and denigrate themselves, with long-term effects. Even after people know about the chasm, it still takes a long time in therapy to rid themselves of self-abasing thoughts and feelings.
3. Shame over not knowing, without the possibility of feeling reconnected to others and oneself, causes trauma. Because there is no help and no hope of help, feelings of aloneness lead to the realization that one is more or less permanently isolated. Then hope is lost. Consequently, when a person discovers Imprisoned Intelligence, it feels like a revelation.
4. Many people develop, on their own, incredible resilience in figuring out strategies to get around their cognitive problems. These strategies can range from extremely effective to ineffective. Unfortunately, the way around the problem often involves avoiding areas of weakness rather than finding ways to learn in spite of the weakness.

The material presented on the chasm is confusing because it will not be clear when to employ which steps. For example, some clients find it helpful to learn how shame and withdrawal from shame work. Others do not. Unfortunately, there are few straightforward suggestions. For this reason, it is helpful to identify the chasm and appreciate its emotional consequences. Armed with this, the therapist can begin to pick and choose what might be helpful to individuals who struggle with Imprisoned Intelligence.

CONCLUSIONS

A very high-functioning professional man had a word recall problem. Normally, this did not interfere with sessions. The therapist could usually supply the word he was struggling to find and the hour would flow. One day, however, his need for silence was misinterpreted. The clinician thought he needed time to think, but he fell into the chasm. He was furious. He felt the therapist was demeaning him by "putting him on the spot." Rage erupted, but the therapist vigorously denied any intent to shame him. Over a period of several sessions, he was able to talk about the shame and humiliation of not being able to think and verbalize in a timely fashion. Then the therapist could empathize with his sense of excruciating exposure. Because he was extremely bright and in other areas of his life performed in an outstanding manner, his pride could not endure the disappointment and shame of feeling so stupid. In treatment he learned that he did not have to suffer these massive disappointments alone. In time, as his rage diminished, he began to appreciate that his sense of shame was understandable and that it reappeared because of old interactive patterns that erupted when he felt stupid.

Because the relationship had stood the test of time, he could use his shame to reconnect and the therapist could again validate his interest and excitement in his areas of strength. Eventually he learned to use his intelligence to protect his disability. He would say to people, "I need time to think about this" or "Can you help me? I can't think of the word I need." If he encountered people who shamed him, he would protect himself by withdrawing his trust and looking for more appropriate people who could understand that a very bright man might still have a "glitch."

Clearly, helping people adapt to learning deficits is not easy. It is difficult to live with cognitive inconsistencies because people base their self-esteem on their intellectual competence. So, ULD can create enormous frustrations that have implications for treatment. Psychotherapy provides a setting wherein these frustrations can be clarified. Then treatment can provide a sense of connection because now the client feels someone else can understand the critical dimensions of the problem. Because this population is intrinsically intelligent and motivated toward success, creativity and self-motivation are enhanced.

Therefore, when Imprisoned Intelligence causes psychological pain, therapists are needed. Sensitive therapists with clinical multidisciplinary expertise are vital for the proper analysis of the combined cognitive and emotional factors in ULD—for example, to help identify previous emotional pain or help people face their cognitive deficits.[*]

To help adults who have suffered from ULD, a bridge needs to be created between learning disability specialists (who are not trained psychotherapeutically) and psychotherapists (who are not trained in learning disabilities) in areas of theory and practice. The goals of the two disciplines are different, but to treat this population, an interface is vital. Although LD specialists help with recognition of LD, skill-building, and ways around the problem, they are not trained to help people with the emotional ramifications of LD. Unless their emotional problems are addressed, people may be too embarrassed and ashamed to benefit from LD specialists.

Throughout the course of psychotherapy, people come to understand that wrestling with these invisible deficits is an unfolding process that never ends. People learn that they need to learn *how* to learn differently—that there is more than one way to skin a cat. Confusion is replaced with a (not necessarily easy to live by) sense of order.

People change their outlook, their expectations of themselves, and their capacities to use others in fruitful ways. They develop a new sense of cohesion and coherence. Personal histories are reinterpreted. For example, there can be a new understanding about how, in order to learn, one may have "manipulated" other people. Also, blame of parents and teachers can shift because the individual now realizes that no one knew about ULD. Conflicts about individual responsibility in specific learning situations can be reexamined and understood. For example, the individual can now ask, "Can I not learn or do I not want to learn?" People can be uncomfortably jealous because others who do not suffer from this problem can intellectually perform so flawlessly and easily.

---

[*]The findings in this study corroborate Fred Levin's (1991) work regarding the need for interdisciplinary research.

In essence, psychotherapy allows the following process to unfold:

- Learning about ULD brings relief and validation.
- People understand that they have suffered silently due to confusion, lack of knowledge, and unwarranted attacks on their motivation.
- The deficit plus the chasm affects self-esteem.
- The inability to learn as others do in areas of weakness causes grief.
- A different personal definition of learning evolves over time.
- People learn to modify perfectionistic goals through the interaction with appropriate mentors.
- People must adopt different learning techniques, which can be extremely painful.
- There is a feeling of connection with others who have similar problems.
- Through this process, people gain a new understanding of themselves; for instance, they may see themselves as survivors of an era when understanding of cognitive deficits was poor.

As people work through their grief, they adapt to their new self-knowledge. There is a sense of coming to terms with oneself. Individuals learn to compensate differently. For example, some people in this study are very proud of their ability to understand the ramifications of ULD and create successful learning strategies for themselves both at school and at work. They no longer need their previous compensations to avoid embarrassment. The pain does not disappear, but the problem is seen within a greater context of self.

Chapter 11

Historical Review

When so many people are affected, why has the topic of adults with ULD received so little attention? A brief historical overview may help clarify the cultural and political conditions that have helped create this dearth of information.

The field of learning disabilities was born of concern for intelligent children whose needs were not being met in school (Strauss and Lehtinen, 1947). It was assumed that children would outgrow their disabilities (Blakeslee, 1991; Bruck, 1987; Buchanen and Wolf, 1986; Gajar, 1992; Gerber, 1994; Vogel, 1989). Under that assumption, the literature focused only on children. It is now clear that many children retain their disabilities in adulthood (Frauenheim, 1978). Margaret Rawson (1977) followed a population of school-age children for twenty years and found that their dyslexia stayed with them. It took many years for anyone to realize that learning disabilities could be an adult affliction. Vogel (1989) states that "the manifestations of learning disabilities, though they may change, persist into adulthood, even among those who have above-average intelligence and who have completed advanced degrees" (p. 112).

In the 1970s, as the first generation of children identified as learning disabled grew up (Vogel, 1985), colleges began to take on the problem. Historically, colleges have taken the lead in research, but their purpose was practical: they wanted to test the knowledge and aptitude of students with LD to decide whether they should be admitted to college programs, and determine how to meet the educational needs of the students while maintaining the educational standards of the institution. Treatment was not their focus.

One factor that enhanced interest in adult LD was the passage of a federal law in 1973, Bill 504 (Vogel, 1985, p. 179), which mandates equal access to educational institutions for handicapped individuals.

Colleges, therefore, were compelled to set up learning disability programs. This created a need for a literature of learning disabilities, because college counselors were now concerned with diagnosis and intervention. The focus was on identification, assessment, and educational interventions (Adelman and Taylor, 1986; Cohen, 1983; Vogel, 1985; Wren and Segal, 1985). These topics remained the focus of LD research throughout the 1980s.

Also in the 1980s, a literature developed that explained severe versus subtle pathology. The research subjects were psychiatric patients whose learning disabilities were discovered during diagnostic evaluation. Using a diagnosis of minimal brain damage, this literature created a medical model (Bellak, 1978, p. 75; Greenspan, 1978; Murray, 1979) in which the learning disabilities were viewed as tangential to the psychiatric diagnosis. Since these patients were often extremely troubled, this research gave no information about high-functioning people who suffer from subtle effects of ULD.

In addition, few professionals have written about severe learning disabilities in adults who have problems with functioning in life (Interagency Committee on Learning Disabilities, 1987; Gerber and Kelley, 1984; Gottesman, 1994; Rourke, Young, and Leenaars, 1989). This work focuses on transitions to adulthood and problems involving lifestyle and vocation. Discussion centers on solutions and therapies (particularly occupational therapy) for practical problems such as inability to hold a job; but emotional variables are overlooked (White, 1992; Koziol, 1987).

In 1992 Gajar conducted a review of research involving adults with learning disabilities. He concluded that literature about the emotional needs of LD adults was practically nonexistent and more research was needed. He spoke of a "paucity of articles addressing the adult with learning disabilities within the community setting" (p. 509).

WHY LD IS SO DIFFICULT TO SPOT

Why are so many people unaware that they are learning disabled? First, schools began identifying LD students twenty years ago. Public Law 94-142, which mandated schools to diagnose and address LD, did not pass until 1977. Any adult who finished school before that time had no opportunity for diagnosis and treatment (Gerber and Reiff, 1991; Ryan and Price, 1992; Cannon, 1996). Estimates that 10 to 15 percent of the U.S. population have LD are probably accurate (Malcom, Polatajko, and Simons, 1990; Levin, 1991).

Second, diagnosing and understanding the interacting variables of ULD can be tricky. The group is extremely heterogeneous (Johnson and Blalock, 1987; Vogel, 1985). Important variables may include the patient's constitution, psychological state, environmental input, and stage of development, all interfacing and interacting with one another (Palombo, 1991; Buchholz, 1987). Furthermore, intelligent people learn how to compensate for their deficits, so though they may still feel that they are struggling, the LD remains invisible (Buchholz, 1987). The following are the subdivisions or categories of symptoms that indicate LD.

CATEGORIES OF SYMPTOMS

It is difficult to define LD and categorize LD sufferers because many have multiple handicaps that are invariably idiosyncratic (Patton and Polloway, 1982, p. 83; Pennington, 1991, p. 3). Furthermore, symptoms run the gamut from mild to severe (Ross, 1987) and may even vary within the individual from day to day (Vogel, 1985, p. 183).

How can the abstract, heterogeneous characteristics of LD be organized into practical categories that are useful in the context of adult life? The legal definition created in 1997 states:

> The term specific learning disability means those children who have a disorder in one or more of the basic psychological processes involved in understanding or in using language, spoken or written, which disorder may manifest itself in imperfect ability to listen, think, speak, read, write, spell, or to do mathematical calculations including conditions such as perceptual disabilities, brain injury, minimal brain dysfunctions, dyslexia, and developmental aphasia.
>
> Disorders not included. The term does not include a learning problem that is primarily the result of visual, hearing, or motor disabilities, of mental retardation, of emotional distur-

bance, or of environmental, cultural, or economic disadvantage. (34CFR300,7(c)(10))[*]

However, there is little consensus on this issue, and academics and clinicians have categorized and defined LD in a number of different ways.

Generally, experts agree that learning disabilities are obstacles that constrict broad areas of adult functioning such as "(a) achievement; (b) language processing and cognitive deficits; (c) occupational adjustment; and (d) social adjustment" (Ross, 1987, p. 5).

Affected individuals show mild to severe deficits in the areas of basic skills, language, memory, auditory processing, visual perception, and directionality (Gottesman, 1994). The problem with these general definitions is that they create overly broad categories that are of limited explanatory usefulness.

Other clinicians use a computer model of the brain to explain LD. Silver, in *The Gifted Learning Disabled Student* (1994), describes how the brain takes in information through the five senses. Learning is divided into steps that involve input, integration, memory, and output. According to Silver, learning disabilities primarily interfere with the process of creating meaning from the information taken in, storing this meaningful material, or outputting it.

Another strategy has been to divide learning disabilities into verbal and nonverbal disabilities. Verbal disabilities involve cognitive deficits in language, including symbols such as numbers. Such deficits are usually discovered in school (Lieberman, 1987) although their impact extends throughout the life span. Johnson and Blalock describe the different types of verbal disabilities; see their book *Adults with Learning Disabilities* (1987) for more detailed information.

To understand the verbal versus nonverbal distinction, it is important to note that some people do not communicate primarily through language. Language and meaning are not interchangeable. When verbal communication is disturbed, the result can be an inability to make friends and keep jobs, but people who have nonverbal strengths may enjoy success in fields that value nonverbal skills, such as the arts, graphic design, music, or athletics. For example, Einstein was apparently not such an excellent speaker but his power for conceptualizing

---

[*]Author's note: CFR stands for Code of Federal Regulations.

nonverbally was obviously in a class by itself (Patten, 1973; Thompson, 1971).

Another verbal learning disability deals with expression. Some people have considerable trouble saying what they want to say. Either speech or writing can be affected. They can understand when they are listening, but when they talk, read, or write they run into obstacles. For others, the problem involves dyslexia, the inability to take in, decode, and perceive information visually because the sounds associated with language are not correctly processed in the brain (Pennington, 1991, p. 58). A person with dyslexia might not be able to correctly take down telephone messages or comprehend written instructions for using a VCR.

The second category, nonverbal learning disabilities, is difficult to discern. Nonverbal learning disorders show themselves in disturbances of spatial orientation, body image, facial recognition, visual/spatial/motor organization, social interaction and analytic problem solving (Johnson, 1987b).

There is some agreement that nonverbal learning disabilities cause the greatest problems for adults in personal, social, and occupational realms (Patton and Polloway, 1982; Johnson, 1987b). Apparently, these disabilities impact partly by disturbing comprehension of time and space (Ross, 1987).

What are some of the practical, day-to-day difficulties that adults with nonverbal learning disabilities encounter? Johnson and Blalock (1987, p. 44) describe people who are verbally adept, yet cannot organize their lives and frequently lose their way. Some people are unable to make appropriate plans for themselves because of an inability to prioritize. Some cannot self-monitor and therefore are unable to identify their own mistakes. Others cannot take in more than one kind of information at the same time and become frustrated and angry. Ross elaborates:

> Adults with learning disabilities of this type are likely to get lost easily, even in familiar places; to be either late or unusually early for appointments; or to lose track of time while absorbed in a task. They may also have trouble recognizing faces and interpreting nonverbal communication; making it more difficult for them to interact appropriately with others. (1987, pp. 5, 6)

When nonverbal learning disabilities interfere with normal interactions, social cues are bypassed. People may have trouble reading others' body language and facial expressions or they may not use their bodies well and end up looking clumsy. Setting a clock radio becomes difficult or impossible. Others who cannot organize or prioritize will have homes that are perpetually a mess. Thus, lack of organization skills can not only impede efficiency at work, it can damage relationships and quality of life. Those who are lucky have secretaries or efficient family members who can help them get organized.

This section will conclude by describing another perspective on LD, one which refreshingly includes the firsthand subjective experiences of successful learning disabled adults (Butler, 1994; Mautner, 1984; Stein, 1987; Strauss, 1978). This literature does not attempt to define and categorize LD, but describes what it is like to live with learning disabilities.

For example, the editors of the *Journal of Learning Disabilities* featured a moving personal account by N. L. Stein (1987). They prefaced the article by stating:

> We publish articles *about* people with learning disabilities, but not often enough by people *with* learning disabilities. (p. 409, emphasis mine)

Far too often, LD literature tends not to consult the experts: the people with the disabilities. In their writings, Reiff, Gerber, and Ginsberg (1993) try to bridge this gap by focusing on the experiences of adults with LD. They say:

> The voices of successful adults with learning disabilities are essential for understanding what *can* be accomplished and which kinds of approaches lead to success; in contrast, traditional perspectives have focused largely on what could *not* be achieved. (p. 124, emphasis mine)*

---

*Reiff, Gerber, and Ginsberg wrote a thoughtful book called *Exceeding Expectations* (1997), which highlights the perseverance and difficulties successful adults with ULD experience.

LIFE SPAN DEVELOPMENT

Although the literature on adults with ULD is scant (Gerber and Kelly, 1984; Kafka, 1984; Kaplan and Shachter, 1991) there is interest in learning disabilities and life span development (Polloway, Smith, and Patton, 1988). Researchers are beginning to look at the impact of learning disabilities over the course of a lifetime (Buchholz, 1987; Pickar, 1986; Orenstein, 1992). Goals seen through the lens of a life span will appear different than goals merely for academic achievement (Johnson and Blalock, 1987; Gerber and Kelly, 1984) or achievements in personal, social, and vocational competency (Gottesman, 1994; Basch, 1988; Lutwik, 1983; Patton and Polloway, 1982). Lieberman (1987) states:

> Society at large tends to be more tolerant than school. Handicapped individuals are able to fade into the adult world and lead satisfactory and even fulfilled lives. They would abhor the idea of someone coming along and even suggesting that they were handicapped in some way. Their worst memories in life may be that being handicapped was thrust upon them in school. (p. 64)

Some individuals bypass or compensate for their learning disabilities and lead a "normal" life. As Lieberman (1987) says, "learning disabilities in adults is meaningful only if it helps people live" (p. 64). For others, learning disabilities are a source of suffering. Ryan and Price (1992) explain:

> There are numbers of adults who are undiagnosed as having this handicap yet who now face problems of life adjustment without the knowledge that they are, indeed, bright enough to achieve, but are inefficient and ineffective when learning and applying knowledge. (p. 6)

Chronic failure leaves a developmental imprint that influences both internal perceptions and perceptions of the world (Buchholz, 1987; Gensler, 1993; Kafka, 1984; Koziol, 1987). Individuals can grow up experiencing the self as damaged (Buchholz, 1987; Garber, 1989), struggling with feelings of alienation, heightened self-exposure, serious self-esteem problems, feelings of humiliation, and fear of failure. The specter of of these experiences creates anticipation anxiety, interfering with the capacity to try, which results in a loss of spontaneity (Gensler, 1993). Individuals learn to live with a chronic state of low-level anxiety and become increasingly withdrawn. Furthermore, if they cannot easily take in information in an organized way, interactions with others will be compromised (Buchholz, 1987; Malcolm, 1990). For example, an infant who does not have the capacity to organize visual input comfortably may not have an interactive smiling response, which enhances development and allows the infant to form ties with caregivers (Lichtenberg, 1983; Kraus, McGee et al., 1996).

MORE TO BE LEARNED

How are clinicians to understand the emotional ramifications of living with LD and ULD? More information is badly needed. So little is known (Johnson and Blalock, 1987; Bigler, 1992; Gerber, 1994; Kaplan and Shachter, 1991; Polloway, Smith, and Patton, 1988; Levin, 1991; Palombo, 1991; Vail, 1989). Even literature about adults with obvious, clearly diagnosed learning disabilities is sorely lacking—in part, because LD as a formal field of study is only a little over thirty years old and did not emerge until the 1960s. The term "learning disability" was created specifically as an umbrella so that many disciplines could interface and interact with each other (Cruickshank and Johnson, 1975; Johnson and Myklebust, 1971; Lerner, 1981; Siegel and Gold, 1982). The fields of education, medicine, psychology, and language are all contributors. The youth of the field, coupled with its multidisciplinary nature, has complicated things enormously. For example, even the definition of learning disabilities has evoked controversy (Vogel, 1989). It took years for people from different disciplines to approach a consensus on a definition (Hammill, 1990).

Furthermore, there is a tendency to think of learning and emotions in different camps. Kirk and Gallaher (1979, p. 184) elaborate on this division. They observe that the medical profession identifies but does not necessarily cure severe problems, that psychologists study behavioral characteristics, and that educators provide interventions. This division has not created a backdrop amenable to the investigation of subjective experiences. It is difficult to justify researching the emotional consequences of learning disabilities when no firm definition of learning disability even exists. Reiff, Gerber, and Ginsberg cogently observe that the "insider's perspective" is missing when decision makers struggle with the definition of learning disabilities (1993, p. 115).

In introducing an article by Deci and Chandler (1986), Adelman and Taylor, as guest editors for the *Journal of Learning Disabilities*, observed that "basic psychological concepts [are] not widely discussed in the LD field" (1986, p. 399). Because the various disciplines (neurology, cognitive psychology, behavioral psychology, and socioemotional psychology) are unwilling to collaborate, LD sufferers, as well as those with other "interdisciplinary" psychological disorders, often do not receive adequate treatment (Deci and Chandler, 1986; Bartoli, 1990).

Kaplan and Shachter (1991) state that "virtually no research has dealt with adults with undiagnosed learning disabilities, whose problem often goes unrecognized by therapists" and that "such disabilities may represent a core issue in treatment, even when patients present with other difficulties" (p. 196). White (1992) reviewed the literature on adults with diagnosed LD and concluded that although it was clear that many adults have trouble adjusting, "of all the areas of adjustment that were investigated in the studies reviewed, social adjustment got the least amount of attention" (p. 454).

There are practical consequences of living with learning disabilities. The standards set by the world often cannot be easily and comfortably met. Cohen (1985), an expert on college students with LD, states: "Although there are many children with learning problems who are not learning disabled, there are virtually no learning disabled children or adolescents who do not evidence significant psychological conflicts and concerns" (p. 177). Adulthood does not guarantee resolution of these painful states. Gensler (1993) maintains that the influence of LD "continues into adulthood in a person's cognitive style, use of defenses, interpersonal relations, character, self-image, and career development" (p. 673).

Researchers and clinicians who listen to the experiences of LD adults are acutely aware of this emotional fallout (Haufrecht and

Berger, 1984; Scheiber and Talpers, 1987). In their writing, these professionals repeatedly emphasize the need for mental health services for LD sufferers (Anderson, 1974; Blakeslee, 1991; Brier, 1994; Cox, 1977; Gajar, 1992; Gottesman, 1994; Johnson and Blalock, 1987; Malcolm, 1990; Palombo, 1985; Rawson, 1977; Rosenberger, 1988; Ross, 1987; Schechter, 1974; Shane, 1984; Vogel, 1989). The problem becomes more complicated when adults do not realize that they have learning disabilities (Ryan and Price, 1992; Schulman, 1984, Rothstein, 1988). In summary, many professionals have attested that LD in adults is a phenomenon that not only deserves more research, but calls for significantly more mental health services than are currently available.

Clearly, learning disabilities, whether diagnosed or undiagnosed, strongly influence the development of character and personality (Kafka, 1984; Garber, 1988). The individual's feelings of competence may be threatened (Basch, 1988). Other aspects of personality maybe negatively affected as well: independence (Kafka, 1984), the capacity to make choices that reflect one's interests, and the ability to compete without undue anxiety (Buchholz, 1987; Cohen, 1985).

EMOTIONAL FALLOUT:
FRUSTRATION

Although many individuals with ULD suffer and learn how to survive, this invisible problem can have lasting effects on personality (Gensler, 1993; Gerber, Ginsberg, and Reiff, 1992) because order and logic seem out of reach (Palombo, 1991). What does it feel like to live with a cognitive deficit? Paul LeClerc, who wrote the foreword in the pamphlet *Dispelling the Myths: College Students and Learning Disabilities* (Garnett and LaPorta, 1991) explains the burden of living with learning disabilities:

> Many of us are sometimes frustrated by our own inability to program a VCR, to sound knowledgeable when speaking to an auto mechanic or hardware sales person, or to fold a road map back to its original shape. All of us know couples that quarrel on trips because one of the pair always takes wrong turns but finds it painfully embarrassing to ask for directions. Such frustrations,

though annoying, are insignificant—but would they be insignificant if our entire futures depended on our mastering that VCR, that map, that maze of highways? How would we feel if we had to achieve that mastery in one hour flat, while 20 people watched us—and if we thought that we alone could not finish the task in the set time? Like the beleaguered driver, would we be too embarrassed to ask for directions? Would we despair of our future?

That learning disabilities are often invisible to oneself and to others compounds emotional struggles (Ryan and Price, 1992; Schulman, 1984). White (1985) says "Millions of others [adults] struggle with the sometimes overwhelming trials of daily life without knowing why they are different from their friends and neighbors or how to overcome their problems" (p. 231). Furthermore, the later the diagnosis, the greater the chance for self-deficits (McGlynn, 1983). For example, if one has motor coordination problems or is clumsy, this problem can seriously affect self-esteem (Weil, 1978, p. 477). Deficiencies in language can interfere with social interactions and create barriers to empathically resonating with others (Gottesman, 1994).

Unless deficits such as these are understood within the context of an individual's overall intellect, expectations of high achievement can cause serious frustration. When expectations are thwarted, frustration follows, which may eventually lead to trauma. How does frustration manifest itself in intelligent but uneven learners? This frustration can include the following four discrete categories:

1. Working harder than others but achieving less
2. Uneven learning polarities: unexplained failures along with successes
3. Constricted potential: intelligence with no place to go
4. Character denigration

These four factors create the painful emotional ramifications of ULD. Others have written about these problems, and the following four sections introduce this literature to the reader.

Frustration from Working Harder
and Achieving Less

Not surprisingly, it is frustrating to work much harder than others and accomplish much less. Wren and Segal (1985) write about the difficulties of living up to seemingly impossible standards without knowing why they are so impossible, when they seem easy for others.

Frustration from Uneven Learning:
Unexplained Failures in the Face of Other Achievements

When people are used to success, an unexpected failure is confusing, frustrating, or even anguishing. Vogel (1985) discusses what she calls "Intra-Individual" differences and describes how difficult it can be to live with the polarities of cognitive discrepancies. Donna Shalala, when she was Chancellor of the University of Wisconsin-Madison in 1991, beautifully highlighted some of the problems discrepant learners face:

> Few lawyers are abashed because they are not invited to sing at the Met; few sculptors are concerned by their inability to do statistics. And few of us think they should be. We take for granted that no one needs to do everything well. On the other hand, many people hold firmly to the idea that the college student—by virtue of being in college—should be omni-competent: able to learn with equal facility French, calculus, the elementary backstroke, English composition, and a lab science. And it is certainly true that most students can do this. But some students, despite their obvious intellectual competence, seem unable to. . . . In the past, those whole learning patterns were oddly discrepant—those who could learn some things well and other things only with great difficulty—were generally discouraged from continuing their education. (Shalala, 1991, p. ii)

Federal legislation has made it easier to cope in college. Yet intellectual discrepancies still pose difficult problems for students in college (Ryan and Price, 1992; Schulman, 1986; Wilson, 1993). Individuals with ULD write poignantly about this in self-reports (Stein, 1987; Mautner, 1984; Strauss, 1978; McMahill, 1993). Vogel (1985) elaborates:

Students with learning disabilities usually have areas of difficulty that contrast sharply with other areas where they excel
. . . . Each LD student has a unique combination of strengths
and weaknesses, but in every case the deficits make learning
especially difficult. . . . Often, their learning disabilities are
inconsistent or sporadic causing problems one day but not the
next. Similarly, they may cause problems in only one specific
area, or they may surface in many areas.

The striking unevenness of their [LD college student's] abilities which often tends to be exaggerated with maturity. . . .
What they did well as children they seem to do even better,
perhaps even exceedingly well as adults, while their functioning in areas of weakness becomes even more dramatically discrepant. (p. 183)

Frustration from Constricted Potential: Intelligence with No Place to Go

People with LD struggle with unexpressed intelligence. When
people know they are bright but cannot achieve, they become very
frustrated (Wren and Segal, 1985; Wren, Adelman, Pike, and Wilson
1987). Margaret Rawson (1977), comments on her 1968 study of
fifty-six bright dyslexic boys. In this 1977 paper, she writes about the
frustrations dyslexic children face when their language disabilities sabotage their potential. Rawson quotes a patient: "For years I've had this
feeling that I've been able to use only a third of my mental powers.
The other two-thirds just roll and tumble around in my head going
nowhere . . . confusing, frustrating . . ." (p. 193). In 1968, Silver,
reviewing Rawson's 1968 study concurred, saying, that "although the
study is not scientifically rigorous, it clearly indicates that children with
high scores on intelligence tests, coming from professional homes, are
not exempt from the problems of language disability" (p. 220). Johnson and Blalock (1987) and Vail (1989) both conclude that more
information is needed if we wish to help gifted LD students actualize
their potential.

Frustration over Character Denigration

When ULD interferes with achievement, traumatic stereotypic denigration from others (being called lazy, stupid, etc.) can follow. Charles

Madigan (1994) of the *Chicago Tribune*, although not speaking about LD, wrote an interesting article called "Welfare Finger-Pointing." He said that "society often determines stereotypes" and that "ever since the 19th Century . . . the assumption has been that those who don't make it in the USA were simply those who didn't try hard enough. . . . There remains an assumption that anyone who is good can achieve anything, even though that clearly is not true" (p. 1).

People with ULD can surely relate to these statements. Unexplained learning failures can cause individuals to be inappropriately judged and scrutinized (Wilson, 1983; Brazelton, 1980; Buchholz, 1987; Buchholz and Mishne, 1983). Bateman (1996) notes:

> The difficulties in identifying students who have learning disabilities include the persistent predisposition of some teachers to believe they could do it if only they would work harder (or if they had a better attitude, etc.). (pp. 37-38)

EMOTIONAL FALLOUT: TRAUMA

Individuals with ULD often grow up experiencing themselves as damaged (Buchholz, 1987; Cohen, 1985). When achievement falls far short of potential, the following psychological repercussions are common: alienation, heightened self-exposure, serious self-esteem problems, humiliation, fear of failure, and social problems (Lichtenberg, 1983; Buchholz, 1987; McGlynn, 1983; Cohen, 1985; Johnson and Blalock, 1987). This emotional fallout (Scheiber and Talpers, 1987, p. 13) can reflect anxiety, fear of discovery, depression, or anger. Cohen (1985) attests to the widespread nature of emotional fallout in LD children: "Although there are many children with learning problems who are not learning disabled, there are virtually no learning disabled children or adolescents who do not evidence significant psychological conflicts and concerns" (p. 177).

Gensler (1993) wrote a very thoughtful paper about the impact of ULD on defenses, interpersonal relations, character, self-image, and career development. When fear of humiliation and exposure makes LD sufferers afraid to try, spontaneity is inhibited, and motivation is sabotaged. Shame and withdrawal render them bored with life and increasingly reliant on others (Kafka, 1984).

Not surprisingly, the continual experience of these painful emotional states leaves the LD sufferer prone to depression. Often, school failures impact negatively on students' self-esteem (Kaplan and Shachter, 1991). Cohen (1983) describes why college students with LD are so often clinically depressed: although the students could compensate to some degree, they struggled with foreign languages, math, reading too slowly, sloppy handwriting, spelling discrepancies, and lack of organization.

Galatzer-Levy (1993) believes that many of the devastating emotional effects of LD can be attributed to cognitive difference. The LD brain is simply not structured in the same way as a non-LD brain, which creates "primary variations in the organization of experiences [that] range from the construction of body image to the sequencing of ideas which may be extraordinary in ways that may be evaluated *as maladaptive or creative or both*" (emphasis mine). He elaborates:

> These primary variations in experience take on added personal meaning as the person finds it difficult to negotiate a world largely designed for people whose cognitive organization differs from his own. Depending on the environment's response, the variation is commonly experienced as a defect and may come to symbolize other feelings of defectiveness, incompleteness, or vulnerability. (Galatzer-Levy, 1993, p. 181)

Perhaps "variations in experience" might also explain some of the personality disorders associated with LD. Rhodes and Jasinski (1990), Wood et al. (1976), and Wood, Wender, and Reimberr (1983) address the interface between learning disabilities and substance abuse. Another more sizable literature examines the interface between learning disabilities and personality disorders (Christman, 1984; Eisen, 1993; Mautner, 1984; Koziol, 1987; Vail, 1989; Cohen, 1983; Kafka, 1984; Levin, 1991; Wilson, 1993).

This historical review is one way of categorizing the literature about adults with learning disabilities. Hopefully, in the future, much more will be learned and others will continue to fill in the gaps.

Chapter 12

Self Psychology
and Imprisoned Intelligence

The goal of this chapter is to provide the reader with a bridge linking self psychology, shame, and Imprisoned Intelligence. Both self psychology and affect theory's concept of shame (explained in Chapter 2) will be used to theorize about Imprisoned Intelligence. The integration of these two theories will help to explain the painful emotional experiences associated with Imprisoned Intelligence. Self psychology is a developmental theory conceived by Heinz Kohut (1971) that explains both growth and constriction of the self. Self psychology makes it possible to understand the consequences of living with ULD. It also offers a lexicon that seems especially appropriate for discussing the emotional consequences of ULD.

Although they do not explicitly address ULD, self psychology and affect theory's concept of shame help explain the suffering of persons with this problem. Sporadic learning failures threaten self-cohesion, and repeated learning failures can create a cycle of shame, despair, and self-denigration. As low self-esteem becomes entrenched, it becomes increasingly difficult to break learning blocks. The painful subjective experiences described by the participants strongly correspond to self psychological descriptions of injury to the self.

LEARNING AND IMPRISONED INTELLIGENCE

To understand the impact of ULD on the self, it is imperative to understand that learning and mental health are very closely entwined.

Learning is enhanced when the student is interested and excited. Learning is a precondition to leading a full life, to enhancing one's potential, and even to survival. Fuqua (1993) states:

> Learning is something we do in school, something we do in therapy, and something we do day to day. It is integral to the very act of living. Without learning we would not adapt or grow, we would become stagnant and rigid . . . we must learn in order to survive and thrive. The process of learning goes beyond structured education settings to the very fabric of our existence. (p. 13)

However, humans are not learning machines who constantly gobble up new information whenever they happen upon it. Learning is best done in a timely fashion so that new knowledge can be integrated with what is already familiar. Fuqua's (1993) comments illuminate this process:

> Yet with all we have to recommend the activity, we still find ourselves resisting the process [of learning] at times. Even as you are reading now with the hope that you will hear something new and enlightening, you must be looking simultaneously for the familiar landmarks of ideas already mastered, signposts pointing toward familiar ground. Too much newness all at once is overwhelming to us, and even when we seek out new knowledge, we find ourselves avoiding the process while simultaneously feeling the urge to pursue it. (p. 14)

Appropriate timing is vital to learning. Furthermore, learning involves flexible use of new information to create a different order in one's brain. Here is Fuqua's (1993) definition of learning:

> Learning is the incorporation of new facts, perceptions, and ideas. It is also the mastery of new processes, styles, and formats of thinking and interacting, both with each other and with the environment. . . . An essential aspect of learning is the addition of something new to an existing structure, producing a necessary change in that structure. The structure that is modified is both the body of knowledge already held by the learner and his self system. What is learned changes what was preexisting. (p. 14)

Learning is a singular internal experience that involves the brain's capacity to change what one knows. Levin (1991) states: "Learning seems to involve some process in which the various learning subsystems of the brain are able to exchange data" (p. 43). Of course, circumstances and encouragement from others also contribute to the learning process. Others can help, but eventually one's own brain needs to do the work if learning is to occur.

ULD creates obstacles that obscure and obstruct the learning process. As one study participant explained, "Learning is like climbing a ladder one step at a time, and for me, there were too many rungs missing." If one wishes to learn but obstacles prevent learning, over time, frustration looms larger and interest shrinks. Without interest, the learning process falters. Interest propels learning and shame prevents it. Interest and shame are powerful forces that act upon the self. To clarify these relationships, self psychological concepts will now be applied to the experience of Imprisoned Intelligence. I will discuss and describe self-states, selfobjects, development, cohesion versus fragmentation, deficits, compensatory structures, and disavowal.

THE IMPACT OF IMPRISONED INTELLIGENCE ON THE SELF AND SELFOBJECTS

In uneven learners, Imprisoned Intelligence is a blow to their sense of self. In areas of strength they perform very well, and they expect themselves to perform just as well in areas of weakness. When learning failure occurs, they experience a shameful cognitive freeze and withdrawal that impacts massively on self-esteem. After their initial bewilderment, such individuals report that they soon learn not to count on others for help with their learning problems. They then become discouraged, their interest in learning wanes, and the lonely struggle with defeat causes them to shamefully withdraw. They assume that the problem is their fault, and they attack themselves. For these individuals, the absence of empathic others results in profound loss of self-esteem.

Self psychological theory offers a powerful explanation of what is taking place here. According to self psychology, the developing self needs certain empathic responses from others to remain healthy and intact. If all goes well with the developing self, the adult can appropriately use others to maintain a sense of well-being, cohesion, self-enhancement, and sustenance.

Empathy is crucial to the developing self. It is the capacity to think and feel oneself into the inner world of another person (Kohut, 1984). In other words, one must attempt to understand someone else's feelings even when they do not match one's own. For example, I may hate to fly but might get excited when others tell me about *their* excitement when flying; I may not be interested in art, but, to propel the development of my child's self-esteem, he needs me to understand his excitement about the pictures he paints.

The self of the very young child relies almost exclusively on the parent's ability to be empathically nurturing and responsive. When this happens, the child's self is reinforced, and he feels "all together." Kohut calls this a feeling of cohesion (Kohut, 1977). When a child's needs are empathically fulfilled, caregivers are providing what Kohut calls "selfobject" functions.

THE IMPACT OF IMPRISONED INTELLIGENCE ON DEVELOPMENT

The development of the self involves three evolving transferences to selfobjects: idealization, mirroring, and twinship. These transferences create a world of self/selfobject experiences in which ambitions and ideals can grow and flourish (Baker, 1987; Lieb, 1990). Often ambitions and ideals are contradictory, and this creates tensions in the self. Kohut (1977) described contradictions between ambitions and ideals as producing a "tension arc." A tension arc is: ". . . the abiding flow of actual psychological activity that establishes itself between the two poles of the self; i.e., a person's basic pursuits toward which he is 'driven' by his ambitions and 'led' by his ideals" (p. 180). The cohesive self uses ideals to direct ambitions. The goals set by one's ambitions and ideals are accomplished by use of one's talents and skills (Kohut, 1984).

Skills must be learned and talents must be developed. Therefore, if an undiagnosed learning disability interferes with the flowering of talents and the learning of skills, the cohesive self is compromised. For example, a college student who has good ideas but writes very slowly may become terribly frustrated and do poorly during an in-class essay test. Taken alone, this incident is not devastating, but when students have similar experiences throughout their entire academic career, they may suffer considerably. When talents and skills are blocked, emotional growth and fulfillment are also blocked. Palombo (1979) describes the psychological state of a child whose learning and achievement has been repeatedly blocked:

> Such a child [with learning disabilities] would begin to feel baffled recognizing that something is very wrong with him. He may feel narcissistically injured and withdraw from those around him or may compensate for the inadequacy and vulnerability by symptomatic behavior such as unmodified grandiosity or omnipotence. He may immure himself within a wall of narcissistic self-investment which isolates him even further from the environment. (p. 37)

In other words, the child becomes ashamed, withdraws his or her interest in the world and ends up investing in only unmodified grandiosity.

Self psychology's focus on three developmental lines can help us understand how ULD prevents the blossoming of potential. In the following sections on idealizing, mirroring, and twinship transferences, you will see how undiagnosed learning disabilities compromise development in intelligent people.

Idealization

The idealizing transference involves relating to a selfobject that one admires and perceives to be flawless and all-powerful. From basking in the selfobject's perfection and power, the individual feels protected. In adulthood, the transformed idealizing transference no longer demands that the selfobject appear perfect and all-powerful; rather, it describes a relationship with an admired other, such as a mentor. However, in childhood, the selfobject is literally perceived as ideal, perfect, and unconquerable. When the selfobject cannot live up to this impossible standard and makes a mistake that is not too severe, this is an opportunity for optimal frustration and transmuting internalization.

It is a "good enough disappointment," which allows the child to develop self-soothing capacities and a more realistic view of the world.

To learn, children need the feelings of security and safety provided by the idealizable selfobject (Baker, 1987). When teachers and parents (selfobjects) fail to understand their learning problems, children feel uncomfortable and unsafe both at school and at home. This constitutes not an "optimal frustration" but a major selfobject failure: the self-object's perfection, power, and ability to protect is, in the child's eyes, absolutely denied. The selfobject can no longer be trusted as protector. Rather than allowing transmuting internalization and growth, these self-object failures occasion withdrawal, shame, and repression of the transference need.

Because the selfobject (the teacher or parent) does not know about the ULD, the child cannot count on the selfobject to maintain his or her sense of self-worth in the face of school failure. The child no longer feels safe and constantly fears being labeled "stupid." Over time, the child abandons all hope of receiving help. The tragedy is that parents and teachers with good intentions are not aware that the child's needs are not being met.

Furthermore, it is difficult to learn in an antagonistic setting. Not surprisingly, students learn more easily from teachers whom they respect and idealize. In turn, parents and teachers feel pride when children learn. Genuine pride in the child's capabilities is difficult to maintain when the child appears to be working below capacity. Parents and teachers also blame themselves for the child's failures.

The following scenario is common: A teacher works with a ULD child who appears to learn nothing. The teacher becomes frustrated. Because the child's problem is not identified, the teacher feels help-less, and her pride in her teaching abilities is wounded. The teacher feels ashamed and withdraws. The child becomes aware that the teacher is disappointed in him. In the face of the teacher's impotence, the child is forced to see that his teacher cannot help or protect him. The idealization process that promotes learning is then curtailed.

Mirroring

Mirroring is the experience of having one's value and worth reflected in the eyes of a caregiver (selfobject). Appropriate mirroring of early grandiosity evokes the child's self-confidence and interest, which propels achievement and learning. Conversely, when appropriate mirroring is not available, the child's grandiose self is repressed and stagnates at a primitive level. Then the grandiose self cannot be modulated by input from the world (Shane, 1984). Children with Imprisoned Intelligence often lack appropriate mirroring because their caregivers cannot mirror good traits that they do not see.

Almost all uneven learners know they are intelligent, but feel that exposing their intelligence to new learning is too risky. The saying "pride goeth before a fall" is pertinent here. Good enough disappointments (optimal frustrations) encourage flexibility and creativity. For example, a child who fails his spelling test because he did not memorize the words that week can, with some encouragement from his parents or teacher, get an A the following week. However, if the child has a memory recall problem, he will not only dread spelling but will also be reluctant to write papers that would further expose his inability to spell. In many cases, he will refuse to do work or will do it in a haphazard manner. Then he can always tell himself, "I could have done better if I tried." Children learn not to expose their intelligence if the chasm is lurking. Therefore, ambitions remain primitive and grandiosity is unneutralized.

In usual circumstances, if selfobjects modulate the omniscience of young children through appropriate and tolerable experiences of disappointment (optimal frustrations), the demands of the grandiose self are lessened, ambitions become realistic, and children learn how to regulate themselves (Kohut and Wolfe, 1978). Tolerable disappointments do not cut off interest, but allow children to learn from failure.

When children suffer from ULD, both parents and child know that the child is not pleasing the parent, and appropriate mirroring fails to occur. For example, a father who has an interest in Little League may not mirror a child with perceptual motor problems that prevent him from catching a ball.

No learner can know it all, but what would be considered minor failures by other children may trigger fragmentation in a student who has unmodulated, impossible expectations—an outcome of a primitive grandiose self—because the student has never learned to handle small disappointments.

Those who have ULD learn about their own primitive grandiosity after diagnosis. They have to confront their overblown expectations of easy learning and perfection when they face their areas of weakness. It is not easy to face deficiencies previously disavowed to protect grandiose expectations. However, the process of confronting and treating LD allows persons to remobilize development, modulate unrealistic expectations, and eventually enjoy a firm self-esteem based on genuine understanding of their gifts and deficits.

Twinship

Children have a powerful need to feel a part of their class. They want to fit in. This need is a manifestation of the twinship transference. When children suffer from ULD, they experience themselves as "different" without knowing why. They may have trouble finding friends in class. When they do not feel like valued members of the class, children may become more afraid of exposing their learning difficulties. They become fearful and afraid to try. Other children may notice their weakness and single them out for teasing.

Of course, ULD children are not alone in feeling left out, friendless, or persecuted at school. Schoolchildren can be inordinately cruel, and the objects of cruelty are not only those who seem to be stupid, but also smart kids, ugly kids, poor kids, shy kids, kids who are bigger or smaller than the norm, or kids who are vulnerable in any way. Any child who is habitually teased or excluded is likely not only to have trouble learning, but to feel depressed, anxious, and miserable.

Children with ULD may be quite successful at avoiding teasing. Often these children are so practiced at concealing and compensating for their deficits that they appear to fit in perfectly with the class. However, despite their appearance of normality, the children know themselves to be different, and may feel even more anguished about having to pretend. Whether they give the appearance of fitting in or not, they continue to feel isolated.

Furthermore, children who are aware that in their areas of weakness they cannot compete with peers feel ashamed, disconnected, isolated, and alone. They withdraw and become subject to chasm experiences. As with the other transference needs, when children's need for twinship is not met, their pain snowballs. Their feelings of isolation and exclusion interfere with learning, and their failure to learn increases their hopelessness and isolation.

As one might imagine, development is often arrested along all three lines simultaneously. For instance, a child will not look up to a teacher who cannot help him, so the teacher offers little mirroring and the child does not feel like a valued member of the class. Alternately, the child may be popular with his peers (meeting his twinship needs), but exasperate the teacher, frustrating his needs for mirroring and for an idealizable selfobject. A child who has some needs met is in a better position to develop a core of vitality and hopefulness that will allow him to compensate for deficits. The child whose needs are frustrated across the board is less able to maintain adequate self-esteem, develop creative compensations, or withstand fragmentation.

IMPRISONED INTELLIGENCE AND DEFICITS

When ULD sufferers cannot learn something that they think they should be able to learn, they experience the failure as a deficit or lack: something is missing. This feeling resembles the depletion states described in self psychological literature. The term *depletion* describes the state of "something being missing" in one's psychological make-up. It is an awareness of an emptiness or a deadness inside one's self and a yearning for others who might facilitate feeling alive again (Palombo, 1985b).

While self psychology emphasizes emotional deficits, the field of learning disabilities emphasizes cognitive deficits. Both deal with "lacks": the former presumes a lack of responsiveness from selfobjects; the latter presumes a lack of endowment. Although some self psychological literature addresses cognitive deficits (Kohut, 1971, 1977; Tolpin, 1980), the psychoanalytic assumption is that lack of appropriate nurturing and resultant self-deficits are the primary problem (Palombo, 1979).

To understand the psychological world of the ULD sufferer, both kinds of deficits are crucial considerations. A typical scenario might be: a cognitive deficit causes the child to fail to meet the caregiver's expectations, perhaps by receiving poor grades. As a result, the caregiver is angry, frustrated, or disappointed and can no longer nurture the child adequately, which makes the child's Imprisoned Intelligence even more pronounced. A cognitive deficit is almost always accompanied by a lack of support and nurturing.

Deficit leads to deficit. Fortunately, the pattern does not continue indefinitely. Participants reported that a new pattern is set in motion by testing. The process looks something like this: (1) The cognitive deficit results in Imprisoned Intelligence. Adverse emotional reactions follow, including shame and withdrawal. Aspects of development are constricted. (2) Development is remobilized after testing and diagnosis. Suddenly, there are new possibilities for dealing with learning problems. The tendency to withdraw diminishes because the deficits are now identified and there is hope for remediation.

Innate cognitive deficits may not be preventable, but emotional deficits are. Early testing and diagnosis seem to offer strong protection against developing later, ULD-related emotional problems. Individuals who are tested and diagnosed at a young age do not exhibit low self-esteem (Kosarych-Coy, 1984); they develop effective compensations and function at an age-appropriate level. Their success is partly due to the fact that they have a vocabulary with which to understand their deficits. Language allows the experience to be put into a context in which words define problems and explanations. Then solutions are a possibility. One successful man in this study who grew up with a verbal learning disorder explained why a lexicon is important to him:

> I didn't have a mechanism for dealing with the teachers who wanted to see me as stupid, who found me frustrating, who reacted very negatively to my inability to spell and to write well . . . . and to be honest, I think there are an awful lot of anal-compulsive people out there who see it as their job as to get Johnny to spell it right and don't have a particular model to have a mind, to help [them] to learn to think. So it would have been very useful for me and my parents to have this rhetoric to deal with the teachers.

IMPRISONED INTELLIGENCE, SHAME, AND FRAGMENTATION: THE CHASM

There are striking similarities between (1) fragmentation, (2) shame, and (3) the experiences of the chasm. The three terms describe a single experience that is the result of insufficient compensations and defenses in combination with a fragile self. Fragmentation can occur in individuals who have not developed self-soothing capacities and are therefore vulnerable and dependent upon selfobjects to perform selfobject functions (mirroring, idealization, twinship). When the selfobject fails to perform its function, the individual is massively disappointed and subject to fragmentation states.

People with undiagnosed learning disabilities may have a greater propensity for severe fragmentation. Because they are unable to understand their LD, compensatory structures fail them more often. When compensatory structures fail, fragmentation and low self-esteem seem to whirl out of control. Fragmentation, then, is very similar to the chasm. Compare a description of fragmentation on the left to a participant's description of the chasm on the right.

FRAGMENTATION	**CHASM**
Patients describe this [fragmentation] in a variety of ways. Some feel that they are falling apart; some that they are lost in space without any supply of oxygen; others that they are treading water in the middle of the ocean with nothing solid to touch, no one nearby, and ever-present danger of sharks; still others feel dead. (Baker and Baker, 1987)	I had a chasm of no knowledge, just this place inside of me that, you know. . . . It was an emptiness. You know, like, if you were to draw a picture of my body, that there was this great space that other people had filled up, that I didn't.

To avoid chasm experiences, the individual may avoid situations that have triggered feelings of fragmentation in the past. For instance, a ULD student who receives an A with negative comments about spelling or neatness may feel no accomplishment, but experience only the crush of defeat as earlier school traumas are revisited. Fuqua (1993) elaborates:

> A person with a sense of self-cohesion feels lively, effectual, and confident. A person who is fragmented complains of listlessness, disorganization, inability to concentrate or think straight, feelings of depletion, and difficulty following through on things. Sometimes, she also feels enraged. The universal urge in the psyche is to try to reinstate a sense of cohesion whenever it is disrupted. (p. 15)

A perpetual feeling of insecurity is associated with fragmentation/ chasm. Because wildly fluctuating self-experiences are triggered by environmental demands, sufferers can never depend on feeling good or stable for any given period of time. Their self-states may vacillate between cohesion and fragmentation on a daily basis. For example, a slow reader may feel cohesive before a test because she has prepared and knows the answers. Her self-esteem plummets during and after the test because she did not have enough time to show her knowledge. Therefore, her suffering is twofold: not only does she have to withstand the chasm itself, but she is constantly in a state of fearful apprehension. She never knows when something will come along to threaten her cohesion. Unlike a cohesive self, she does not have "the sense of continuity of the self in time" (Kohut, 1984, p. 65). The pain of this state may be hard to grasp for those who have not experienced it, but it is a problem of ontological scope: one's very existence feels tenuous and uncertain.

Self-cohesion is a necessary precondition for learning. When people have cohesive selves, they are invested in themselves and interested in their world. When people are fragmented, thought processes freeze and interest withers away (Nathanson, 1987). The chasm then is the nucleus around which pain and low-esteem coalesce. It affects many areas of experience and can seriously inhibit learning.

Even after testing, persons have to repeatedly face the chasm to make headway against their learning problems. Sometimes they also endure or fear ridicule from the world. Despite these struggles, most persons with ULD are able to progress in their careers and lives without a catastrophic loss of self-esteem. Perhaps their success is due to strong compensatory structures, or the self-regard they gain by mastering discouragement and hardship (Gerber and Reiff, 1991). Additional research is necessary to determine when and why the chasm is experienced, as well as how it is laid to rest.

IMPRISONED INTELLIGENCE AND EMOTIONAL DISTANCING: DISAVOWAL

Most people cannot tolerate swinging from cohesion to fragmentation that seems to occur without rhyme or reason. To protect themselves, they learn to distance themselves from their pain. One way to achieve the desired distance from emotions is through disavowal. Disavowal is knowing a painful fact but feeling nothing. The fact itself is not repressed, but the emotions surrounding it are. Basch (1998) describes how disavowal works:

> [Disavowal] blocks the formation of a bond between perception and affect. . . . [It] is directed toward danger from the external world. Disavowal, by preventing the formation of an affective link between a potentially traumatic experience and the affect it would ordinarily be expected to arouse, minimizes that experience's importance for the self system, for, though acknowledged, *what is not affectively charged* can be disregarded. (pp. 124-125, emphasis mine)

Take, for example, a civil service worker who reads slowly but needs to pass an exam to get a promotion. After each attempt the exam is returned with a failing grade. Because the stakes are high, when the worker sees the grade, he feels nothing but emptiness and adopts an "I-don't-care" attitude. Only later do the shame and disappointment hit.

Imprisoned Intelligence is often accompanied by disavowal. Many people accept the fact that they are different, but until the diagnosis, they have no emotional reaction. Because they are vulnerable, they organize their world by rationalizing their differences as simply a way of life. In other words, disavowal is a step beyond frustration: when frustration can no longer be tolerated, it is replaced by a feeling of nothingness.

The Testing: Interrupting Disavowal

Diagnostic testing interferes with the disavowal associated with ULD by facilitating: (1) attempts to change and confront inadequate ways of compensating, (2) the process of working through grief, and (3) enhanced communication within the self and with others.

Confronting Previous Compensations

One area that is challenged is individuals' pride in their independence—previously a compensation that allowed them to maintain self-esteem in the face of unsupportive teachers and parents. As discussed before, in the past, because no one was there to help, survivors learned to figure things out for themselves and created ingenious compensations for their ULD. For years, an independent stance may have served them well. Now, pride and self-sufficiency may no longer be adequate solutions; testing indicates a disability, best handled not by independent effort, but by consulting professionals and allowing them to help. One person reported:

> I learned that I operate in some areas on a third-grade level. I did go for tutoring for a while, but I quit because it was much easier to be a doctoral student than it was to be working with phonics. It was too hard. I couldn't do it. It was easier, you know, back on campus, being a doctoral student.

In other words, this brilliant person found it too difficult to live (even temporarily) in a world where she felt so stupid.* Confronting pride in one's independence with the need to be dependent to learn in areas of difficulty corresponds with Kohut's concept of archaic grandiosity. The feeling that "there's nothing wrong with me and I can do whatever I want if I only try hard enough" is challenged by the testing. People learn that some things cannot be done at all, and some things will take a great deal of effort. Testing, although illuminating, also constitutes a narcissistic injury.

For example, when people with LD first learn to deal with their deficits, their weakness becomes painfully clear. At first, learning is awkward, painfully slow, and difficult. This insults their pride in their intelligence, because learning in their areas of strength is so easy, and that is what they expect of themselves in every arena. When expectations of easy learning are confronted by reality, the chasm can follow. One young woman with dyslexia said that before her diagnosis, she

---

*Here is an example that shows where self psychology diverges from my findings. Kohut's description of compensatory structures suggests that once the structures become integrated, they continue to provide a valuable source of self-enhancement. This is not necessarily the case for ULD sufferers. The compensatory structures that stood them in good stead before the diagnosis are not always appropriate for continued use. They may need to be examined, reevaluated, and sometimes discarded by the individual after the diagnosis.

compensated for her extremely slow reading by asking lots of questions in class. When she got to college, however, this method of learning annoyed the professor. After her diagnosis, she had to focus on keeping quiet and taking notes. Needless to say, it was very difficult. Not only did she have to endure the chasm until new skills were in place, but she had to give up a comfortable solution.

The contrast between attitudes before and after testing exemplifies how, to protect oneself from further painful exposure, one's pride goes underground. Grandiose expectations are split off and unavailable for selfobject modulation.

Ironically, before diagnosis, it is this unmodified grandiosity that propels people to compensate creatively for their Imprisoned Intelligence. After diagnosis, primitive grandiosity was neutralized. Interestingly, this was not accomplished gradually through transmuting internalizations, but by facing a disappointment immediately and all at once.

Grief

As discussed in the section on treatment, grieving occurs when grandiose expectations are denied by reality. It is truly difficult to understand that no matter how smart you are, areas of learning that seem easy to others can be difficult to impossible. But over time, as people learn new strategies, they also learn to modify their grandiose expectations. One aspect of reconciliation is understanding that learning takes time.

Those who have silently suffered with Imprisoned Intelligence move from naiveté to maturity; even in the face of the difficult transitions described above, they did not lose hope. After the diagnosis, things change: words and feelings begin to come together and make sense. The problem does not go away but becomes integrated into one's concept of self.

Enhanced Communication with Self and Others

Almost everyone interviewed felt relieved to be able to label what they knew but could not verbalize until the diagnosis. When empathic failures occur due to others' misunderstanding of ULD, there is now a vocabulary with which to explain the failure. Verbalization also interferes with disavowal by creating a link between cognition and affect where there was none before. Until the diagnosis of a learning disability, there are no words with which to examine this disavowed state; after diagnosis there is a lexicon of words to describe ULD experiences.

Disavowal can be seen on a broader scale as well. For example, prior to diagnosis, the world ignores a person's cognitive problems and the associated psychological ramifications.* After diagnosis, if allowed an opportunity to communicate their feelings to a sympathetic ear, people can then move away from a defensive fragmenting position toward compensatory strategies. This is the maturation process that I have called reconciliation.

Also, armed with new information, individuals can reinterpret their personal history. Mentors, when available, are able to rekindle idealization when the mentor is aware of both the individual's strengths and disabilities. Parents who did not have the knowledge to help their child with the ULD can now offer support to their adult offspring who is struggling to live with the disability. Intellectual strengths and disabilities can be seen as a whole. Hope, therefore, is rekindled.

Learning about narcissistic deficits and the psychological treatment of ULD will be beneficial to this population. This research only begins to answer questions about how defensive structures are replaced by compensatory structures. In psychoanalytic terms, how does structuralization occur? Is it always an unconscious process? Also, is there a difference between high and low achievers in compensatory structure formation? Why do some people with serious disabilities achieve while others do not? Perhaps Kohut's concept of vigor (1977, p. 100) provides a clue. Levin's (1991, p. 43) ideas about interhemispheric connections may offer another explanation. Other environmental variables may come into play as well, such as parental judgment of academic success and failure. Perhaps the type of compensatory structure determines success. So much needs to be learned

---

*Kohut alluded to such experience when he suggested that his critics may have disavowed the intensity of the self-selfobject relationships because these relationships challenged the goal of self-autonomy (1984, p. 61).

about this new field of inquiry. A real need to bridge the disciplines and learning disabilities and psychology. Kohut's concepts enhance the bridging of these two fields.

In conclusion, I have attempted to show that attention to that part of the tension arc called talents and skills plays a decisive role in self-development. When talents are not enhanced and skills are not developed, psychological problems can arise. Although deficits can be filled in with compensatory structures, this process will not occur easily in the circumstances of ULD. Undiagnosed learning disabilities lead to empathic breaks (within oneself and with others) that cause shame and intellectual constriction. People become afraid to try because they cannot tolerate unexplained failures. This is Imprisoned Intelligence.

CONCLUSIONS

One of Kohut's crucial achievements was to introduce and promote understanding of concepts such as fragmentation, grandiosity, and compensation. He also created a view of development based upon an empathic understanding of transference needs. Perhaps more important, he created a lexicon with which to discuss the phenomena that he observed. Clinicians may agree or disagree with his ideas, but with his words, they can carry on a discourse which would not otherwise be possible. Imprisoned Intelligence also creates a lexicon, and it is my hope that the new language can be used by others to create a dialogue. There is so much to be learned about this new field of inquiry, and a real need exists to bridge the disciplines of learning disabilities and psychology. Kohut's concepts give us tools that enhance the building of these bridges.

Self psychology, with its emphasis on deficits and self-esteem, provides an appropriate context in which to study Imprisoned Intelligence because (1) Kohut's concept of cohesion is a necessary component in learning; (2) fragmentation, of which shame is a component, makes it very difficult or impossible to learn; and (3) learning involves optimal frustration—the capacity to tolerate, over long periods of time, small, progressive disappointments.

Clearly, the emotional consequences of ULD become psychotherapeutic issues. The detailed personal accounts of the subjective stories of adults with ULD have produced my concept of Imprisoned Intelligence. Though many learning problems are environmentally based, many are innate, and the two call for different treatment strategies. My clinical experience suggests that a psychodynamic psychotherapy, informed by knowledge about learning disabilities, can be successful with this population. Self psychology is an especially useful psychodynamic model, since many of these individuals seem to suffer from "self problems": low self-esteem, repressed archaic grandiosity, empty depression, and tendency to extreme shame states and fragmentation states.

Furthermore, adults with ULD feel that their psychological development has been compromised by the lack of awareness of their disabilities. Baker (1987) concurs that a needless tragedy of Imprisoned Intelligence can occur. He states:

> With exceptional responsiveness, they [children with learning disabilities] can learn well and do not develop secondary narcissistic vulnerabilities. More often, the disability is not understood, and the child develops poor self-esteem and a tendency to avoid schoolwork. Thus, a parent might respond more than satisfactorily to a typical child but be unable to meet the needs of a special child. (p. 449)

Early interventions could prevent the problems that stem from unidentified learning disabilities. It could be so helpful if school personnel such as classroom teachers and school social workers could be trained to identify and help children with undiagnosed learning disabilities. Kohut (1985, p. 39) stated that although psychoanalytic principles cannot explain innate endowments, one cannot ignore their impact on the self's capacity for creativity. Innate deficits influence self-states.

Kohut's conceptualization of compensatory structures also offers considerable insight into the experiences of adults with innate deficits. Rather than being incapacitated by inadequate self-nurturing responses, many people with ULD (in and out of awareness) have creatively and ingeniously developed ways of compensating for their learning disabilities. Unfortunately, because no one knew, more adaptive compensations were not available. Though compensations often allow individuals to function adequately, they are probably nowhere near optimal, and in some circumstances they take a psychological toll. Perhaps, since 20 percent of adults suffer from ULD, Kohut was actually treating more people with undiagnosed learning disabilities than he may have appreciated.

Finally, the understanding of how individuals not only survive difficult and adverse conditions but go on to build fulfilling lives and careers is just beginning. This is because the ability to think and learn surely involves the self, and the self's relationship to learning is now coming under the microscope. One's innate capacity to think and learn, as well as the emotional consequences of this capacity, are surely issues of self.

Referral Sources

The following list is for the reader's perusal. While I cannot guarantee the content of the Web sites, they offer starting places for one's own research. I find the sites for nonprofit national organizations to be especially helpful; they generally offer sound information, and many have links to a variety of other resources. Beware of Web sites that try to sell you something. The information they offer may be less than impartial.

Children and Adults with Attention Deficit Disorder (CHADD)
National nonprofit, parent-based organization with information on ADD, ordering materials, local information, and events.
http://www.chadd.org

Dyslexia, the gift (Positive aspects of dyslexia)
http://www.dyslexia.com/

Dyspraxia Foundation
http://www.emmbrook.demon.co.uk/dysprax/homepage.htm

Hidden Handicaps Support Group
http://www. geocities.com/HotSprings/Spa/2320

Individuals with Disabilities Education Act 1997—legal information about amendments
http://www.ed.gov/offices/OSERS/IDEA/

The International Dyslexia Association
8600 LaSalle Road
Chester Building, Suite 382
Baltimore, MD 21286-2044
410-296-0232   Fax 410-321-5069
E-mail infor@interdys.org
http://www.interdys.org

Language-Based Learning Disability: Remediation Research
http://www-ld.ucsf.edu/

LD Pride Online
http://www.ldpride.net

LDOnline
http://www.ldonline.org/

Learning Disabilities Association of America
4156 Library Road
Pittsburgh, PA 15234
412-341-1515
http://www.ldanatl.org

A medical solution to dyslexia
http://www.dyslexiaonline.com/

National Attention Deficit Disorder Association
This nonprofit organization's Web site focuses on information related to helping adults with attention deficit disorder learn to live
successfully with their ADD.
http://www.add.org

National Center for Learning Disabilities Inc.
381 Park Ave. South, Suite 1401
New York, NY 10016
212-545-7510 or 888-575-7373   Fax 212-545-9665
http://www.ncld.org/

National Information Center for Children and Youth with Disabilities
NICHCY is a national information and referral center that provides
information on disabilities and disability-related issues for families,
educators, and other professionals. Their special focus is children
and youth (birth to age 22).
http://www.nichcy.org

NLDline
http://www.nldline.com

Office of Special Education and Rehabilitative Services—U.S. Department of Education
http://www.ed.gov/offices/OSERS/

San Diego branch of the International Dyslexia Association
http://www.dyslexiasd.org/

Smart But Stuck: About Learning Disabilities and Imprisoned Intelligence
   This is my Web site. It attempts to give the reader a mini-version of this book. It introduces some of the psychological consequences that can go along with undiagnosed learning disabilities and gives some concrete suggestions for how to help oneself.
http://www.imprisonedintelligence.com

Tara's NLD Jumpstation
(someone's private Web page—but rather interesting)
http://www.geocities.com/HotSprings/Spa/7262/

University of Kansas Center for Research on Learning
http://www.ku-crl.org/

University of Pennsylvania Student Action Group—Helping to Educate About Alternative Learning
http://dolphin.upenn.edu/~heal/

Recommended Reading

Gerber, P.J. and Reiff, H.B. (1991). *Speaking for themselves: Ethnographic interviews with adults with learning disabilities.* Ann Arbor, MI: The University of Michigan Press.

Goleman, D.E. (1994). *Emotional intelligence: Why it can matter more than IQ.* New York: Bantam Books.

Lelewer, N. (1994). *Something's not right.* Action, MA: VanderWyk and Burnham.

Reiff, H.B., Gerber, P.J., and Ginsberg, R. (1997). *Exceeding expectations: Successful adults with learning disabilities.* Austin, TX: Pro-Ed.

Schmitt, A. (1992). *Brilliant idiot: An autobiography of a dyslexic.* Intercourse, PA: Good Books.

Schwarz, J. (1994). *Another door to learning: True stories of learning disabled children and adults, and the keys to their success.* New York: Crossroads.

Vail, P.C. (1981). *Emotion: The on/off switch for learning.* Rosemont, NJ: Modern Learning Press.

Wren, C.L. (2000). *Hanging by a twig: Understanding and counseling adults with learning disabilities and ADD.* New York: W. W. Norton & Co.

Bibliography

Abrams, J. C. (1980). A psychodynamic understanding of the emotional aspects of learning disorders. In B. Keogh (Ed.), *Advances in special education: A research annual. Perspectives on applications, 2* (pp. 29-50). Greenwich, CT: JAI Press.

Adelman, H. and Taylor, L. (1986). Introduction to Deci, E. L. and Chandler, C. L. The importance of motivation for the future of the ld field. *Journal of Learning Disabilities, 19*(10), 399.

Anderson, C. (1974). The brain-injured adult: An overlooked problem. In R. E. Weber (Ed.), *Handbook on learning disabilities: A prognosis for the child, the adolescent, the adult* (pp. 217-241). Englewood Cliffs, NJ: Prentice-Hall.

Baker, H. S. (1987). Underachievement and failure in college: The interaction between intrapsychic and interpersonal factors from the perspective of self psychology. In S. C. Feinstein (Ed.), *Adolescent Psychiatry, Vol. 14* (pp. 441-460). Chicago: The University of Chicago Press.

Baker, H. S. and Baker, M. N. (1987). Heinz Kohut's self-psychology: An overview. *American Journal of Psychiatry, 144*(1), 1-9.

Bartoli, (1990). On defining learning and disability: Exploring the ecology. *Journal of Learning Disabilities, 23*(10), 628-631.

Basch, M. F. (1980). *Doing psychotherapy.* New York: Basic Books.

Basch, M. F. (1988). *Understanding psychotherapy: The science behind the art.* New York: Basic Books.

Basch, M. F. (1992). *Practicing psychotherapy: A casebook.* New York: Basic Books.

Bateman, B. (1996). Legal definitions and the juvenile delinquency-learning disability linkage. *LDA Newsbriefs, 31*(1), 37-38.

Baum, S., Renzulli, J., and Hebert, T. (1994). Reversing underachievement: Stories of success. *Educational Leaderships, 52*(3), 47-52.

Bellak, L. (1978). *Psychiatric aspects of minimal brain dysfunction in adults.* New York: Grune and Stratton.

Bigler, E. D. (1992). The neurobiology and neuropsychology of adult learning disorders. *Journal of Learning Disorders, 25*(8), 488-506.

Blakeslee, S. (1991). Study ties dyslexia to brain flaw affecting vision and other senses. *The New York Times*, September 15, p. 1.

Bollas, C. (1983). Expressive uses of the countertransference: Notes to the patient from oneself. *Contemporary Psychoanalysis, 19*(1), January, 1-34.

Brazelton, B. T. (1980). Neonatal assessment. In S. I. Greenspan and G. H. Pollock (Eds.), *The course of life: Psychoanalytic contributions toward understanding personality development* (pp. 203-205). Adelphi, MD: National Institute of Mental Health.

Bresslau, N. (1990). Does Brain Dysfunction Increase Children's Vulnerability to Environmental Stress? *Archives of General Psychiatry, 47*(1), 15-21.

Brier, N. (1994). Psychological adjustment and adults with severe learning difficulties: Implications of the literature on children and adolescents with learning disabilities for research and practice. *Learning Disabilities: A Multidisciplinary Journal, 5*(1), 15-27.

Bruck, M. (1987). The adult outcomes of children with learning disabilities. *Annals of Dyslexia: An Interdisciplinary Journal of The Orton Dyslexia Society, 37*, 252-262.

Buchanen, M. and Wolf, J. S. (1986). A comprehensive study of learning disabled adults. *Journal of Learning Disabilities, 19*(1), 34-38.

Buchholz, E. S. (1987). The legacy from childhood: Considerations for treatment of the adult with learning disabilities. *Psycholanalytic Inquiry, 7*(3), 431-452.

Buchholz, E. and Mishne, J. (1983). *Ego and self psychology: group interventions with children, adolescents, and parents.* New York: Jason Aronson.

Buchsbaum M. S., Haier, R. J., Sostek, A. J., Weingartner, H., Zahn, T. P., Siever, L. J., Murphy, D. L., and Brody, L. (1984). Attention dysfunction and psychopathology in college men. *Archives of General Psychiatry, 4*(42), 354-360.

Butler, W. D. (1994). Learning disabilities information. Reproduced in *The National Networker: Quarterly Newsletter for Adults Who Have a Learning Disability,* PO Box 32611, Phoenix AZ 85064-2611.

Cannon L. (Ed.). (1996). Learning disabilities and juvenile justice: Evidence of failure for persons with learning disabilities. Report of the summit on learning disabilities, 1994. *LDA Newsbriefs 31*(1), 21.

Christman, D. C. (1984). Notes on learning disabilities and the borderline personality. *Clinical Social Work Journal, 12*(1), 18-30.

Chuaeoan, H. (1997). He was my hero. *Time Magazine,* January 27, p. 25.

Cohen, J. (1983). Learning disabilities and the college student: Identification and diagnosis. *Adolescent Psychiatry: Developmental and Clinical Studies, 11,* 177-198.

Cohen, J. (1985). Learning disabilities and adolescence: Developmental considerations. *Adolescent Psychiatry: Developmental and Clinical Studies, 12,* 177-196.

Cox, S. (1997). The learning-disabled adult. *Academic Therapy, 13*(1), 79-86.

Cruickshank, W. and Johnson, G. O. (1975). *Education of exceptional children and youth.* Englewood Cliffs, NJ: Prentice-Hall.

Deci, E. L. and Chandler, C. L. (1986). The importance of motivation for the future of the l.d. field. *Journal of Learning Disabilities, 19*(10), 587-594.

Eisen, M. R. (1993). The impact of the learning-disabled child on the family. In K. Field, E. Kaufman, and C. Saltzman (Eds.), *Emotions and learning reconsidered: International perspectives* (pp. 126-138). New York: Gardner Press.

Elson, M. (1986). *Self psychology in clinical social work.* New York: W. W. Norton.

Frauenheim, J. G. (1978). Academic achievement characteristics of adult males who were diagnosed as dyslexic in childhood. *Journal of Learning Disabilities, 11*(8), 21-28.

Freud, S. (1891). *On aphasia* (E. Stengel, Trans.). New York: International Universities Press.

Freud, S. (1917). Mourning and melancholia. In E. Jones (Ed.) and J. Riviere (Trans.). *Sigmund Freud: Collected papers*. The International Psychoanalytical Library, Number 10., Vol. 4. (152-170). New York: Basic Books.

Fuqua, P. B. (1993). A model of the learning process based on self psychology. In K. Field, E. Kaufman, and C. Saltzman (Eds.), *Emotions and learning reconsidered: International perspectives* (pp. 13-33). New York: Gardner Press.

Gajar, A. (1992). Adults with learning disabilities: Current and future research priorities. *Journal of Learning Disabilities, 28*(8), 507-519.

Galatzer-Levy R. M. (1993). When you're stupid and things don't work right: Notes from the analysis of an adolescent boy with a learning disability. In K. Field, E. Kaufman, and C. Saltzman (Eds.), *Emotions and learning reconsidered: International perspectives* (pp. 171-186). New York: Gardner Press.

Garber, B. (1988). The emotional implications of learning disabilities: A theoretical integration. *The Annual of Psychoanalysis, A Publication of the Institute for Psychoanalysis, 16* (pp. 111-128). Madison, CT: International Universities Press.

Garber, B. (1989). Deficits in empathy in the learning-disabled child. In K. Field, B. Cohler, and G. Wool (Eds.), *Learning and education: Psychoanalytic perspectives* (pp. 617-637). New York: International Universities Press.

Gardner, H. (1983). *Frames of mind: The theory of multiple intelligences.* New York: Basic Books.

Garnett K. and LaPorta, S. (1991). Dispelling the myths. *College students and learning disabilities.* Hunter College/National Center for Learning Disabilities, 99 Park Avenue, Sixth Floor, New York, NY 10016.

Gensler, D. (1993). Learning disability in adulthood: Psychoanalytic considerations. *Contemporary Psychoanalysis, 29*(4), 673-691.

Gerber, P. J. (1994). Researching adults with learning disabilities from adult-development perspective. *Journal of Learning Disabilities, 27*(1), 6-9.

Gerber, P. J., Ginsberg, R., and Reiff, H. (1992). Identifying alterable patterns in employment success for highly successful adults with learning disabilities. *Journal of Learning Disabilities, 25*(8), 475-487.

Gerber, P. J. and Kelley, R. H. (1984). Learning disabilities and social skill development: Research-based implications for the developmental life-span. In W. M. Cruickshank and J. M. Kliebhan (Eds.), Early adolescence to early adulthood: Selected papers from the 20th International Conference of the Association for Children and Adults with Learning Disabilites (pp. 69-77). Syracuse, NY: Syracuse University Press.

Gerber, P. J. and Reiff, H. B. (1991). *Speaking for themselves: Ethnographic interviews with adults with learning disabilities.* Ann Arbor, MI: The University of Michigan Press.

Goldberg, A. (1990). *The prisonhouse of psychoanalysis.* Hillsdale, NJ: Analytic Press.

Goldberg, A. (1994). *The end of inquiry.* Presentation given at the meeting of the Chicago Psychoanalytic Society, September 27, 1994.

Goldberg. C. (1991). *Understanding shame.* Northvale, NJ: Jason Aronson, Inc.

Goleman, D. (1995). *Emotional intelligence.* New York: Bantam Books.

Gottesman, R. L. (1994). The adult with learning disabilites: An overview. *Learning Disabilities: A Multidisciplinary Journal, 5*(1), 1-14.

Greenspan, S. (1978). Principles of intensive psychotherapy of neurotic adults with minimal brain dysfunction. In L. Bellak (Ed.), *Psychiatric aspects of minimal brain dysfunction in adults* (pp. 161-175). New York: Grune and Stratton.

Hammill, D. (1990). On defining learning disabilities: An emerging consensus. *Journal of Learning Disabilities, 23*(2), 74-84.

Haufrecht, B. and Berger, P. C. (1984). Adult psychosexual disorders: An integrated approach. *Social Casework, 65*(8), October, 478-485.

Hinshelwood J. (1917). *Congenital word blindness.* London: H. K. Lewis.

Interagency Committee on Learning Disabilities. (1987). *Learning disabilities: A report to the U. S. Congress.* Washington, DC: U.S. Department of Health and Human Services.

Johnson, D. (1987a). Principles of assessment and diagnosis. In D. Johnson and J. Blalock (Eds.), *Adults with learning disabilities* (pp. 9-30). New York: Grune and Stratton.

Johnson, D. (1987b). Nonverbal learning disabilities. *Pediatric Annals, 16*(2), 133-141.

Johnson D. J. and Blalock, J. W. (1987). *Adults with learning disabilities.* New York: Grune and Stratton.

Johnson, D. and Myklebust, H. (1971). *Learning disabilities: Educational principles and practices.* New York: Grune and Stratton.

Kafka, E. (1984). Cognitive difficulties in psychoanalysis. *Psychoanalytic Quarterly, 53*(4), 533-550.

Kaplan C. P. and Shachter (1991). Adults with undiagnosed learning disabilities: Practice considerations. *Families in Society: The Journal of Contemporary Human Services, 72*(4), 195-201.

Kaufman, R. (1989). The inability to learn in school: The role of early developmental deficiencies in learning disabilities. In K. Field, B. Cohler, and G. Wool (Eds.), *Learning and education: Psychoanalytic perspectives* (pp. 559-615). Madison, CT: International Universities Press.

Keogh, B. (1988). The future of the learning disability field. In S. Chess, A. Thomas, and M. Hertzig. (Eds.), *Annual progress in child psychiatry and child development* (pp. 207-219). New York: Brunner/Mazel.

Kirk, S. and Gallagher, J. (1979). *Educating exceptional children.* Boston: Houghton Mifflin.

Kohut, H. (1971). *The analysis of the self.* New York: International Universities Press.

Kohut, H. (1977). *The restoration of the self.* New York: International Universities Press.

Kohut, H. (1984). *How does analysis cure?* Chicago: The University of Chicago Press.

Kohut, H. (1985). *Self psychology and the humanities: Reflections on a new psychoanalytic approach.* C. B. Strozier (Ed.) New York: W. W. Norton and Co.

Kohut, H. and Wolfe, E. S. (1978). The disorders of the self and their treatment: An outline. *International Journal of Psychoanalysis, 59*(4), 413-423.

Kosarych-Coy, J. M. (1984). A study of the self-concepts of community college students identified as learning disabled. *Dissertation Abstracts International, 45*(5), 1299A.

Kozoil, L. F. (1987). Learning disorders—Food for clinical thought. *Clinical Review, 1*(2), 1-2.

Kraus, N., McGee, T. J., Carrel, T. D., Zecker, S. G., Nicol, T. G., and Koch, D. B. (1996). Auditory neurophysiologic responses and discrimination deficits in children with learning problems. *Science, 273*(5277), 971-973.

Krystal, H. (1988). *Integration and self healing.* Hillsdale, NJ: Analytic Press.

Landers, A. (1997a). "The streets are full of easily lost people." *Chicago Tribune,* January 6, Tempo Section 5, p. 3.

Landers, A. (1997b). "No clue when it comes to some faces." *Chicago Tribune,* March 25, Tempo Section 5, p. 3.

Lerner, J. (1981). *Learning disabilities: Theories, diagnosis, and teaching strategies.* Boston: Houghton Mifflin.

Levin, F. M. (1991). *Mapping the mind.* Hillsdale, NJ: London Analytic Press.

Levin, F. M. (1995). Psychoanalysis and knowledge: Part 1. The problem of representation and alternative approaches to learning. In J. A. Winer (Ed.), *The Annual of Psychoanalysis* (pp. 95-116). Hillsdale, NJ: The Analytic Press.

Levin, F. M. (1997). Some thoughts on attention. *Samiksa, Journal of the Indian Psychoanalytic Society, 51,* 23-30.

Levin, F. M. (1998). Mind and brain: Attempting to bridge our understanding of conscious and unconscious processes. *Samiksa, Journal of the Indian Psychoanalytic Society, 52,* 39-48.

Levin, F. M. (In press). *Psyche and brain: The biology of talking cures.* Madison, CT: International Universities Press.

Levin, F. M. and Kent, E. W. (1995). Psychoanalysis and knowledge: Part 2. The special relationship between psychoanalytic transference, similarity judgment, and the priming of memory. In J. A. Winer (Ed.), *The Annual of Psychoanalysis* (pp. 117-130). Hillsdale, NJ: The Analytic Press.

Lewin, T. (1996). College toughens its stance on learning disabilities aid. *The New York Times National,* February 13, p. 1.

Lichtenberg, J. (1983). The psychoanalytic situation and infancy. In J. Lichtenberg (Ed.), *Psychoanalysis and infant research* (pp. 183-214). Hillsdale, NJ: The Analytic Press.

Lichtenberg, J. (1988). Infant research and self psychology. In A. Goldberg (Ed.), *Frontiers in self psychology: Progress in self psychology* (pp. 59-64). Hillsdale, NJ: The Analytic Press.

Lieb, P. (1990). The origins of ambitions. In A. Goldberg (Ed.), *The realities of transference: Progress in self psychology.* Hillsdale, NJ: The Analytic Press.

Lieberman, L. M. (1987). Is the learning disabled adult really necessary? *Journal of Learning Disabilities, 20*(1), 64.

Lutwik, N. (1983). Countertherapeutic styles when counseling the learning disabled college student. *Journal of College Student Personnel, 24*(4), 321-324.

Madigan, C. M. (1994). Welfare finger-pointing: Society often determines stereotypes. *Chicago Tribune,* February 20, Perspective, p. 1.

Malcolm, C. B., Polatajko, H. J., Simons, J. (1990). A descriptive study of adults with suspected learning disabilities. *Journal of Learning Disabilities, 23*(8), 518-520.

Mautner, T. S. (1984). Dyslexia—My "invisible handicap" *Annals of Dyslexia: An Interdisciplinary Journal of The Orton Dyslexia Society, 34,* 299-311.

McGlynn M. J. (1983). Differences in self-concept in learning disabled versus non-learning disabled adults. *Dissertation Abstracts International, 44*(3), 711-A.

McMahill, V. (1993). Learning disabilites and self-esteem. *LDA Newsbriefs, 26*(6), 22.

Moore B. E. and Fine, B. D. (1990). *Psychoanalytic terms and concepts.* New Haven and London: American Psychoanalytic Association and Yale University Press.

Murray, M. (1979). Minimal brain dysfunction and borderline personality adjustment. *American Journal of Psychotherapy, 33*(3) (July), 391-403.

Muslin, H. L. and Val, E. R. (1987). *The psychotherapy of the self.* New York: Brunner/Mazel Publishers.

Nathanson, D. (1987). A timetable for shame. In D. L. Nathanson (Ed.), *The many faces of shame* (pp. 1-64). New York: The Guilford Press.

Orenstein, M. (1992). Imprisoned intelligence: The discovery of undiagnosed learning disabilities in adults. *Psychological Abstracts,* AAD98-16334, 58-11, p. 6243.

Palombo, J. (1979). Perceptual deficits and self-esteem in adolescence. *Clinical Social Work Journal, 7*(1), 34-61.

Palombo, J. (1985a). The treatment of borderline neurocognitively impaired children: A perspective from self psychology. *Clinical Social Work Journal, 13*(2), 117-128.

Palombo, J. (1985b). Depletion states and selfobject disorders. *Clinical Social Work Journal, 13*(1), 32-49.

Palombo, J. (1988). Adolescent development: A view from self psychology. *Child and Adolescent Social Work, 5*(3), 171-186.

Palombo, J. (1991). Neurocognitive differences, self cohesion, and incoherent self narratives. *Child and Adolescent Social Work, 8*(6), 449-472.

Patten, B. M. (1973). Visually mediated thinking: A report of the case of Albert Einstein. *Journal of Learning Disabilities, 6*(7), 415-420.

Patton, J. R. and Polloway, A. A. (1982). The learning disabled: The adult years. *Topics in Learning Disabilities, 2*(3), October, 79-87.

Pennington, B. F. (1991). *Diagnosing learning disorders: A neurological framework.* New York, London: The Guilford Press.

Pickar, D. (1986). Psychosocial aspects of learning disabilities: A review of research. *Bulletin of the Menninger Clinic, 50*(1), 22-32.

Pollock, G. H. (1961). Mourning and adaptation. *International Journal of Psychoanalysis, 42,* 341-361.

Polloway, E. A., Smith, J. D., and Patton, J. R. (1988). Learning disabilities: An adult developmental perspective. *Learning Disability Quarterly, 7*(2), 265-272.

Poznanski, E. (1979). Handicapped children. In S. Harrison and J. Noshpitz, J. (Eds.), *Basic handbook of child psychiatry* (pp. 641-650). New York: Basic Books.

Rawson, M. (1968). Developmental language disability: Adult accomplishments of dyslexic boys. Paper. Baltimore, MD: Johns Hopkins Press.

Rawson, M. (1977). Dyslexics as adults: The possibilities and the challenge. *Bulletin of the Orton Society: An Interdisciplinary Journal of Specific Language Disability,* XXVII, 193-197.

Reiff, H., Gerber, P. J., and Ginsberg, R. (1993). Definitions of learning disabilities from adults with learning disabilities: The insiders' perspective. *Learning Disability Quarterly, 16*(2), 114-125.

Reiff, H., Gerber, P J., and Ginsberg, R. (1997). *Exceeding expectations: Successful adults with learning disabilities.* Austin, TX: PRO-ED.

Rhodes, S. and Jasinski, D. R. (1990). Learning disabilities in alcohol-dependent adults: A preliminary study. *Journal of Learning Disabilities, 23*(9), 551-556.

Rosenberger, J. (1988). Self psychology as a theoretical base for understanding the impact of learning disabilities. *Child and Adolescent Social Work, 5*(4), 269-280.

Ross, A. O. (1977). *Learning disability: The unrealized potential.* New York: McGraw-Hill.

Ross, J. M. (1987). Learning disabled adults: Who are they and what do we do with them? *Lifelong Learning: An Omnibus of Practice and Research, 11*(3), 4-8.

Rothstein, A. (1998). Neuropsychological dysfunction and psychological conflict. *The Psychoanalytic Quarterly, 67*(2), 218-240.

Rothstein, A., Lawrence, B., Crosby, M., and Eisenstadt, K. (1988). *Learning disorders: An integration of neuropsychological and psychoanalytic considerations.* Madison, CT: International Universities Press.

Rourke, B. P., Young, G. C., and Leenaars A. A. A. (1989). Childhood learning disability that predisposes those afflicted to adolescent and adult depression and suicide risk. *Journal of Learning Disabilities, 22*(3), 169-175.

Ryan, A. G. and Price, L. (1992). Adults with LD in the 1990s. *Intervention in School and Clinic, 28*(1), 6-20.

Schechter, M. D. (1974). Psychiatric aspects of learning disabilities. *Child Psychiatry and Human Development, 5*(2), 67-77.

Scheiber, B. and Talpers, J. (1987). *Unlocking potential: College and other choices for learning disabled people—a step-by-step guide.* Bethesda, MD: Scheiber and Adler.

Schulman, S. (1984). Psychotherapeutic issues for the learning disabled adult. *Professional Psychology: Research and Practice, 15*(6), 34-39.

Schulman, S. (1986). Facing the invisible handicap. *Psychology Today, 20*(2), February, 58-61.

Schwartz, J. (1992). *Another door to learning: True stories of learning disabled children and adults, and the keys to their success.* New York: The Crossroad Publishing Company.

Schwartz, M., Gilroy, J., and Lynn, G. (1976). Neuropsychological and psychosocial implications of spelling deficit in adulthood: A case report. *Journal of Learning Disabilities, 9*(3), 144-148.

Shalala, D. (1991). Foreword. In K. Garnett and S. LaPorta, *College students and learning disabilities* (p. ii). New York: Hunter College National Center for Learning Disabilities.

Shane, E. (1984). Self psychology: A new conceptualization for the understanding of learning disabled children. In P. E. Stepansky and A. Goldberg (Eds.), *Kohut's legacy* (pp. 191-201). Hillsdale, NJ: The Analytic Press.

Shaprio, J., Loeb, P., and Bowermaster, D. (1993). "Separate and Unequal" *U.S. News and World Report,* 12/13/93 p. 46-60.

Siegel, E. and Gold, R. (1982). *Educating the learning disabled.* New York: Macmillan.

Silver, L. (1968). More than twenty years after: A review of developmental language disability. Adult accomplishments of dyslexic boys. *The Journal of Special Education, 3*(2), 219-222.

Silver, L. (1979). Minimal brain dysfunction syndrome. In J. D. Noshpitz (Ed.), *Basic handbook of child psychiatry, Volume II.* New York: Basic Books.

Silver, L. (1981). The relationship between learning disabilities, hyperactivity, distractibility, and behavioral problems. *Journal of the American Academy of Child Psychiatry 20*, 385-397.

Silver, L. (1984). Emotional and social problems of children with developmental disabilities. In R. Weber (Ed.), *Handbook on learning disabilities* (pp. 97-120). Englewood Cliffs, NJ: Prentice-Hall.

Silver, L. (1989a). Learning disabilities. *Journal of the American Academy of child Psychiatry, 20*, 309-313.

Silver, L. (1989b). Psychological and family problems associated with learning disabilities: Assessment and intervention. *Journal of the American Academy of Child and Adolescent Psychiatry, 28*(3), 319-325.

Silver, L. (1994). What are specific learning disabilities? In center for talented youth (CTY). The Johns Hopkins University (Eds.), *The gifted learning disabled student* (pp. 25-28). Baltimore, CT: CTY Publications and Resources.

Silver, L. and Brunsetter, R. W. (1987). Learning disabilities: Recent advances. In J. D. Noshpitz (Ed.), *Basic handbook of child psychiatry, Volume 5* (pp. 354-361). New York: Basic Books.

Stein, L. K., Mendel, E. D., and Jaboley, T. (1981). *Deafness and mental health.* New York: Grune and Stratton.

Stein N. L. (1987). Lost in the Learning Maze. *Journal of Learning Disabilities, 20*(8) August/September, 409-441.

Stern, D. (1985). *The interpersonal world of the infant.* New York: Basic Books.

Strauss, A. A. and Lehtinen, L. E. (1947). *Psychopathology and education of the brain-injured child.* New York: Grune and Stratton.

Strauss, R. (1978). Richard's story. *Bulletin of the Orton Society: An interdisciplinary Journal of Specific Language Disability, 18*, 181-185.

Thompson, L. (1971). Language disabilities in men of eminence. *Journal of Learning Disabilities, 4*(1), 113-121.

Tomkins, S. (1987). Shame. In D L. Nathanson (Ed.), *The many faces of shame* (pp. 133-161). New York: The Guilford Press.

U.S. Government Code of Federal Regulations. Learning disability. (34CFR300, 7(c)(107).

U.S. Office of Education. (1977). Definition and criteria for defining students as learning disabled. *Federal Register, 42*(250), 65083, Washington, DC: U.S. Government Printing Office.

Vogel, S. (1985). Learning disabled college students: Identification, assessment, and outcomes. In D. Duane and C. Leong (Eds.), *Understanding learning disabilities: International and multidisciplinary views.* NY: Plenum Press.

Vogel, S. (1989). Special considerations in the development of models for diagnosis of adults with learning disabilities. In L. B. Silver (Ed.), *The assessment of learning disabilities: Preschool through adulthood* (pp. 111-134). Boston: College Hill.

WBEZ (1996). Commercial for Epson Printers, May 3, WBEZ National Public Radio.

Webster's New Collegiate Dictionary (1981). Springfield, MA: G. & C. Merriam Co.

Weil, A. P. (1978). Maturational variations and genetic-dynamic issues. *Journal of the American Psychoanalytic Association, 26*(3), 461-491.

White, W. J. (1985). Perspectives on the education and training of learning disabled adults. *Learning Disability Quarterly, 8*(3) summer, 231-235.

White, W. J. (1992). The postschool adjustment of persons with learning disabilities: Current status and future projections. *Journal of Learning Disabilities, 25*(7), 448-456.

Wilson, N. O. (1993). Learning disabilities and the general public. *LDA Newsbriefs, 28*(4), LDA, 4156 Library Road, Pittsburgh, PA 15234.

Wolf, E. (1988). *Treating the self: Elements of clinical self psychology.* New York: The Guilford Press.

Wood, D., Reimberr, F. W., Wender, P. H., and Johnson, G. E. (1976). Diagnosis and treatment of minimal brain dysfunction in adults: A preliminary report. *Archives of General Psychiatry, 33*(12), 1453-1460.

Wood, D., Wender, Ph. H., and Reimberr, F. W. (1983). The prevalence of attention deficit disorder, residual type, or minimal brain dysfunction, in a population of male alcoholic patients. *American Journal of Psychiatry, 140*(1), 95-98.

Wren, C., Adelman, P., Pike, M. B., and Wilson, J. L. (1987). *College and the high school student with learning disabilities: The student's perspective.* Project Learning Strategies, DePaul University, 2323 Seminary, Chicago, IL 60614.

Wren, C. and Segal, L. (1985). College Students with learning disabilities: A student's perspective. Carol T. Wren, Director, Project Learning Strategies, DePaul University, 2323 Seminary, Chicago, IL 60614.

Wurmser, L. (1987). Shame: The veiled companion of narcissism. In D. L. Nathanson (Ed.), *The many faces of shame* (pp. 64-92). New York: The Guilford Press.

Index

HAWORTH Social Work Practice in Action
Carlton E. Munson, PhD, Senior Editor

SOCIAL WORK: SEEKING RELEVANCY IN THE TWENTY-FIRST CENTURY by Roland Meinert, John T. Pardeck and Larry Kreuger. (2000). "Highly recommended. A thought–provoking work that asks the difficult questions and challenges the status quo. A great book for graduate students as well as experienced social workers and educators." *Francis K. O. Yuen, DSW, ACSE, Associate Professor, Division of Social Work, California State University, Sacramento*

SOCIAL WORK PRACTICE IN HOME HEALTH CARE by Ruth Ann Goode. (2000). "Dr. Goode presents both a lucid scenario and a formulated protocol to bring health care services into the home setting. . . . This is a must-have volume that will be a reference to be consulted many times." *Marcia B. Steinhauer, PhD, Coordinator and Associate Professor, Human Services Administration Program, Rider University, Lawrenceville, New Jersey*

FORENSIC SOCIAL WORK: LEGAL ASPECTS OF PROFESSIONAL PRAC-TICE, SECOND EDITION by Robert L. Barker and Douglas M. Branson. (2000). "The authors combine their expertise to create this informative guide to address legal practice issues facing social workers." *Newsletter of the National Organization of Forensic Social Work*

HUMAN SERVICES AND THE AFROCENTRIC PARADIGM by Jerome H. Schiele. (2000). "Represents a milestone in applying the Afrocentric paradigm to human services generally, and social work specifically. . . . A highly valuable resource." *Bogart R. Leashore, PhD, Dean and Professor, Hunter College School of Social Work, New York, New York*

SOCIAL WORK IN THE HEALTH FIELD: A CARE PERSPECTIVE by Lois A. Fort Cowles. (2000). "Makes an important contribution to the field by locating the practice of social work in health care within an organizational and social context." *Goldie Kadushin, PhD, Associate Professor, School of Social Welfare, University of Wisconsin, Milwaukee*

SMART BUT STUCK: EMOTIONAL ASPECTS OF LEARNING DISABILI-TIES AND IMPRISONED INTELLIGENCE by Myrna Orenstein. (2001). "A trail-blazing effort that creates an entirely novel way of talking and thinking about learning disabilities. There is simply nothing like it in the field." *Fred M. Levin, MD, Training Supervising Analyst, Chicago Institute for Psychoanalysis; Assistant Professor of Clinical Psychiatry, Northwestern University, School of Medicine, Chicago, IL*

CLINICAL WORK AND SOCIAL ACTION: AN INTEGRATIVE APPROACH by Jerome Sachs and Fred Newdom. (1999). "Just in time for the new millennium come Sachs and Newdom with a wholly fresh look at social work. . . . A much-needed uniting of social work values, theories, and practice for action." *Josephine Nieves, MSW, PhD, Executive Director, National Association of Social Workers*

SOCIAL WORK PRACTICE IN THE MILITARY by James G. Daley. (1999). "A significant and worthwhile book with provocative and stimulating ideas. It deserves to be read by a wide audience in social work education and practice as well as by decision makers in the military." *H. Wayne Johnson, MSW, Professor, University of Iowa, School of Social Work, Iowa City, Iowa*

GROUP WORK: SKILLS AND STRATEGIES FOR EFFECTIVE INTERVENTIONS, SECOND EDITION by Sondra Brandler and Camille P. Roman. (1999). "A clear, basic description of what group work requires, including what skills and techniques group workers need to be effective." *Hospital and Community Psychiatry* (from the first edition)

TEENAGE RUNAWAYS: BROKEN HEARTS AND "BAD ATTITUDES" by Laurie Schaffner (1999). "Skillfully combines the authentic voice of the juvenile runaway with the principles of social science research." *Barbara Owen, PhD, Professor, Department of Criminology, California State University, Fresno*

CELEBRATING DIVERSITY: COEXISTING IN A MULTICULTURAL SOCIETY by Benyamin Chetkow-Yanoov. (1999). "Makes a valuable contribution to peace theory and practice." *Ian Harris, EdD, Executive Secretary, Peace Education Committee, International Peace Research Association*

SOCIAL WELFARE POLICY ANALYSIS AND CHOICES by Hobart A. Burch. (1999). "Will become the landmark text in its field for many decades to come." *Sheldon Rahan, DSW, Founding Dean and Emeritus Professor of Social Policy and Social Administration. Faculty of Social Work, Wilfrid Laurier University, Canada*

SOCIAL WORK PRACTICE: A SYSTEMS APPROACH, SECOND EDITION by Benyamin Chetkow-Yannov. (1999). "Highly recommended as a primary text for any and all introductory social work courses." *Ram A. Cnaan, PhD, Associate Professor, School of Social Work, University of Pennsylvania*

CRITICAL SOCIAL WELFARE ISSUES: TOOLS FOR SOCIAL WORK AND HEALTH CARE PROFESSIONALS edited by Arthur J. Katz, Abraham Lurie, and Carlos M. Vidal. (1997). "Offers hopeful agendas for change, while navigating the societal challenges facing those in the human services today." *Book News Inc.*

SOCIAL WORK IN HEALTH SETTINGS: PRACTICE IN CONTEXT, SECOND EDITION edited by Toba Schwaber Kerson. (1997). "A first-class document . . . It will be found among the steadier and lasting works on the social work aspects of American health care." *Hans S. Falck, PhD, Professor Emeritus and Former Chair, Health Specialization in Social Work, Virginia Commonwealth University*

PRINCIPLES OF SOCIAL WORK PRACTICE: A GENERIC PRACTICE APPROACH by Molly R. Hancock. (1997). "Hancock's discussions advocate reflection and self-awareness to create a climate for client change." *Journal of Social Work Education*

NOBODY'S CHILDREN: ORPHANS OF THE HIV EPIDEMIC by Steven F. Dansky. (1997). "Professional sound, moving, and useful for both professionals and interested readers alike." *Ellen G. Friedman, ACSW, Associate Director of Support Services, Beth Israel Medical Center, Methadone Maintenance Treatment Program*

SOCIAL WORK APPROACHES TO CONFLICT RESOLUTION: MAKING FIGHTING OBSOLETE by Benyamin Chetkow-Yanoov. (1996). "Presents an examination of the nature and cause of conflict and suggests techniques for coping with conflict." *Journal of Criminal Justice*

FEMINIST THEORIES AND SOCIAL WORK: APPROACHES AND APPLICATIONS by Christine Flynn Salunier. (1996). "An essential reference to be read repeatedly by all educators and practitioners who are eager to learn more about feminist theory and practice: *Nancy R. Hooyman, PhD, Dean and Professor, School of Social Work, University of Washington, Seattle*

THE RELATIONAL SYSTEMS MODEL FOR FAMILY THERAPY: LIVING IN THE FOUR REALITIES by Donald R. Bardill. (1996). "Engages the reader in quiet, thoughtful conversation on the timeless issue of helping families and individuals." *Christian Counseling Resource Review*

SOCIAL WORK INTERVENTION IN AN ECONOMIC CRISIS: THE RIVER COMMUNITIES PROJECT by Martha Baum and Pamela Twiss. (1996). "Sets a standard for universities in terms of the types of meaningful roles they can play in supporting and sustaining communities." *Kenneth J. Jaros, PhD, Director, Public Health Social Work Training Program, University of Pittsburgh*

FUNDAMENTALS OF COGNITIVE-BEHAVIOR THERAPY: FROM BOTH SIDES OF THE DESK by Bill Borcherdt. (1996). "Both beginning and experienced practitioners . . . will find a considerable number of valuable suggestions in Borcherdt's book." *Albert Ellis, PhD, President, Institute for Rational-Emotive Therapy, New York City*

BASIC SOCIAL POLICY AND PLANNING: STRATEGIES AND PRACTICE METHODS by Hobart A. Burch. (1996). "Burch's familiarity with his topic is evident and his book is an easy introduction to the field." *Readings*

THE CROSS-CULTURAL PRACTICE OF CLINICAL CASE MANAGEMENT IN MENTAL HEALTH edited by Peter Manoleas. (1996). "Makes a contribution by bringing together the cross-cultural and clinical case management perspectives in working with those who have serious mental illness." *Disability Studies Quarterly*

FAMILY BEYOND FAMILY: THE SURROGATE PARENT IN SCHOOLS AND OTHER COMMUNITY AGENCIES by Sanford Weinstein. (1995). "Highly recommended to anyone concerned about the welfare of our children and the breakdown of the American family." *Jerold S. Greenberg, EdD, Director of Community Service, College of Health & Human Performance, University of Maryland*

PEOPLE WITH HIV AND THOSE WHO HELP THEM: CHALLENGES, INTEGRATION, INTERVENTION by R. Dennis Shelby. (1995). "A useful and compassionate contribution to the HIV psychotherapy literature." *Public Health*

THE BLACK ELDERLY: SATISFACTION AND QUALITY OF LATER LIFE by Marguerite Coke and James A. Twaite. (1995). "Presents a model for predicting life satisfaction in this population." *Abstracts in Social Gerontology*

BUILDING ON WOMEN'S STRENGTHS: A SOCIAL WORK AGENDA FOR THE TWENTY-FIRST CENTURY edited by Liane V. Davis. (1994). "The most lucid and accessible overview of the related epistemological debates int he social work literature." *Journal of the National Association of Social Workers*

NOW DARE EVERYTHING: TALES OF HIV-RELATED PSYCHOTHERAPY by Steven F. Dansky. (1994). "A highly recommended book for anyone working with persons who are HIV positive. . . . Every library should have a copy of this book." *AIDS Book Review Journal*

INTERVENTION RESEARCH: DESIGN AND DEVELOPMENT FOR HUMAN SERVICE edited by Jack Rothman and Edwin J. Thomas. (1994). "Provides a useful framework for the further examination of methodology for each separate step of such research." *Academic Library Book Review*

CLINICAL SOCIAL WORK SUPERVISION, SECOND EDITION by Carlton E. Munson. (1993). "A useful, thorough, and articulate reference for supervisors and for 'supervisees' who are wanting to understand their supervisor or are looking for effective supervision." *Transactional Analysis Journal*

ELEMENTS OF THE HELPING PROCESS: A GUIDE FOR CLINICIANS by Raymond Fox. (1993). "Filled with helpful hints, creative interventions, and practical guidelines." *Journal of Family Psychotherapy*

IF A PARTNER HAS AIDS: GUIDE TO CLINICAL INTERVENTION FOR RELATIONSHIPS IN CRISIS by R. Dennis Shelby. (1993). "A welcome addition to existing publications about couples coping with AIDS, it offers intervention ideas and strategies to clinicians." *Contemporary Psychology*

GERONTOLOGICAL SOCIAL WORK SUPERVISION by Ann Burack-Weiss and Frances Coyle Brennan. (1991). "The creative ideas in this book will aid supervisors working with students and experienced social workers." *Senior News*

SOCIAL WORK THEORY AND PRACTICE WITH THE TERMINALLY ILL by Joan K. Parry. (1989). "Should be read by all professionals engaged in the provision of health services in hospitals, emergency rooms, and hospices." *Hector B. Garcia, PhD, Professor, San Jose State University School of Social Work*

THE CREATIVE PRACTITIONER: THEORY AND METHODS FOR THE HELPING SERVICES by Bernard Gelfand. (1988). "[Should] be widely adopted by those in the helping services. It could lead to significant positive advances by countless individuals." *Sidney J. Parnes, Trustee Chairperson for Strategic Program Development, Creative Education Foundation, Buffalo, NY*

MANAGEMENT AND INFORMATION SYSTEMS IN HUMAN SERVICES: IMPLICATIONS FOR THE DISTRIBUTION OF AUTHORITY AND DECISION MAKING by Richard K. Caputo. (1987). "A contribution to social work scholarship in that it provides conceptual frameworks that can be used in the design of management information systems." *Social Work*

Order Your Own Copy of
This Important Book for Your Personal Library!

SMART BUT STUCK
Emotional Aspects of Learning Disabilities and Imprisoned Intelligence

_____ in hardbound at $34.95 (ISBN: 0-7890-1466-1)

_____ in softbound at $24.95 (ISBN: 0-7890-1467-X)

COST OF BOOKS_____

OUTSIDE USA/CANADA/
MEXICO: ADD 20%_____

POSTAGE & HANDLING_____
(US: $3.00 for first book & $1.25
for each additional book)
Outside US: $4.75 for first book
& $1.75 for each additional book)

SUBTOTAL_____

IN CANADA: ADD 7% GST_____

STATE TAX_____
(NY, OH & MN residents, please
add appropriate local sales tax)

FINAL TOTAL_____
(If paying in Canadian funds,
convert using the current
exchange rate. UNESCO
coupons welcome.)

☐ **BILL ME LATER:** ($5 service charge will be added)
(Bill-me option is good on US/Canada/Mexico orders only;
not good to jobbers, wholesalers, or subscription agencies.)

☐ Check here if billing address is different from
shipping address and attach purchase order and
billing address information.

Signature_____

☐ **PAYMENT ENCLOSED: $**_____

☐ **PLEASE CHARGE TO MY CREDIT CARD.**

☐ Visa   ☐ MasterCard   ☐ AmEx   ☐ Discover

Account #_____

Exp. Date_____

Signature_____

Prices in US dollars and subject to change without notice.

NAME _____

INSTITUTION _____

ADDRESS _____

CITY _____

STATE/ZIP _____

COUNTRY _____ COUNTY (NY residents only) _____

TEL _____ FAX _____

E-MAIL_____
May we use your e-mail address for confirmations and other types of information? ☐ Yes   ☐ No

Order From Your Local Bookstore or Directly From
The Haworth Press, Inc.
10 Alice Street, Binghamton, New York 13904-1580 • USA
TELEPHONE: 1-800-HAWORTH (1-800-429-6784) / Outside US/Canada: (607) 722-5857
FAX: 1-800-895-0582 / Outside US/Canada: (607) 772-6362
E-mail: getinfo@haworthpressinc.com
PLEASE PHOTOCOPY THIS FORM FOR YOUR PERSONAL USE.

BOF96

NEW AND INFORMATIVE BOOKS FROM
HAWORTH SOCIAL WORK PRACTICE IN ACTION

CLINICAL PRACTICE WITH FAMILIES
Supporting Creativity and Competence
Michael Rothery and George Enns

NEW!

Presents the most important and useful contemporary ideas in family therapy in a clear, understandable framework, and offers an opportunity to take a structured approach to contemporary theory and understand its implications for practice.

Over 200 Pages!

$69.95 hard. ISBN: 0-7890-1084-4.
$29.95 soft. ISBN: 0-7890-1085-2.
2001. Available now. 254 pp. with Index.

SMART BUT STUCK
REVISED EDITION!

Emotional Aspects of Learning Disabilities and Imprisoned Intelligence, Revised Edition
Myrna Orenstein, PhD

Combining research and twenty case studies, this important book discusses why and how intelligent individuals with learning disabilities are misunderstood and how shame and fear can lead to imprisoned intelligence.
$34.95 hard. ISBN: 0-7890-1466-1.
$19.95 soft. ISBN: 0-7890-1467-X.
2001. Available now. 228 pp. with Index.

THE MENTAL HEALTH DIAGNOSTIC DESK REFERENCE
NEW EDITION!

Visual Guides and More for Learning to Use the Diagnostic and Statistical Manual (DSM-IV-TR)
Second Edition
Carlton E. Munson, PhD

Over 350 Pages!

Written by nationally respected clinician, supervisor, and educator Dr. Carlton Munson, this book will help end clinical gridlock and enable you to improve services to your clients within the context of managed care.
$59.95 hard. ISBN: 0-7890-1464-5.
$24.95 soft. ISBN: 0-7890-1465-3. 2000. 396 pp. with Index.

SOCIAL WORK THEORY AND PRACTICE WITH THE TERMINALLY ILL, SECOND EDITION
NEW EDITION!

Joan K. Parry, ACSW, LCSW, DSW

The ideas and techniques shared in this book can help patients and their loved ones cope with the stress of terminal illness, the dying process, and grief.
$49.95 hard. ISBN: 0-7890-1082-8.
$24.95 soft. ISBN: 0-7890-1083-6. 2000. 160 pp. with Index.

WOMEN SURVIVORS, PSYCHOLOGICAL TRAUMA, AND THE POLITICS OF RESISTANCE

NEW!

Norma Jean Profitt, DSW

Over 200 Pages!

This essential book traces survivors' development over a substantial period of time to find out how these women make sense of their lives and decide to become advocates to stop violence against women.
$49.95 hard. ISBN: 0-7890-0890-4.
$24.95 soft. ISBN: 0-7890-1113-1. 2000. 232 pp. with Index.

SOCIAL WORK

NEW!

Seeking Relevancy in the Twenty-First Century
Roland Meinert, PhD, John T. Pardeck, PhD, and Larry Kreuger, PhD

You will be exposed to issues in social work that normally are not covered in mainline social work literature, such as the use of hypertechnology, the disjuncture of science and social work, and the problems with social work theories.
$39.95 hard. ISBN: 0-7890-0644-8.
$24.95 soft. ISBN: 0-7890-1050-X. 2000. 152 pp. with Index.

HUMAN SERVICES AND THE AFROCENTRIC PARADIGM

NEW!

Jerome H. Schiele

Over 250 Pages!

Describes how the Afrocentric paradigm can be used to identify, explain, and solve fundamental social problems that confront those who seek help from human service professionals and community advocates.
$49.95 hard. ISBN: 0-7890-0565-4.
$34.95 soft. ISBN: 0-7890-0566-2. 2000. 314 pp. with Index.

FORENSIC SOCIAL WORK
NEW EDITION!

Legal Aspects of Professional Practice, Second Edition
Robert L. Barker, PhD, and Douglas M. Branson, JD

"*The authors combine their expertise to create this informative guide to address legal practice issues facing social workers. A must read for master-level students. . . . Offers advice on what to look for when hiring a lawyer.*"
—*Newsletter of the National Organization of Forensic Social Work*
$49.95 hard. ISBN: 0-7890-0867-X.
$24.95 soft. ISBN: 0-7890-0868-8.
2000. 262 pp. with Index.

Over 225 Pages!

SOCIAL WORK IN THE HEALTH FIELD
A Care Perspective
Lois Anne Fort Cowles, PhD

Over 300 Pages!

Addresses such important issues as social worker functions and client problems, interdisciplinary teamwork and other organizational considerations, and ethics and skill requirements. Each subject area clearly and concisely describes and highlights the similarities and differences between social work in the health field and social work practice.
$49.95 hard. ISBN: 0-7890-6033-7.
$29.95 soft. ISBN: 0-7890-0913-7.
1999. 372 pp. with Index.
Includes an Instructor's Manual.

INCLUDES INSTRUCTOR'S MANUAL FREE WITH DESK COPY!

SOCIAL WORK PRACTICE IN HOME HEALTH CARE
Ruth Ann Goode, PhD, LCSW

An easy-to-read "how to practice" approach to social work practice in home health care agencies.
$39.95 hard. ISBN: 0-7890-0483-6.
$24.95 soft. ISBN: 0-7890-0905-6.
1999. 150 pp. with Index.

The Haworth Press, Inc.
10 Alice Street
Binghamton, New York 13904–1580 USA

ADDITIONAL INFORMATIVE BOOKS FROM
HAWORTH SOCIAL WORK PRACTICE IN ACTION

SOCIAL WORK IN GERIATRIC HOME HEALTH CARE
The Blending of Traditional Practice with Cooperative Strategies
Lucille Rosengarten, ACSW, BCD
Based on the author's twenty-five years of social work experience in geriatric home care case management, this book explores improved ways to organize home health care by use of cooperative strategies, and by privileging the social work role.
$39.95 hard. ISBN: 0-7890-0746-0.
$24.95 soft. ISBN: 0-7890-0747-9. 1999. 124 pp. with Index.

SOCIAL WORK PRACTICE IN THE MILITARY
Over 300 Pages!
Edited by James G. Daley, PhD
"Offers IN-DEPTH COVERAGE of issues such as family violence, substance abuse, combat settings, and managed care's impact on the military."
—Book News, Inc.
$69.95 hard. ISBN: 0-7890-0625-1.1999.
$24.95 soft. ISBN: 0-7890-0626-X. 1999. 358 pp. with Index.

CLINICAL WORK AND SOCIAL ACTION
An Integrative Approach
Jerome Sachs, DSW, and Fred A. Newdom, ACSW
"The authors construct a course in which clinical social workers and classroom instructors can approach client-centered practice without sacrificing core social welfare values."
—Journal of Social Work Education
$49.95 hard. ISBN: 0-7890-0278-7.
$29.95 soft. ISBN: 0-7890-0279-5. 1999. 228 pp. with Index.

GROUP WORK
NEW EDITION!
Skills and Strategies for Effective Interventions, Second Edition
Sondra Brandler, DSW, and Camille P. Roman, MSW
This edition contains excerpts and discussions of case studies that will serve as valuable references that may be applied to your own experiences.
$49.95 hard. ISBN: 0-7890-0710-X.
$34.95 soft. ISBN: 0-7890-0740-1.
1999. 348 pp. with Index.
Over 300 Pages!

CALL OUR TOLL-FREE NUMBER: 1-800-429-6784
US & Canada only / 8am–5pm ET; Monday–Friday
Outside US/Canada: + 607–722–5857
FAX YOUR ORDER TO US: 1-800-895-0582
Outside US/Canada: + 607–771–0012
E-MAIL YOUR ORDER TO US:
getinfo@haworthpressinc.com
VISIT OUR WEB SITE AT:
http://www.HaworthPress.com

TEENAGE RUNAWAYS
Broken Hearts and "Bad Attitudes"
Laurie Schaffner, PhD (cand.)
"DEFLATES MISCONCEPTIONS that runaways are incorrigible delinquents, and reveals that many teenage runaways leave home in search of safety and freedom from abusive physical, sexual, or emotional treatment."
—Book News, Inc.
$59.95 hard. ISBN: 0-7890-0550-6.
$19.95 soft. ISBN: 0-7890-0892-0.
1999. 171 pp. with Index.
Features numerous interviews.

CELEBRATING DIVERSITY
Coexisting in a Multicultural Society
Benyamin Chetkow-Yanoov, DSW
"Offers both theoretical analysis and PRACTICAL SUGGESTIONS FOR WORKING WITH DIFFERENCES."
—The Other Side
$39.95 hard. ISBN: 0-7890-0437-2.
$14.95 soft. ISBN: 0-7890-0438-0.
1999. 114 pp. with Index.
Features tables and figures.

SOCIAL WELFARE POLICY ANALYSIS AND CHOICES
Over 350 Pages!
Hobart A. Burch, PhD
The knowledge you'll gain from its pages will enable you to understand and evaluate individual policy issues and choices by exploring the possible choices, the effects and implications of each alternative choice, and the factors that influence each choice.
$89.95 hard. ISBN: 0-7890-0602-2.
$34.95 soft. ISBN: 0-7890-0603-0.
1999. 381 pp. with Index.
Features appendixes and a bibliography.
Includes an Instructor's Manual.

PRINCIPLES OF SOCIAL WORK PRACTICE
Over 200 Pages!
A Generic Practice Approach
Molly R. Hancock, MSW
"Lays out basic principles of practice and describes methods to integrate them into concrete contexts. . . . Seeks ethical, personal, and methodological principles that can be used with flexibility in different applied contexts—whether in practice with families, couples, groups, organizations, or communities."
—Journal of Social Work Education
$69.95 hard. ISBN: 0-7890-6024-8.
$27.95 soft. ISBN: 0-7890-0188-8.
1997. 261 pp. with Index.
Includes an Instructor's Manual.

WE'RE ON THE WEB!
VISIT OUR WEB SITE AT:
http://www.HaworthPress.com